Brigid Benson is a bestselling author with a heartfelt passion for journeys and connections, a sparky sense of curiosity and strong, deep roots in Scotland. Her previous books include 52 *Weekends by the Sea*, 52 *Weekends in the Country* and *North Coast Journey: The Magic of Scotland's Northern Highlands*.

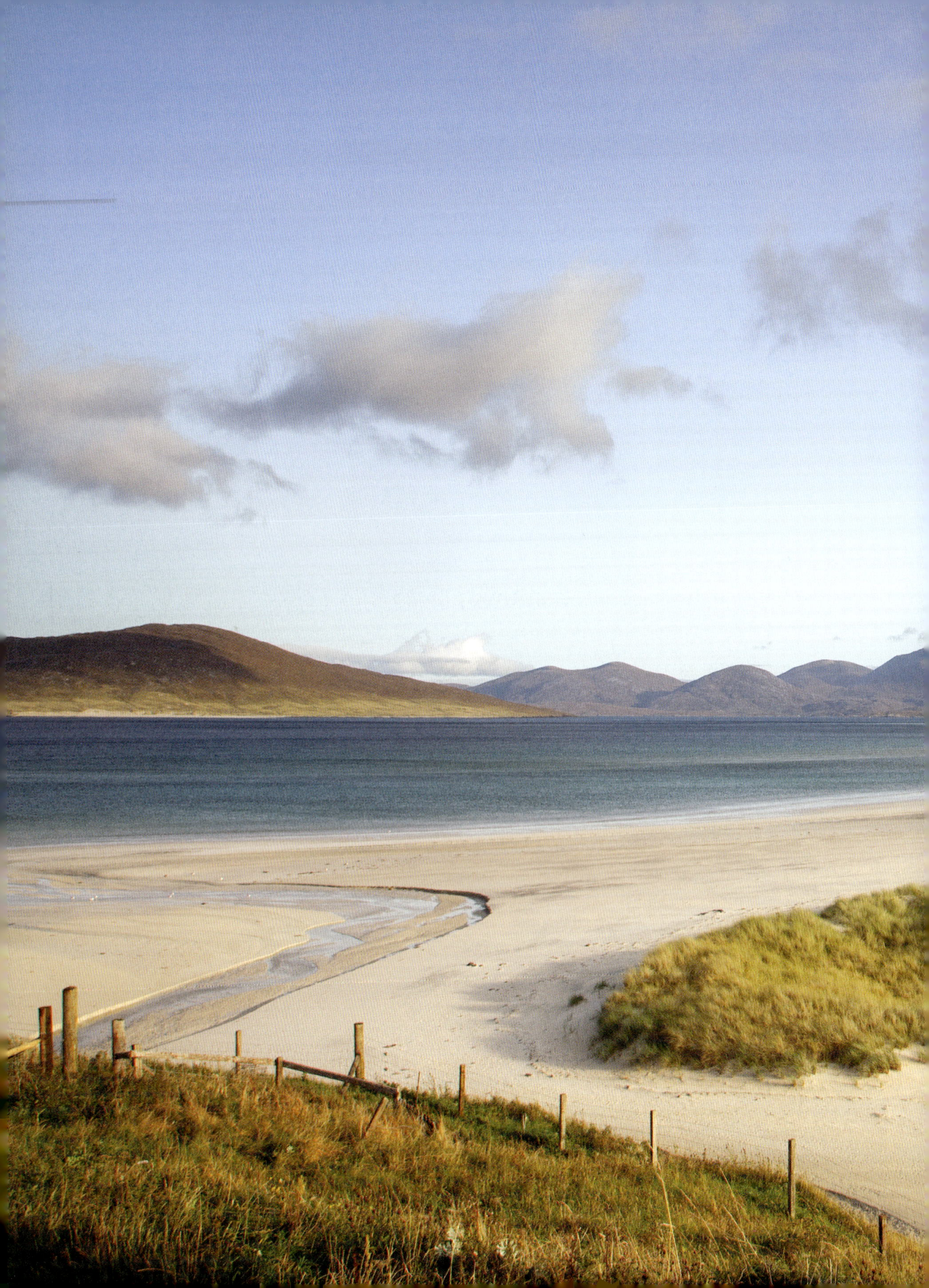

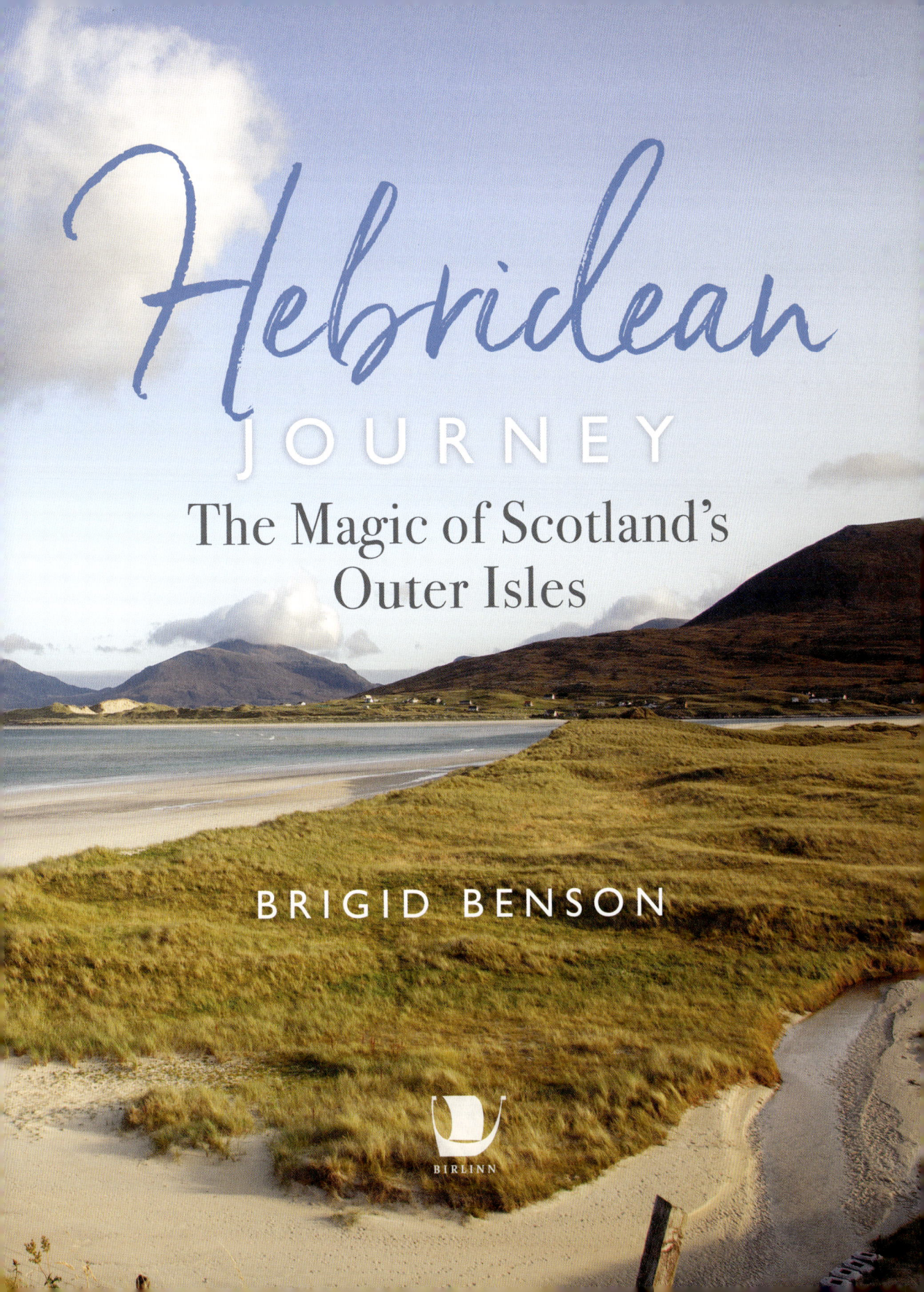

Hebridean
JOURNEY
The Magic of Scotland's Outer Isles

BRIGID BENSON

BIRLINN

First published in 2022 by
Birlinn Limited
West Newington House
10 Newington Road Edinburgh
EH9 1QS

www.birlinn.co.uk

Copyright © Brigid Benson 2022

All photography by Brigid Benson
www.brigidbenson.com
@brigid_benson

Maps designed and produced by Lovell
Johns Ltd. Contain Ordnance Survey data.
© Crown copyright and database right 2022

The moral right of Brigid Benson be identified
as the author of this work has been asserted by
her in accordance with the Copyright, Designs
and Patents Act 1988

All rights reserved. No part of this publication
may be reproduced, stored or transmitted in any
form without the express written permission of
the publisher

Every effort has been made to ensure this book
is as up to date as possible. Some details,
however, are liable to change. The author and
publisher cannot accept responsibility for any
consequences arising from the use of this book

ISBN: 978 1 78027 770 7

British Library Cataloguing-in-Publication Data
A catalogue record for this book is available
from the British Library

Designed and typeset by Mark Blackadder

Printed and bound by PNB Latvia

May your spirit dance to the *ceòl na mara*
May your heart know the delight of island-going
BB

For Muriel and David, with my love

Contents

Acknowledgements	9
Introduction	13
Overview map	23

Part 1 Lewis and Harris

Map	26
Stornoway to Skigersta	27
Across Barvas Moor to the Butt of Lewis	36
Time Travels to Callanish and Beyond	44
The Eye Peninsula	55
Map	60
Over the Atlantic to Great Bernera	61
Uig and the Western Shore	65
Map	74
Around the East Coast Sea Lochs to Tarbert	74
To Scalpay	86
The Huisinis Road	90
Map	96
The Golden Road to the East	96
The Remarkable Sound of Harris	105
Wondrous West Coast Harris Beaches	110

Part 2 Berneray and North Uist

Map	118
The Seals, Sands and Stones of Berneray	118
Across the Causeway to Lochmaddy	124
Lochmaddy to Baleshare	131
The Coast Road from Clachan to Udal	136

Part 3 Grimsay and Benbecula

Map	148
The Boats, Lobsters and Wool of Grimsay	148
To Atmospheric Benbecula	153

Part 4 South Uist and Eriskay

Map	162
The Shrines, Shores and Silent Weaver of South Uist	163
The Hebridean Island that Won Margaret Fay Shaw	168
Irresistible Eriskay	180

Part 5 Barra and Vatersay

Map	192
To Barradise and Beyond	193
Vatersay	205

List of Illustrations	213
Ways to Visit and Useful Addresses	215
Index	221

Acknowledgements

We are waves of the same sea, leaves of the same tree, flowers of the same garden
SENECA

Much of this book was researched and written during a time of world-changing significance. In the circumstances of a global pandemic, love and kindness came to the fore and got so many people through. The immense courage and determination of teams working throughout the NHS have been an inspiration, likewise the massive contribution of all kinds of other key workers, seen and unseen. I dedicate *Hebridean Journey* to all those magnificent people committed to doing their very best for everyone. I thank you with all my heart.

The love and support I have received while creating this book through challenging times has been simply beautiful. I am so grateful to family, friends, colleagues and complete strangers who have all contributed in their own special way.

I honour especially the radiance of my mum, Muriel Benson, née Topp, and David Christopher Potter, two hugely influential and loving people in my life who died in 2022. Their inspirational light will forever illuminate my journeys.

To name everyone who has contributed in some way would fill too many pages; I am unable to do that but my thanks are huge nonetheless.

Working with the fantastic team at Birlinn Books is a joy. I am immensely appreciative of their vision, warmth, care and enthusiasm, and I thank Hugh, Andrew, Deborah, Mark, James, Anita, Yasmine and the terrific sales, media, events and marketing teams especially.

I invite all the hardworking teams at Caledonian MacBrayne to please take a bow for their important work on the ferry lifelines between islands and the mainland. I am grateful to Andrew MacNair and Laura

Wohlegemuth especially. Here's to the kindness of Peter Urpeth and Rob McKinnon, John, Ishbel and all the team at Ravenspoint, Anne Wilson and Cubby too. Special thanks go to Barbara MacDonald in South Uist and Donald Macdonald in Lewis for allowing me to take their portrait while hard at work with their sheep in the hills.

To lovely Veronica and Donnie in Barra, thank you for sharing so much so generously. I will treasure always our fabulous island walks and breezy seashore picnics under glittering stars.

To the Society of Authors, which has provided so much encouragement to writers in hard times, thank you immensely for all you do for all of us.

Last, but certainly not least, the gratitude I feel for the enduring kindness and warm welcome of the people of the Outer Hebrides islands through the years is huge; thank you with all my heart.

Tapadh leibh

Brigid Benson

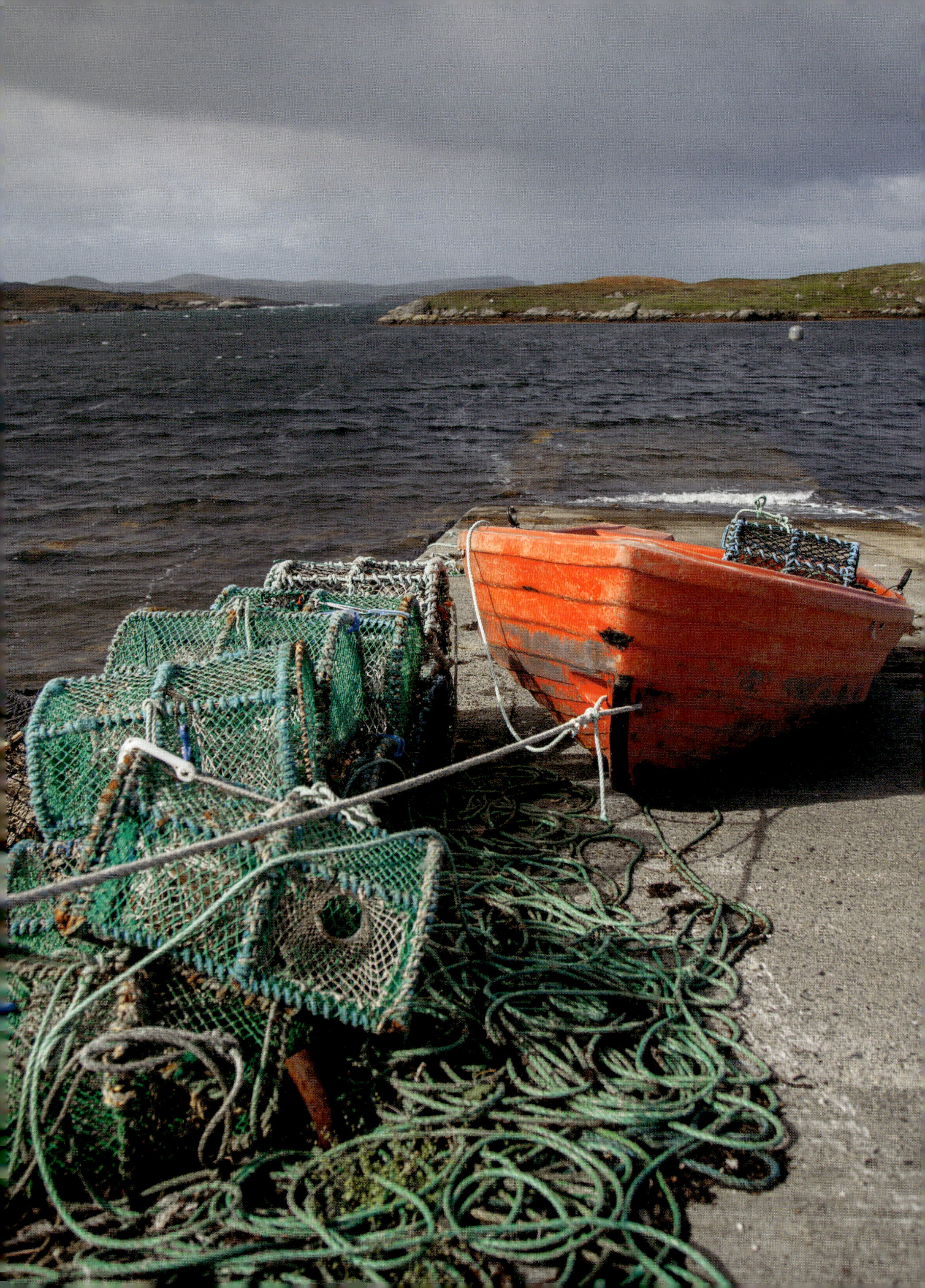

Introduction

Welcome and thanks for being here! I am honoured to share my experience of the Outer Hebrides with you. I feel passionate about these far-west Atlantic islands and vibrant communities on the rim of Europe, and I am blessed to know them well.

The magnificent archipelago, known traditionally as the Long Island, extends 130 miles from the Butt of Lewis to the shores of Vatersay. My journey begins in Stornoway, regarded as the capital of the Outer Hebrides. Getting to know the historic harbour town in the Isle of Lewis is an immensely rewarding foundation for any trip through the island chain.

From Stornoway, the adventure builds, layer upon layer. Each isle on the rocky thread is a unique environment, imbued with stories, traditions and challenges. Vibrant communities are embracing and managing change to shape a positive future. Each island is distinct, yet some aspects of Hebridean life resound through them all and it feels important to introduce a few of them here.

Island Life

At the risk of stating the obvious, it is impossible to experience the Outer Hebrides without experiencing the sea. The sea touches everything. The Atlantic Ocean to the west and the Minch to the east exert enormous influence. Tides dictate ferry sailings, aircraft flights, boat trips and sandy crossings to offshore islands. Clean, deep waters provide harvests of fish and seafood for the table. Seaweed serves as an ingredient in foodstuffs and pharmaceutical products and nourishes thin sandy soil. Mysterious ancient monuments, burial grounds and chapels perch at the ocean edge with tantalising views to neighbouring isles and far horizons. Prior to roads, bridges and causeways, scattered communities travelled the briny highway in boats expertly designed for rocky clefts and wild open swell. The flotsam and jetsam that washes ashore from distant lands continues to be repurposed with imagination. Nothing is wasted on an island.

    For me, one of the great joys of the Outer Hebrides is the immersion in Gaelic, the first language of the islands, however English is widely spoken too, and so conversing is rarely a problem. Scots Gaelic is a gloriously evocative tongue and, to me, the opportunity to hear it spoken, or sung, is a wonderful and unmissable treat. The complex language is rich in rhythm and fluid in spelling, with a long history of being passed down through the generations by word of mouth. Soon after English forces defeated Jacobites at the Battle of Culloden, the Act of Proscription in 1746 introduced a new education system that outlawed Gaelic. Contemporary efforts to halt decline of the language include the opportunity for children to learn Gaelic at school, with courses for adults also. Shapeshifting is part of the heritage of the Gaelic language and, though pesky at times, on discovery of several variations of spelling for a place name, or a person, for example, these alternatives speak to the enduring spirit of the language through historic persecution.

    Traditional Gaelic songs evolved to accompany everyday tasks; they provided rhythm for spinning, rocking cradles, making tweed cloth, rowing boats and digging wet slabs of peat from the moor. More poignant laments like a 'A Pheigi a Ghràidh' recall the agonising choice of leaving

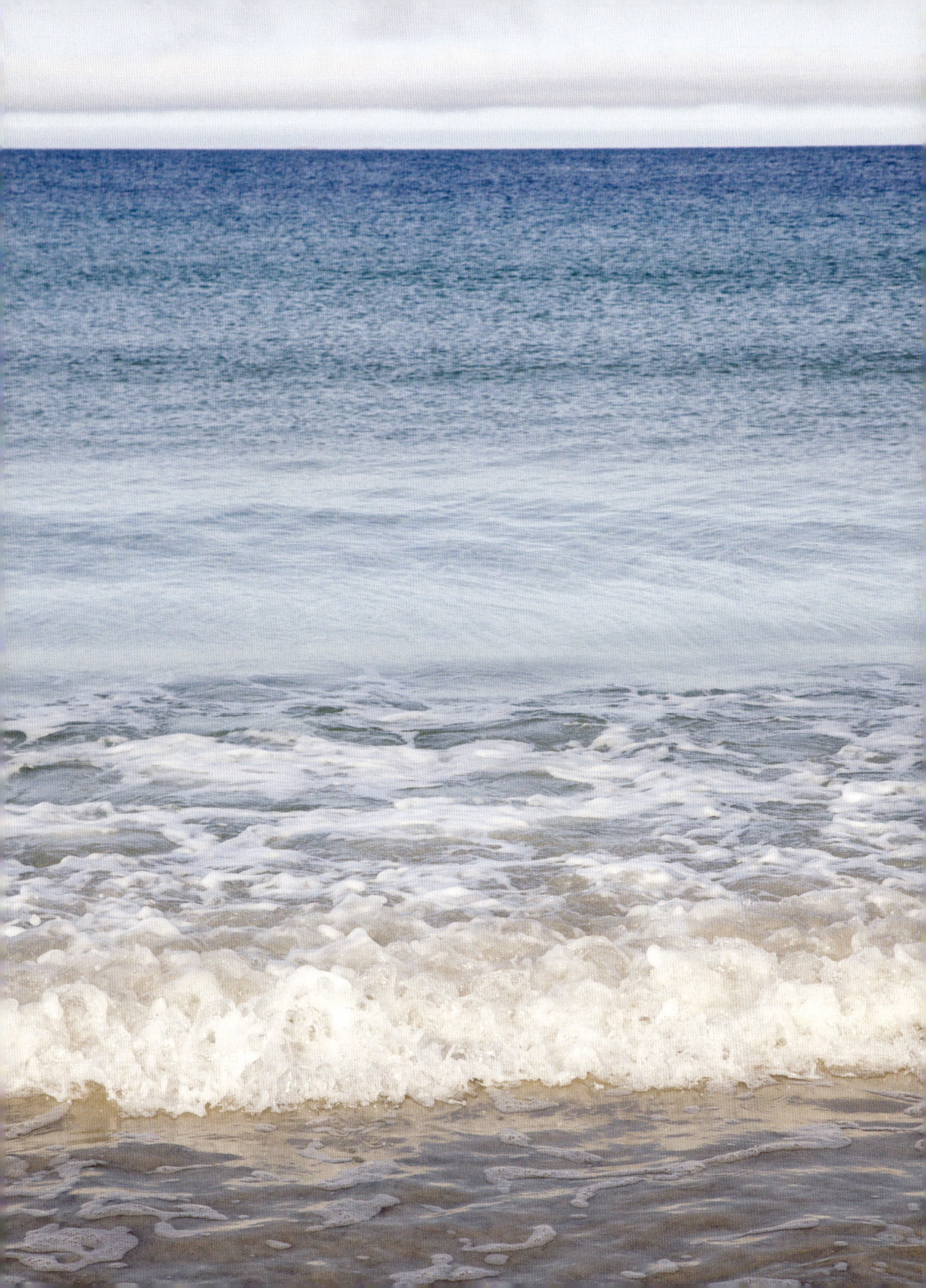

loved ones to seek work abroad. A favourite sung by women waulking the tweed cloth was '*Cha Tied Mi Do Dh'Fhear Gun Bhata*' or 'I'll Not Go With a Man Who Doesn't Have His Own Boat'. The runaway success of Stornoway band Peat and Diesel reflects their witty ability to reference brilliantly, in lyric and tune, the experience of contemporary island life with sparks of tradition.

Gaelic expressions honour moods and sounds of the sea beautifully. *Gair na mara* suggests the laughter of the waves, *nualan na mara* describes them lowing, like cattle. In Gaelic Catholic communities, the sea is described as *cuilidh Moire*, the treasury of the Virgin Mary. Fishers returning to the shore reported *Dh'iarr a mhuir a bith ga tadhal*, the sea wanted to be visited. In Gaelic, white-crested waves are described as flying gulls, *tha an fhaoileag air a' mhuir*. At the Samhain fire festival to celebrate the start of a new year on 31 October, islanders made simple offerings to the sea spirit Seonaidh, or Shony, in the hope of abundant fish to nourish them and seaweed to fertilise their fields.

The sea brings people to island shores, not least the Vikings who arrived around AD 800 and occupied the Outer Hebrides for some 500 years. The Old Norse legacy lingers in place names and in genetic material. In 2019, a study of volunteers revealed people in the Outer Hebrides had 9 per cent levels of Norwegian ancestry. Many islanders feel more affinity with Scandinavia than parts of the British Isles.

The sea takes people away, too. Economic migration has dispersed islanders throughout the world, sometimes in desperate circumstances against their will. Island estate owners cleared families from the land onto emigrant ships in the late 1800s. The exodus of 600 people from across the Outer Hebrides in April 1923 was, in many respects, more hopeful, yet the void left by young men and women seeking brighter futures when steamships SS *Metagama* and SS *Marloch* sailed from Stornoway and Lochboisdale to Canada scarred the islands deeply.

Economic forecasts for the next 30 years suggest the outmigration of young people remains a threat to the well-being of the Outer Hebrides. Islanders want the choice to remain or to leave but when the overheated property market in scenic areas collides with a shortage of sustainable year-round employment, those with so much to offer have no alternative but to settle elsewhere. Reversing this crisis is an urgent priority.

Land in community ownership supports islanders to make progressive change while honouring significant traditions. The communities of Lewis, Harris, Berneray and North Uist observe the Sabbath as a valued holy day of solemnity, according to the Fourth Commandment. The tradition is respected by non-churchgoers too, out of consideration for their friends and neighbours. Visitors are advised strongly to be aware of this and make plans accordingly; most fuel stations, food outlets and shops are closed on Sundays, however the communities of South Uist, Eriskay, Barra and Vatersay are more active.

Throughout the Outer Hebrides, crofting has undergone much change and is no longer the backbone of community life. A crofting township was defined traditionally as a minimum of four men and their families, working the land, raising livestock and, where possible, harvesting the sea. Around them grew a community of more crofters, boat-builders, shoemakers, shopkeepers, net makers, and other essential trades. The impact of a township losing anyone to war, emigration and tragedies at sea was immense.

Crofting derives from the Gaelic *croit*, meaning 'enclosed land'.

Smallholders worked alone for seasonal labours like ploughing, harrowing and sowing seeds, and came together in community teams to harvest crops, haul boats out of the water, gather sheep for shearing and cut slabs of heavy wet peat to dry through summer on the moor for use as fuel in winter. The most productive partnerships worked towards a target of cutting and stacking 1,000 peats a day, arranging them painstakingly to dry on the moor in scouring winds before returning weeks later to turn them over. Peat-cutting for fuel continues and each slab is handled at least twice before it is taken home for winter fuel, much shrunken and with little flame but great heat.

In spring women and young children traditionally went with the cattle to the moor, or pastures in the hills, while the men and older children tended crops, repaired dwellings and renewed thatched roofs. This transhumance tradition permitted grazing land in the township to recover while the family cow produced plentiful milk and fattened up on lush fresh growth. The women and children lived in shielings or *àirighean*, simple stone buildings with turf roofs built beside a source of fresh water. Here they made stores of butter and cheese for winter. The flit at the end of the summer saw the community and livestock regroup in the township.

Full-time crofters are rare now; many islanders work several jobs. It is not unusual to hear crofting described as an expensive hobby. Calls for legislative reform to address the crisis of absentee crofters, neglected croft land and sales of former crofts at eye-watering prices beyond the reach of local people grow ever louder.

GOOD TO KNOW

For anyone considering a visit to the Outer Hebrides, I hope these insights gleaned over many years and through all seasons will prove useful.

Kindness abounds in the islands, and communities warmly welcome intrepid and considerate visitors. Popular tourist routes include The Hebridean Way long-distance itinerary for walkers and cyclists through ten magnificent islands, and the Hebridean Whale Trail.

In whatever way you choose to discover the moors, sea lochs, white

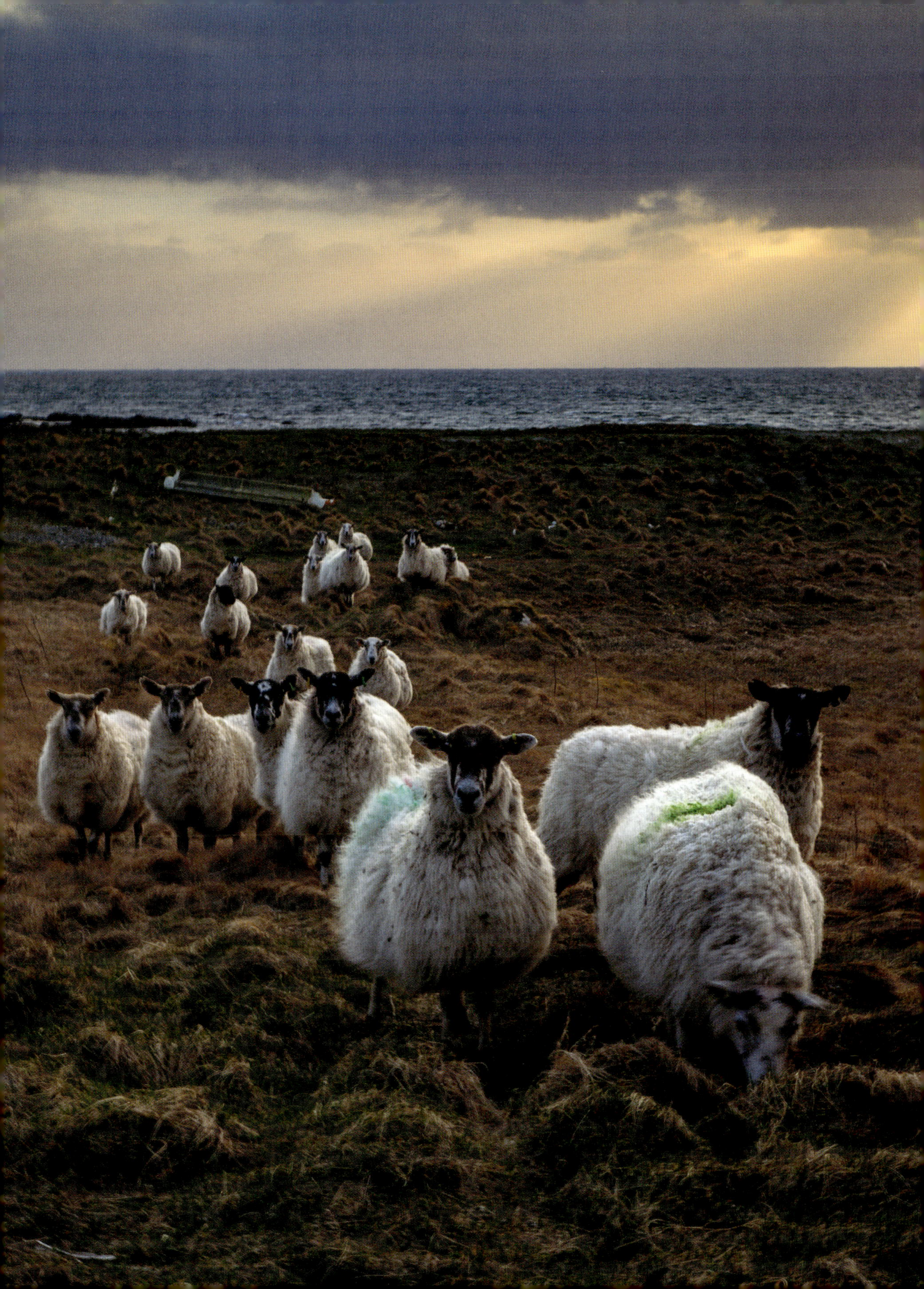

sand beaches, rugged coast, dramatic uplands, wildflower machair, tidal islets and mind-blowing archaeological sites, please resist any temptation to hurtle around, skimming the surface and ticking off a list. Far more rewarding to travel gently and connect more deeply. The experience is life affirming and rewarding.

I feel that full and frank disclosure of the weather is an important responsibility, but please, don't let that put you off visiting because the elemental drama and speed of change is awesome. The Outer Hebrides archipelago is shaped by a maritime climate. The great ocean gap of 3,000 miles between the west coast of Lewis and neighbours across the Atlantic is a playground for dynamic weather systems that make landfall in many guises. Some are ponderous and overstay their welcome, others are balmy or ferocious and fleeting. With high rainfall and strong gales, the islands are among the windiest places in Europe and the shores are among the most vulnerable. Rugged parts of mainland Scotland may boast four seasons in a day, but the islands trump that easily with four seasons an hour.

The extraordinary climate is a wise and magnificent teacher. I have learned acceptance, flexibility and resilience when plans have changed suddenly because ferries were detained and causeways closed due to high seas and strong winds. The Gaelic proverb *Am fear a bhios fada aig an aiseag, gheibh e thairis uaireigin* affirms that there may well be a long wait at the ferry, but the crossing will happen sometime.

Island weather is an invitation to seize life by the moment, to make the most of early mornings and long light nights, and to remember that the storm will pass. Through a learning curve of cursing and swooning, I have grown to appreciate the moods and seasons of the wild Atlantic seaboard and I feel so grateful for it.

The roller coaster may deter travellers seeking solid sunshine, but intrepid souls are rewarded massively with unforgettable experiences: fast-moving storms seen off by glorious sunshine, pink glowing sunsets on the Atlantic, scarlet sunrises on the Minch, huge cloudscapes, mesmerising merry dancers of the aurora borealis, glittering galaxies in skies untainted by light pollution and long summer days of warmth and midnight sun.

To prepare for this rare feast, it is best to dress appropriately. Waterproof jackets and boots repay the investment. Trekking sandals are ideal for adventures across mile upon mile of spectacular white shell beaches. With respect to island beasties, a midge head net is unglamorous but effective.

A great backpack is invaluable to stash binoculars, detailed maps, sun cream, a towel for impromptu swims, and food and drink. Take a head torch to explore caves and experience night-time strolls in remote places without streetlights. Walking poles are handy for the hills and useful for testing the depth of seawater channels on expeditions to tidal islands. Surfboards, bodyboards, stand-up paddleboards, kayaks and kites are always fun.

Studies reveal that the mild and damp Hebridean climate provides ideal conditions for infected ticks which cause Lyme disease, so be sure to carry a tick remover. For bad-weather delays, the creature comforts of a good book, tasty treats, cosy car rug and flask of hot chocolate help get me through.

Many island roads are narrow single-track carriageways with passing places. Please be aware fully of how passing places are designed to be used before you set off because these routes are lifelines to scattered communities. The smooth flow of traffic is critical for everyday activities of work, school, medical appointments and more. Moreover, the driver behind may be a coastguard, doctor or voluntary firefighter who is not

HEBRIDEAN JOURNEY

in an official vehicle. When slow-moving holiday traffic fails to use passing places properly, or refuses to pull over and allow other vehicles to overtake, the impact harms the community at large. Please do recognise the importance of learning how to use passing places promptly and appropriately before you embark on your trip. Your kindness and consideration will be appreciated.

Your Hebridean adventure awaits, and I wish you much happy island-going.

Apply Handbrake
And Switch Off Engine

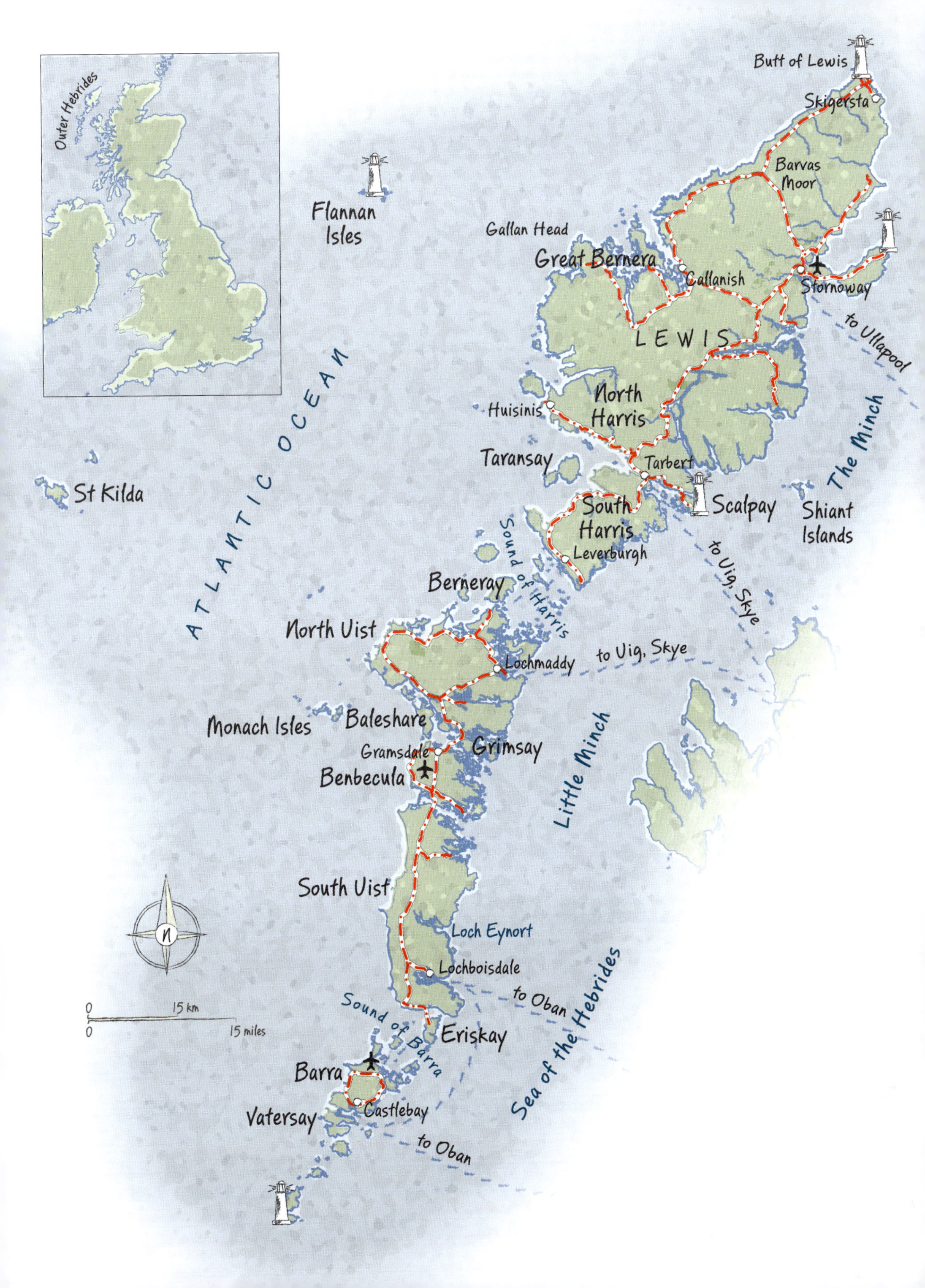

Outer Hebrides
Butt of Lewis
Skigersta
Barvas Moor
Flannan Isles
Gallan Head
Great Bernera
Callanish
Stornoway
LEWIS
to Ullapool
North Harris
Huisinis
ATLANTIC OCEAN
The Minch
Taransay
Tarbert
St Kilda
South Harris
Scalpay
Shiant Islands
Sound of Harris
Leverburgh
to Uig, Skye
Berneray
North Uist
Lochmaddy
to Uig, Skye
Monach Isles
Baleshare
Grimsay
Gramsdale
Benbecula
Little Minch
South Uist
n
Loch Eynort
Lochboisdale
to Oban
Sound of Barra
0
15 km
0
15 miles
Eriskay
Sea of the Hebrides
Barra
Castlebay
Vatersay
to Oban

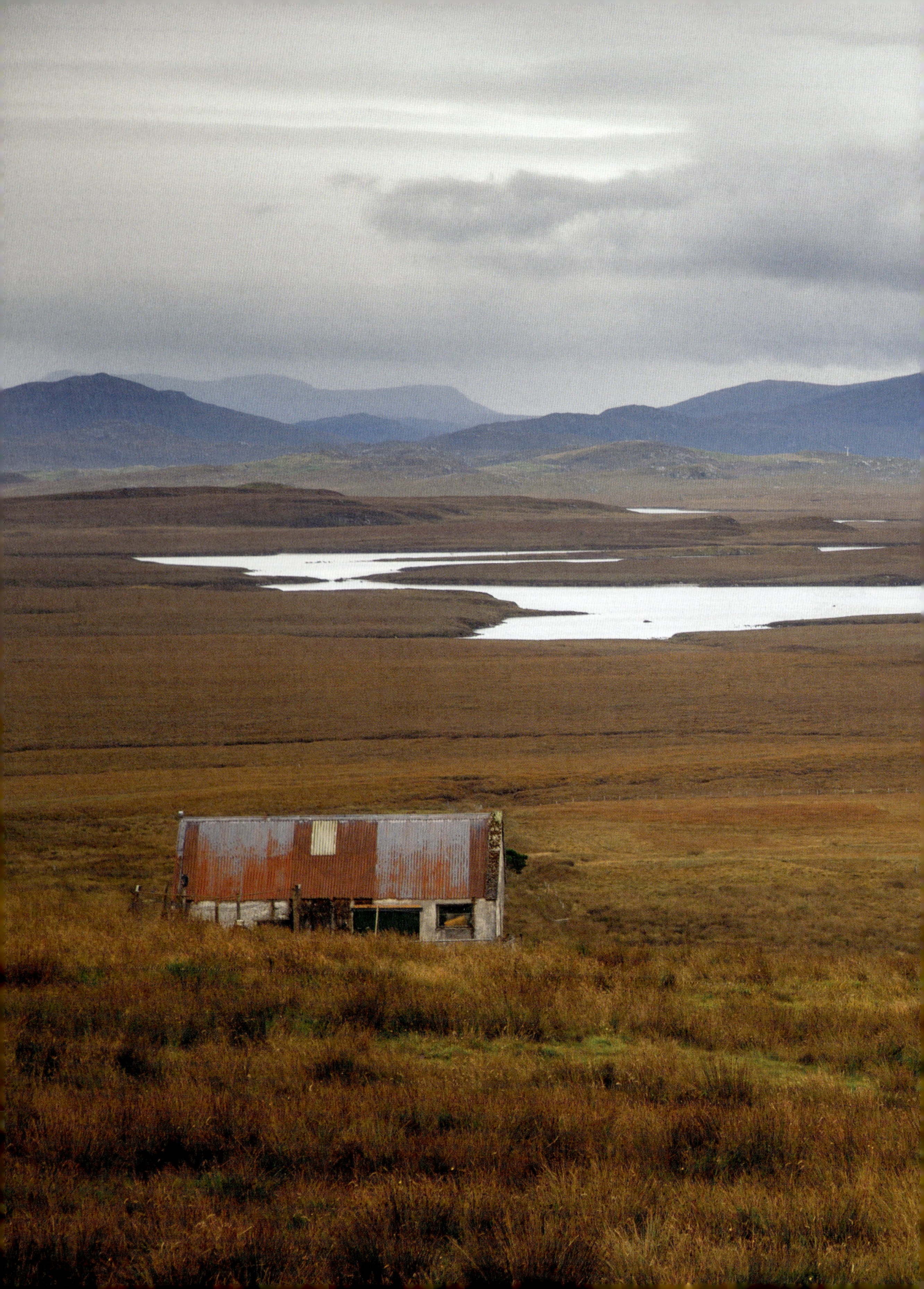

PART ONE
Lewis and Harris

Butt of Lewis
Eoropie
Dun Eistean
Traigh Shanndaigh
Knockaird
Habost
Port of Ness
Aird Dell
Lionel
Skigersta
Melbost Borve
Filiscleitir
Borve
0
5 km
0
5 miles
Clach an Truseil
Shader
Steinacleit
A857
Barvas
Barvas Moor
Arnol
Tom Mor Urrahag
Bragar
Shawbost
Tolsta Head
Tolsta
A858
B895
Gearrannan
Aird Liamisiadair
A857
Carloway
Loch Carloway
Ben Bragar
Lewis
Back
Coll
Brevig
Tiumpan Head
Tolsta Chaolais
Broad Bay
Loch Roag
Portnaguran
Aird Tong
Portvoller
Breasclete
Shulishader
Sheshader
Callanish
Stornoway
Garrabost
Eye Peninsula
Bayble
Knock
Achamore
A859
Arnish Moor
Arnish Point
to Ullapool
The Minch

Stornoway to Skigersta

Sailing by Caledonian MacBrayne ferry from Ullapool on the northwest coast of mainland Scotland to Stornoway on the island of Lewis is a very special way to arrive in the capital of the Outer Hebrides.

Island-going feels a rite of passage. The ferry, belly full of passengers, vehicles, livestock and other island necessities, steams from the shelter of Loch Broom to the open water of the Minch. On a gentle day, cavorting dolphins and diving white gannets may escort the vessel through the blissful Summer Isles archipelago backed by the iconic mountains of Assynt; the thrill is wonderful. On stormy winter crossings when ferocious gales summon mighty walls of water, the sense of adventure tends to dissipate into lurching nausea. Happily, Stornoway is but a couple of hours away.

On the approach to the largest settlement in the Outer Hebrides, the ferry rounds the stumpy lighthouse and former coastal battery at Arnish Point before executing an impressive churning white-water reverse to berth at the ferry terminal. The loudspeaker invitation to disembark heralds a flood to the exit doors, and the excited sense of arrival is palpable.

The Outer Hebrides archipelago is known alternatively as the Long Island and Innse Gall, meaning 'The Island of Strangers', a Gaelic reference to Norse settlers whose legacy percolates still. The number of inhabited islands in the group has fallen steeply; many are empty of people through circumstances of extreme hardship. Mailboats no longer call but crofters from neighbouring islands ferry sheep across for lush summer grazing and day trippers land in search of paradise beaches and romantic ruins. Experts arrive to assess flora, fauna, the impact of climate crisis and the archaeology of lost communities.

Dreadful times have left deep scars throughout the islands. Entire communities were uprooted during the Highland Clearances, which began in the mid to late 18th century. Estate owners dispossessed agricultural tenants of their land and homes to make way for the more lucrative business of sheep farming. Families were funnelled forcibly onto crowded emigrant ships bound for territories in Canada, their passages paid by a laird eager to be rid of them swiftly. Anyone too old or too ill for the hideous voyage was left behind.

War also brought devastation to the Outer Hebrides. The impact of healthy young men and women leaving clachans, or small villages, whose survival depended on collective efforts to harvest the land and sea, caused many crofting communities to collapse. The social and economic devastation caused by the First World War contributed to mass emigration from the islands in the 1920s.

Stornoway grew from fishing village to island capital around the deep natural harbour that attracted foreign attention. Viking settlers arrived from Scandinavia around AD 800 and stayed for 500 years. Oliver Cromwell's troops garrisoned the town in 1653 to see off the threat of Dutch invasion. A more friendly invasion occurred in the late 1800s when fleets of visiting vessels sailed in pursuit of great summer shoals of shiny herring that rose to the surface of the sea after sunset and before dawn. By seven o'clock in the morning, fishing stations all around the basin thronged with jostling boats and crews unloading the catch of silver darlings. Nimble-fingered island women worked in groups of three to gut and clean the fish. The tallest lassie of the trio, with the longest reach, layered them precisely in barrels and salted them for curing.

Through the frenzy of herring season, Stornoway wharves were awash with fishers, teams of skilled lassies, coopers hammering barrels, labourers with horses and carts, and fish merchants negotiating sharp deals. The heavy summer air was pungent with fumes from dozens of kippering houses. Cargo boats sailed back and forth to Liverpool, especially; from there, barrels of cured herring were exported throughout the British empire. Vessels from Russia and countries on the Baltic Sea called for herring too. When the lucrative shiny shoals swam onward, the fleet, lassies, coopers and merchants, followed in hot pursuit, making huge seasonal encampments in the harbours of Lerwick, Wick, Fraserburgh, Eyemouth, Yarmouth and Lowestoft.

The herring export trade collapsed during the Russian Revolution and the First World War, yet the contribution of the oily fish to the growth of Stornoway is reflected in a trio of the silver darlings on the town coat of arms. Today the catch is largely whitefish and shellfish, and fish processing is altogether different.

Public statues of women are regrettably rare, yet two bronze herring lassies by Virginia Hutchison and Charles S. Engebretsen grace the Stornoway quays at North Beach and South Beach, honouring the contribution of the pioneering island women who migrated for work around the British coast.

Traces of the herring boom remain around the town. The site of the former fish mart, built in 1894 to accommodate 250 people employed in the trade, is now the ferry terminal, with distinct architectural echoes of the former incumbent. Today the fleet lands the catch beside the

Beauty Spot

On Stornoway seafront, An Lanntair arts centre is a lively and colourful hub. The airy café offers locally sourced food, art on the walls and great harbour views beyond. The neighbouring former town hall, a gracious turreted building, houses the 'Harris Tweed Story Room'. The exhibition traces the production of the unique island cloth, protected by law to the present day. Low tide in the harbour reveals *Sheol nan Iolaire*, a Scottish War Memorials Project installed on the 100th anniversary of the sinking of HMY *Iolaire*, with the loss of 201 sailors on 1 January 1919, one of the worst peacetime maritime disasters in UK waters. The poignant installation on 280 wooden poles outlining a ship on South Beach, between Pier 1 and Pier 2, honours each of the men on board the *Iolaire* when she sank further along the coast on the Beasts of Holm rocks, desperately close to the shore. Discover the location and more about this catastrophic tragedy on page 55.

modern fish mart close by the ice machine on North Beach Quay.

Happily, the distinctive kippery fug of herrings on tenterhooks still wafts along the shore from the Stornoway Smokehouse on Shell Street. A sweet small shoal by sculptor Sam MacDonald is set into the pavement at the intersection of Cromwell Street and Point Street, and aspects of island fishing communities feature in murals by Iain Brady at Perceval Square and South Beach Street.

Opposite the harbour, in the gracious grounds of Lews Castle, a white marble statue of a woman in flowing robes occupies a plinth beneath an elaborate dome. The James Matheson memorial, erected by his widow, Mary, is a tribute to the man who, according to the inscription, 'added to his Highland possession the Island of Lewis' and set about 'ameliorating the condition of the Inhabitants of that Island'. Some dispute this.

Filthy rich Matheson inspired the character of McDrug in Benjamin Disraeli's novel *Sybil*, published in 1845. The blistering narrative portrays a crisis-ridden Britain of two nations, poor and rich. Disraeli finds the origins of much obscene wealth arises out of immoral dealings. His character McDrug is 'fresh from Canton with a million of opium in each pocket'. James Matheson made his fortune from opium, peddling the narcotic produced in Britain's Indian empire to traders supplying desperately addicted people in China. His vile enterprise sparked the Opium Wars. When Chinese authorities, desperate to end mass heroin addiction, sought to block his dealing, they were crushed by Britain's military might. Chinese ports were forced to accept British traders and the sovereignty of Hong Kong was transferred to the UK.

James Matheson splashed his ill-gotten gains on the acquisition of Lewis in 1844 and determined to have a castle. Work began in 1847 on a scheme that cleared islanders' homes and rerouted long-established highways to make way for the luxury abode. Further developments were impacted by years of blight in the potato harvest that had previously produced a greater volume of food per acre than any other crop. The Victorian laird responded with relief schemes and economic projects to generate work and income for stricken tenants. His industrial schemes included brickworks, harbour developments and an extraordinary mission to distil the natural resource of peat from vast bogs across the island into oil at his showpiece Lewis Chemical Works. The scheme started promisingly but nosedived when cheaper American oil came to market.

James and Mary Matheson were childless, and upon the laird's demise in 1878 his widow supervised the Lewis estate. On Mary's death in 1896 the island went to family members, who put it up for sale in 1918. Community ownership of land was unheard of at the time and so wealthy individuals acquired islands with ease. Enter Lord Leverhulme, a dynamic industrialist, soap magnate and business visionary with barely any understanding of the Hebridean crofting tradition.

The peer arrived in Lewis with revolution in mind. Fixing his sights on the untapped potential of Hebridean waters, he acquired a fleet of trawlers, built overland transport links between Stornoway and outlying island harbours and commissioned processing and canning factories.

Curiosity

Stornoway Museum, in the modern, purpose-built extension to Lews Castle, offers fascinating insights into island life. The elegant, wooded pleasure grounds of specimen trees planted by former lairds are now community owned and free to visit. Enjoy gentle strolls and picnic spots with elevated views through the trees over the town, harbour and newly built Newton Marina for visiting yachts. Robert Alfred Colby Cubbin, a marine engineer from Liverpool, built a well in the grounds to supply his converted steam trawler yacht. On sailing trips to the islands, the eccentric recluse is reported to have enjoyed a diet of buns and cream cakes washed down by spring water, hence the well. Cubbin died aged 49, leaving monies to his mother with instructions to build four new lifeboats, including one for the island of Barra.

People from outlying villages who tramped barefoot across vast tracts of peat moor to visit Stornoway stopped at the Allt na Brog burn running through castle grounds. Here they washed dirty feet and put on the town shoes carried wisely around their neck, safe from the boggy squelch. In translation from Gaelic, Allt na Brog is the 'Shoe Burn'.

In towns across Britain, he established the MacFisheries chain of fishmongers. Leverhulme's misguided expectation was that islanders would wholly subscribe to his fisheries revolution; what he failed to consider was that full-time work in his factories meant abandoning work on the family croft and this was unacceptable, especially to ex-servicemen who went to war with the promise of a plot of land and homes fit for heroes on return. The situation was already tense when the land was not forthcoming after the end of the war in November 1918.

On the outskirts of Stornoway, the imposing Isle of Lewis war memorial rises 85 feet from Cnoc nan Uan hill. A staircase within the Scots baronial tower offers distant views to the four island parishes, Stornoway, Barvas, Lochs and Uig. According to the Imperial War Museum, when the ratio of those killed in war is compared to the census, the islanders of Lewis lost twice as many people as the rest of the British Isles. Despite their service, the surviving war heroes' bounty was not delivered because croft land was in short supply.

While the government procrastinated on its promise, frustrated islanders took matters into their own hands and organised land-grab raids on Leverhulme's estate. Tensions escalated and the government passed the 1919 Land Settlement (Scotland) Act which created the opportunity of compulsory purchase of land for new crofts. When the Board of Agriculture acquired farms on Leverhulme's estate in 1922, the division of land created over 100 new crofts for the community. The 1919 legislation continues to support contemporary community land-buyout projects.

Lord Leverhulme halted his schemes and withdrew from Lewis, granting much of his domain to The Stornoway Trust, founded expressly in 1923 to take on stewardship of the estate. The Trust is Scotland's oldest community landlord, administered by ten trustees with responsibility for 69,000 acres.

The journey from Stornoway to the Bridge to Nowhere at New Tolsta follows the east coast B895 road to reveal the extent of Leverhulme's plan to improve transport between Stornoway and fishing ports in the isolated north-east of the island, and how it came to a shuddering end.

Leaving the harbour town behind, the B895 rounds the muddy estuary where the Laxadale and Blackwater rivers flow into the gaping mouth of Broad Bay. Stealthy fishers from Fideach Angling Club hunt sea trout and salmon in the Steinish and Tong pools while the bright lights of Stornoway Airport illuminate the runway on the opposite shore. The country road visits Aird Tong headland, birthplace of Mary Anne Macleod who left Lewis for New York in 1930 to seek work as a domestic servant. Six years later she married property developer Frederick Trump, one of the most eligible men in the city. Mary's ambition was matched by that of her son Donald, who became the 45th President of the United States in January 2017.

Surfers camp in sandy dunes on Coll beach. Beyond lies Brevig harbour, opened in 1995 to accommodate boats returning from northern fishing grounds, avoiding the alternative perilous route to Stornoway. A poignant memorial cairn honours fishers drowned in the Minch and Broad Bay from 1855 onwards, the year the Statutory Registers of Births, Deaths and Marriages were introduced. Among them is Donald Trump's great, great grandfather, Donald Smith.

Ironically, Brevig's new harbour failed to provide sanctuary; the design caused poor visibility at the entrance and heavy swell after prolonged northerly winds. Extensive remedial works have proved necessary. Signs on the bank of the Gress River remind anglers that Sunday fishing is not permitted. Lewis is a predominantly Protestant island and general respect for the Sabbath day of rest is woven into island life, whether people are religious or not. Between two bridges on the river stands a memorial honouring the Gress land raiders, declaring them 'heroes of the district'. The monument is one of four throughout Lewis; the raiders of Pairc, Aignish and Reef have striking tributes too.

The war memorial at Back is beside the Free Church renowned for the extraordinary sacred tradition of Gaelic psalm singing, a form of indigenous music in Scotland. The congregation repeats lines from the Psalms of David led by the precentor who delivers them solo in Gaelic first. Free expression is encouraged. The haunting sound of this worship ebbs and flows like the sea. The tradition was introduced to permit everyone, including those who cannot read, to participate in their own way.

On approach to Tolsta Head, the B895 climbs high above Tolsta Glen. A branch road slithers steeply to the wooded shore, where, in 1843, five families displaced by the laird from the Pairc district of Lewis

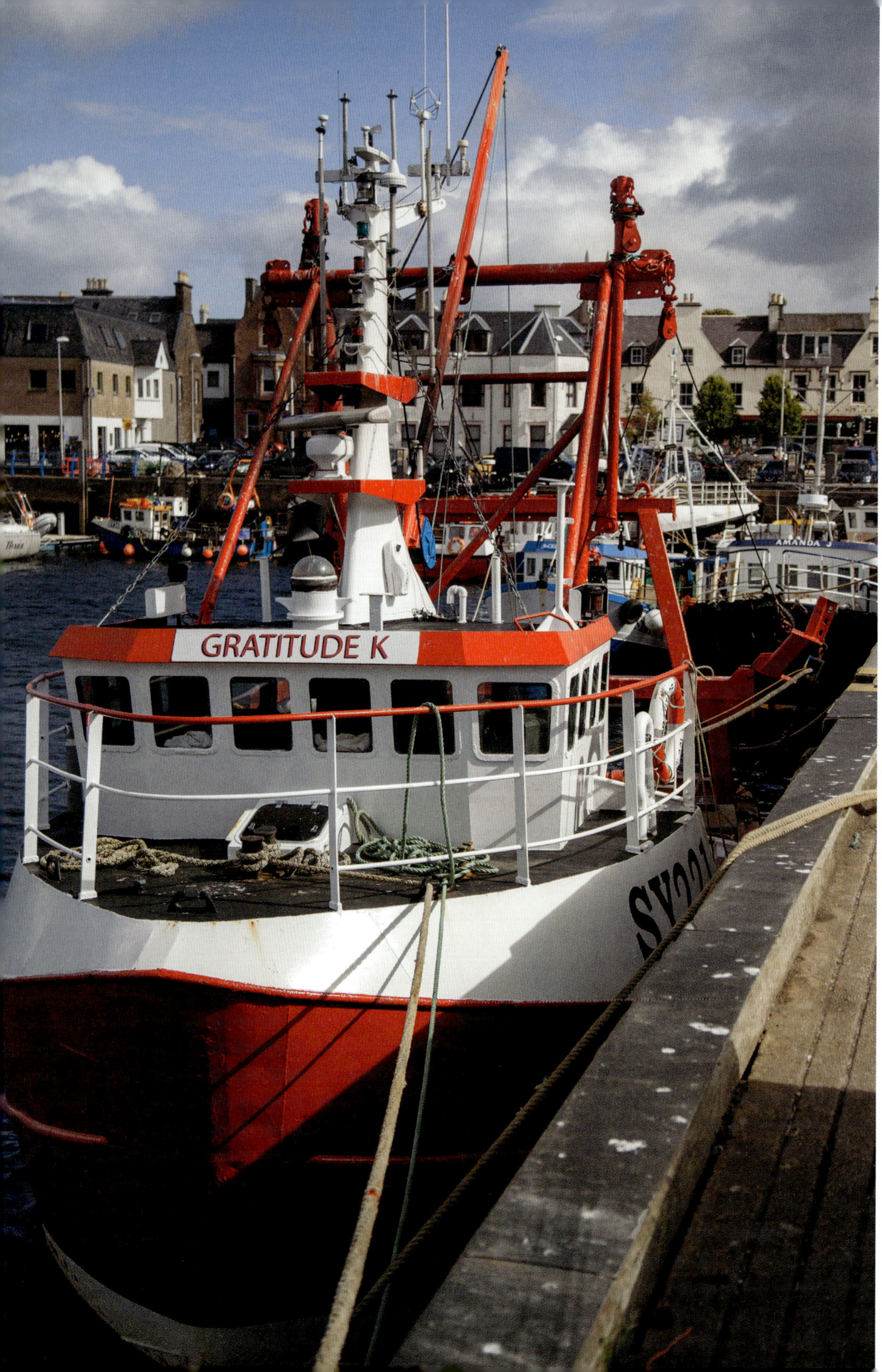
GRATITUDE K
AMANDA J

established a new settlement in the previously uninhabited glen. At North Tolsta the community stores, Buth Tholastaidh, is a great pit stop for post office services, picnic supplies, home-grown plants and recordings by local musicians.

Towards the shore, information panels set the scene for the thrilling Tolsta Heritage Trail to the Port of Ness. Coastal views to Tiumpan Head lighthouse at the tip of the Eye peninsula, beyond Stornoway, are spectacular; the parade of iconic mountains on the north-west mainland is magnificent, especially in snow. A steep lane winds to Giordal beach, more intimate and secluded than Tolsta's famous Traigh Mhor, Gaelic for 'Big Beach'. The aptly named swathe lives up to its name, a massive runway of golden sand perfect for beach rides with the local pony-trekking centre.

Two ancient hillforts overlook the lovely sands of Garry beach, yet the most eye-catching structure in the landscape is the lonely concrete Bridge to Nowhere. The redundant roadway commissioned by Leverhulme was intended to facilitate speedy delivery of fresh fish landed at the Port of Ness to processing factories in Stornoway. When the tycoon's dream died, the bridge became a white elephant. Yet this crossing place is where the Tolsta Heritage Trail truly takes off. The hike through 14 miles of spectacular coastal scenery is exhilarating. The natural fortress of Dun Othail lends further drama along the way, rising nearly 200 feet high, separated from the mainland by a steep ravine called Nicolson's Leap.

The trail reveals how women, children and cattle from Lionel relocated each summer to Filiscleitir where they lived on ancestral grazing land beside the burn in *bothan-àirigh*, or shieling huts, with turf roofs. After winter months indoors, the community summer flit to the moor was a joyous event known as *An Iomraich*. Families trooped and clanked out of the clachan, laden with essentials, pots, pans, bed linen, a few decorative items for homely touches and dry peats for fuel. While precious pastures at home regenerated, the cattle munched shoots of moorland heather. With their plentiful flavoursome milk, the women made butter and cheese, burying the store deep in cool peat for use in winter.

Sadly, the evocative evidence of this Scottish transhumance tradition is disappearing fast. Early stone shielings are tumbled overgrown mounds

Curiosity

Dramatic clifftop ruins near Filiscleitir are the remnants of an extraordinary dream home. John Nicolson emigrated from Lewis to America and became a member of the Plymouth Brethren. He married a wealthy American wife and returned to build Dune Tower, a grand pile with a mission hall known as Dune Chapel. The Filiscleitir shieling community attended summer services here until 1930.

in the moor. Some later wooden huts cling on, weather-beaten and in tatters. Others have been revived with loving care. These moorland retreats offer escape for peace and quiet, or ceilidh nights under the stars.

The Tolsta to Ness Coastal Heritage Trail tracks onward to Lionel, passing a white obelisk on the grassy mound at Meall Geal. The monument honours amateur geologist John Wilson Dougal, the plaque depicting a small rock hammer. The route continues through peat banks carved into the moor by generations of crofting families. Traditionally, going to the peats was a community activity. Folk shared their labour and passed their cutting and stacking techniques, Gaelic stories and songs from one generation to the next. Fires were lit, large kettles filled with fresh water and a handful of tea leaves for communal lunch breaks with home-grown potatoes and freshly caught herrings. Dwindling numbers of islanders work the family peat banks now that alternative fuels are available.

A skinny lane dips to the coast at Skigersta, a name that sounds like a spell, and indeed there is magic at this shore. A fiercely brave, tiny harbour huddles in the cleft of a cliff, staring into the great gaping jaws of the ocean. The courage of the Skigersta fishing community reminds me of David and Goliath. Without adequate space in the snug harbour, a line of hauled-out boats wait patiently on the steep slipway for their return to the sea.

Across Barvas Moor to the Butt of Lewis

To journey through the interior of Lewis is to experience one of the most extensive and intact areas of moorland in the world. Few other places compare, and they are in South America, Russia and New Zealand.

The great spread of Barvas Moor is a rare natural asset of huge value. Peat is the biggest single store of carbon in the UK, comprising the equivalent of 20 years of all UK CO_2 emissions. The precious bog is a boot-sucking squelch of hags and hollows, utterly filthy and exhausting to cross on foot. In sharp contrast, the smooth A857 highway skims the terrain at full speed.

Zooming from Stornoway through miles and miles of treeless expanse to reach the Lewis west side feels a powerful transition. Heralding the North Atlantic Ocean, the Welcome Inn filling station makes a great pit stop for fuel, groceries, newspapers, beer, wine, spirits, and all those handy household bits you didn't know you needed until you saw them. It is also the headquarters of Hebridean Surf, offering tuition and kit to ride outstanding waves.

Barvas has become a hot spot for a rare bird that is a trophy on many a twitcher's list. Male corncrakes fly in from Africa around mid April and disappear promptly into the dense cover of yellow flag iris, cow parsley and nettles. Here they await the arrival of the females. Corncrakes may be notoriously difficult to spot, but the males' crooning gives them away. Their rasping *crex crex* call resounds between midnight and

Curiosity

Lumpy Barvas Ware pottery is made from local clay containing impurities like sand and gravel. Traditionally women shaped plump storage pots known as craggans and fired them gently in the embers of a peat fire before building up the heat. The rustic craggans were dipped in a glaze of milk to make them less porous. With the development of tourism in the Hebrides, enterprising villagers sold distinctive Barvas Ware souvenirs. From the 1860s to the 1930s their designs mimicked finer china tea sets.

Stay well clear of an entirely different kind of firing at Barvas Sands Range. Red flags signal the danger of live firing across an area of land and sea used by the armed forces.

3 a.m., and if the weather is calm some give it laldy through daytime too. With the decline of some traditional crofting methods, the noisy corncrake has suffered habitat loss in the Outer Hebrides. Islanders are working with the RSPB to support the rare birds by maintaining areas of long vegetation for cover and delaying the silage cut until August to protect nests.

From Upper Barvas to the Port of Ness 56,000 acres of coast, agricultural land and moor have been in the community ownership of the Galson Estate Trust since 2007. The Trust manages 22 villages with five main aims: to alleviate poverty; to advance education, training and sustainable development; to provide and improve housing; to develop communication links for the benefit of all the community; and to protect and conserve the environment. The bilingual website, in Gaelic and English, is a rich resource for locals and visitors.

The Clach an Truseil standing stone rises some 20 feet above ground, impressive but lonely since the companion circle of prehistoric stones was dispersed down the centuries into neighbouring fields, walls and buildings. The monolith, reputedly the tallest in Scotland, is dwarfed by new landmarks, a clutch of whirring wind turbines that generate energy for homes across the Galson Estate.

The coast known locally as the west side is especially rich in prehistoric sites. Some yell from the landscape, others are more enigmatic and require great leaps of imagination. The community of Upper and Lower Shader sprawls around roadside Loch an Duin with obvious ruins of an island fort accessed by a stony causeway. The age and origin of the site at nearby Steinacleit is less certain. In the 1920s crofters discovered what was at first considered to be a stone circle, experts now deem it an ancient farmstead.

Cyclists on the Hebridean Way, a great adventure of 185 miles through ten islands, appreciate the civilised comfort of Borve House Hotel. There's further gentle shelter in the colourful burnside garden at nearby Borgh Pottery. Two bridges, old and new, span the Borve

River. The first structure, superseding stepping stones and a ford, was such a novelty that the crofting community used it as a platform for their dances.

Near Melbost Borve shore, a ruined and overgrown chapel, burial ground and holy well are dedicated to St Brigid. In the Celtic tradition, wells are sacred places of flow and healing, they connect our visible world with the sphere of the divine. Brigid's identity emerges from the rare fusion of a pagan fire goddess with a Christian saint, and she is honoured in both spheres. She is especially associated with the Hebrides and oystercatchers, black and white birds with flame-red beaks. They are known in Gaelic as *gille-brìghde*, the 'servant of Brigid' because they guided her coracle safely across the Irish Sea to Hebridean shores where she established sacred sites. The feast day of Christian St Brigid, 1 February, coincides with the pagan fire festival of Imbolc which celebrates goddess Brigid sweeping her wand across the icy land to bring forth the light and new growth of spring.

It was on the North Atlantic shore at Aird Dell that crofter Murdo MacIver unearthed a treasure trove while cutting peat for fuel. Two bronze leaf-shaped swords, from the eighth century, emerged, one after the other, in 1891 and 1892. The rocky west coast becomes more frequently sandy beyond the friendly Cross Inn, a happy hub in the eponymous township. Ferocious storm waves shift and sculpt dunes, and coastal walks are massively exhilarating when the towering swell thunders to shore. The mayhem is unpredictable; stay at a safe distance.

Cross Stores is a wonderful Hebridean institution. Under one roof you'll find groceries, a bottle shop, locally laid eggs, locally made cakes, takeaway food, a gamut of essential household items and a kitchen den where Ness black pudding is made by hand. The origins of the savoury pudding emerge from the ingenuity of crofting families who used every bit of their livestock to ensure they had enough food for winter. Blood, intestines and oatmeal are the foundation of the delicacy flavoured with spices and herbs. The community laundrette and charity shop beside the Cross Stores are especially popular with touring visitors.

Enterprise abounds in island communities. In rural Habost crofter Norman Murray pioneered a lemonade factory and Roderick Murray made *Briosgaidean Roigean*, or Ness Biscuits. Discover their innovations and other aspects of north Lewis life at Comunn Eachdraidh Nis. The modern museum and exhibition space in the former school building is bright and welcoming. Homebaking in the café is a treat, especially on Fridays when afternoon tea is served at tables dressed in white linen. Reservations are advised. A pamphlet offering a self-guided coastal walk of around 90 minutes through the colourful wildflowers and historical features of Habost machair is available from the shop.

This atmospheric northern district of Lewis rewards exploration on foot. Before reaching the Port of Ness, take the road to Eoropie where Traigh Shanndaigh, one of the Hebrides' most spectacular beaches, is backed by one of the Hebrides' most spectacular children's playparks. Swings, slides and tunnels mark the start of the Butt of Lewis Circuit

Walk, a great way to experience the coast and sparse, vibrant, modern community living alongside occasional vintage tractors and traditional peat stacks. Clean North Atlantic air imbued with salty energy is utterly invigorating.

I smile at the memory of a storm-blasted encounter on the hillside above the Eoropie shore with three kindly strangers by the name of Donald. As I walked along their lane, sodden and bulky in my winter gear, barely able to peer through dripping long hair plastered over my face, one of the elderly Donalds quipped on the howling wind, 'What's a glamorous lady like you doing here?' and proceeded to invite me in for warming tea.

The narrow coast road winding to the Butt of Lewis visits sheltered sands at Stoth beach where building materials were landed by boat for the construction of the red-brick lighthouse designed by David Stevenson and built between 1859 and 1862. The tower rises over

Beauty Spot

On wildflower machair overlooking the glorious sands of Eoropie Bay, the Cunndal memorial recalls a devastating tragedy that occurred in March 1885 when the small and remote community lost 12 fishermen in a North Atlantic storm. The youngest was 22, the oldest 62.

HEBRIDEAN JOURNEY

120 feet, a reassuring beacon for vessels rounding the northernmost tip of the Outer Hebrides on shipping routes between the Baltic States, Britain and mainland Europe. The exposed outpost is the start or the end of the Hebridean Way, depending on direction of travel.

Turning inland, the B8014 jogs through narrow strips of croft land. A small gate between two plots opens to a path through a field of sheep. Here the tiny church of St Moluag, in the care of the Episcopal Church, is encircled by stone walls. The peaceful site was one of the most important religious centres in the Outer Hebrides during the 12th to 15th centuries. Irish missionary St Moluag is credited with bringing Christianity to Lewis. The restored chapel remains without electricity. Services are held by candlelight.

Before reaching the Port of Ness, take a moment to appreciate the home of Ness Football Club in the peaty moorland landscape. From a distance, the lovingly tended pitch glows like shining emerald. The team battles the

Curiosity

At Knockaird a track through croft land reaches the Clach Stein standing stones, close by a concrete water tower, and the ruins of Dun Eistean, a medieval island fort atop dramatic sea cliffs. Visitors must cross a caged footbridge over a daunting chasm of churning waves. The wildly exposed outpost of stone-built huts with turf roofs was the stronghold of Clan Morrison. They were certainly made of stern stuff.

elements in shirts as green as the wind-blasted salt-sprayed quadrant.

On approach to the Port of Ness a large barometer in the garden wall of Ocean Villa on the cliff high above the harbour served to inform the fishing community of the changing weather. The Ness Fishery Memorial honours 96 local men who lost their lives at sea between 1835 and 1900. Poignant information panels celebrate the local tradition of longline fishing and commemorate tragedies that shattered the isolated community.

Sulasgeir is a tiny, exposed island, some 40 miles north of the Butt of Lewis. Every August, ten men from Ness maintain the tradition of sailing in a fishing boat to hunt guga on the windswept wave-lashed skerry, which takes its name from the solan goose, or gannet. *Guga* is the Gaelic term for adolescent gannets, plump and unable to fly. The seabirds nest on the rocks and the legally sanctioned hunt permits the killing of 2,000 guga by traditional methods. The salty meat is considered a delicacy in the islands. For the men of Ness, the dangerous weeks on uninhabited Sulasgeir are a historic rite of passage. Witnessing their mothers, partners and children wave them off from the quayside is an extraordinary experience.

HEBRIDEAN JOURNEY

Time Travels to Callanish and Beyond

It is easy to feel like a time traveller in the atmospheric landscape of Lewis, which flows, thrillingly, from one era to another. This route offers spine-tingling sites of extraordinary mystery and world renown.

Achamore is the only village in Lewis that is not beside the sea. Curvaceous hills in Harris and Uig dominate the distant horizon. The sensuous profile, known locally as the Sleeping Beauty, suggests a woman lying on her back. To provide fuel for heating and cooking, local families cut peat from the surrounding moor. By the 1980s the workings of generations exposed the tip of large stones submerged in the dark, wet earth. Some ten years later, further peat cutting revealed the stones were part of a prehistoric circle some 135 feet in diameter. Experts believe the windswept site with elevated views over the lonely moor puddled with lochans was formed originally of 22 standing stones around six feet tall that fell flat through land disturbance.

The A858 highway speeds across the ocean of peat towards Loch Roag, a huge west coast sea loch comprising a host of magical islands. The surrounding shore is studded with further stones and megaliths that orbit mighty Callanish, a unique ceremonial site older than Stonehenge and the pyramids.

Until 1857 the henge at Callanish was also submerged in peat, yet the tips of protruding stones suggested a significant hidden monument. James Matheson, owner of Lewis, commissioned excavations that revealed an imposing central monolith encircled by standing stones and accessed by four avenues of standing stones. Of all the known megalithic monuments in the world, only Callanish is arranged in the form of a cross.

The mysterious design, constructed around 3,000 BC was in use for at least 2,000 years. Sometime after the first thousand years a crypt was added to the base of the central monolith. Thrilling Callanish is the focus of a deeply ritualistic landscape where our ancient forebears may have created an astronomical observatory associated with the moon. At least 15 other sites of standing stones and circles orbit the unique henge.

The energy and the enigma of the Callanish stones attract international visitors all year round. To be alone with them is sensational and

I feel immensely grateful for the experience of an unforgettable autumn evening when, for some little while, quite by chance, it was just the henge and me. As I stood in the centre circle, surrounded by tall ancient stones, sunset rays broke through the day's heavy cloud. Piercing shafts of light hit the rock, conjuring life into glittering mica particles on the surface. Suddenly it seemed I was surrounded by sparkly dance partners at an extraordinary trippy ceilidh. The Callanish Stones Visitor Centre offers many more stories of encounters with the mysterious and awesome ancient megaliths.

The Hebridean Way cycle route tracks the A858 around the shore of Loch Roag to Breasclete, a coastal community with strong links to the distant Flannan Isles some 20 miles west of Gallan Head, the most north-westerly point of Britain. Boats sailed daily from Breasclete to service the construction of a lighthouse on Eilean Mor, the largest of the Flannan Isles, known also as the Seven Hunters. The beacon came into operation in 1899, and within the first year of operation, an eerie tragedy occurred.

On 15 December 1899, the captain of a transatlantic steamship

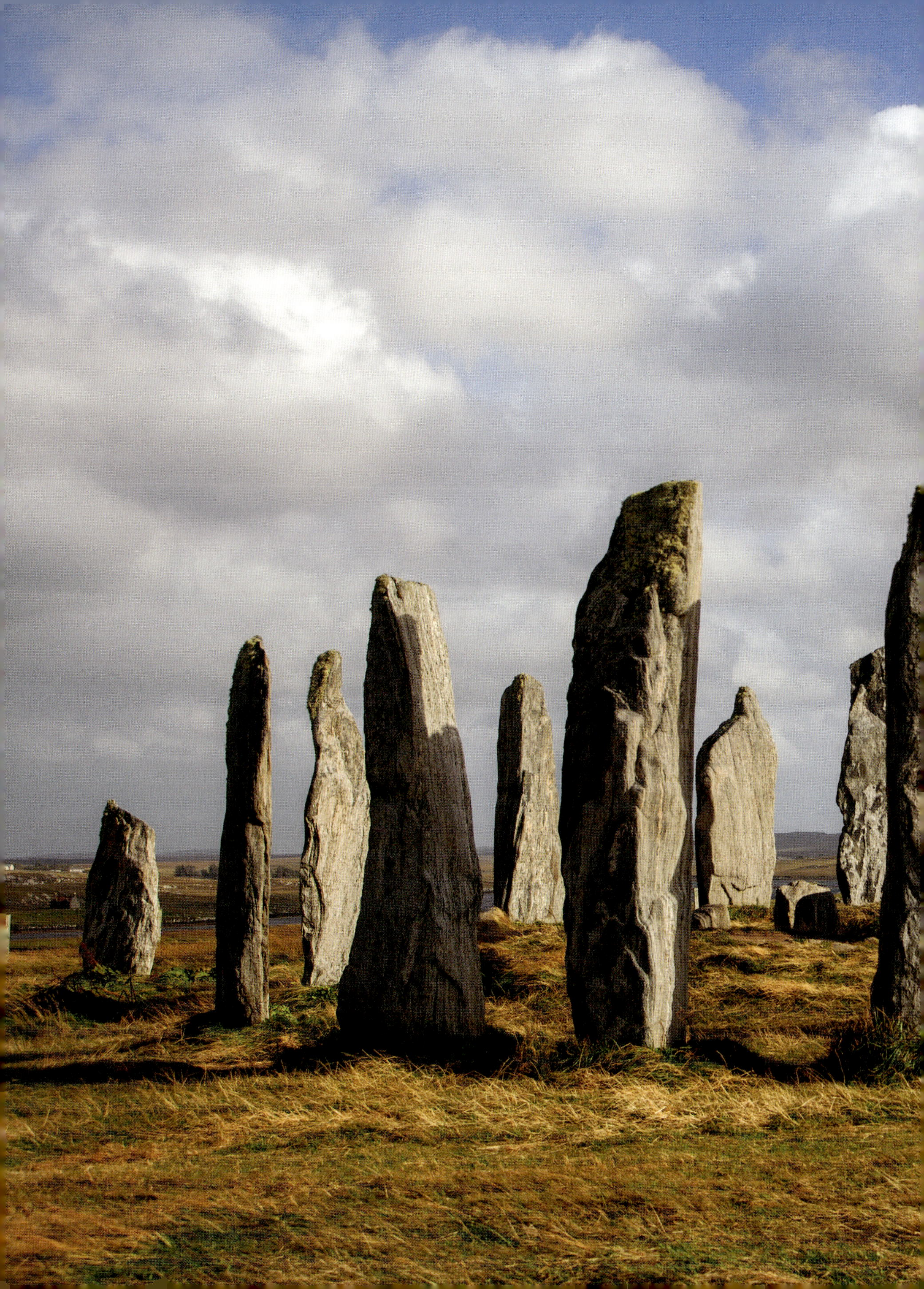

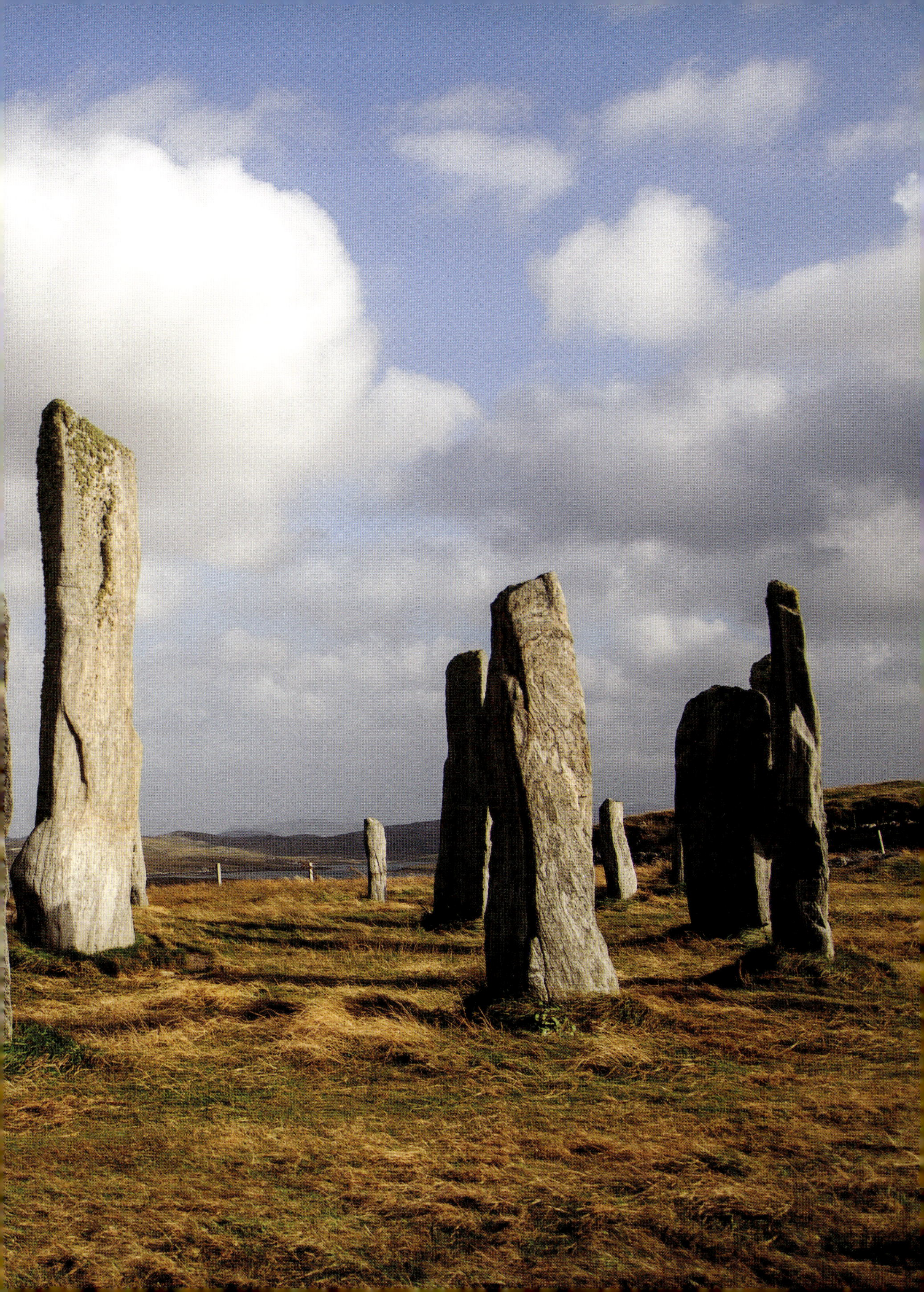

sailing from Philadelphia could not see a light on Eilean Mor and duly reported his concern to port authorities on arrival at Leith. Meanwhile, unaware of the news, the *Hesperus* relief ship sailed from Breasclete to deliver assistant light keeper Joseph Moore for a shift change. His colleague William Ross, another of the regular keepers, was on shore leave after breaking his arm at work. Donald McArthur, an occasional keeper, had replaced him.

On approach to the island, the *Hesperus* crew noted there was no flag raised to indicate landing preparations had been made, which was unusual. The captain sounded the ship's steam whistle without response. The crew fired a rocket, still without response. Landing at the east side, Joseph Moore climbed 163 perilous steps to the clifftop. Calling out the keepers' names his increasingly desperate shouts were met only by the cry of gulls. Within the lighthouse complex, Moore discovered everything in order, though a kitchen chair had been knocked over. In the lamp room the wick was trimmed, and the lenses gleamed. The last entry in the logbook, on 15 December, was without any suggestion of concern. Yet there was no sign of the keepers, James Ducat, Thomas Marshall and Donald McArthur.

Tragically the men were never found. Twisted iron handrails at the west-side landing platform offered clues to their vanishing. Dislodged rocks and contents of a supply box strewn high around the clifftop suggested almighty and deadly rogue waves had swept the keepers away. When the tragedy was made public, rumours of supernatural events abounded. These are explored at the profoundly moving Flannan Isles exhibition in the community centre at Breasclete.

Local opinion suggests that keepers Ducat and Marshall were working to secure equipment in stormy weather, both acutely aware that any loss might result in a deduction from their wages. Indeed, Marshall had previously been fined five shillings for losing his equipment in a gale, a penalty that would impact his family finances considerably. Islanders believe that Donald McArthur raced to them as immense waves smashed the island, knocking over the chair in a desperate hurry. Tragically, he too was taken.

On Breasclete shore, the memorial honouring the brave men is moving, and terrifying. A boulder of Lewisian gneiss represents Eilean Mor graced by a vulnerable lighthouse in the path of a gigantic body

FLANNAN MEMORIAL

Is sinne air ar fagal
Ri faire na soluis
A feitheamh ri dubhar na h-oidhche

This memorial is dedicated to the memory of the N.L.B. Keepers
who died on the 15th December 1900 in pursuit of their duties
James Ducat - Thomas Marshall - Donald Macarthur

Sailm 89:9 "Riaghlaidh tusa onfhadh na fairge;
'n uair a dh'eireas a tonnan, caisgidh tu iad

of water. At the Breasclete shore station, where the keepers' families lived, a decorative plaque above the door depicts a shining beacon with the Latin motto of the Northern Lighthouse board, *In Salutem Omnium*, 'For the Safety of All'.

Having served the lighthouse so faithfully, Breasclete Pier is also the landing place of more recent island businesses. A harvest of high-quality seaweed produced in the supremely clean water of Loch Roag is used in Ishga natural skincare products. The world's largest chemical manufacturer, BASF, also harvests marine products used in natural pharmaceuticals.

Sweet Tolsta Chaolais village, situated between the fresh water of Loch a' Bhaile and the briny of Loch Roag, appeared as the fictional island of Struay for the BBC children's television programme *Katie Morag*, adapted from books by Mairi Hedderwick. The Bonnet Laird walking route visits the community-owned land. The intriguing name refers to traditional headwear choices of crofters and lairds, tenant crofters in caps, known as bonnets, and lairds in deerstalkers. Thus, a bonnet laird is one who wears a bonnet and has a share in the land.

Curiosity

The war memorial beside the Mission House at Tolsta Chaolais is unique for two reasons. While other memorials commemorate the fallen from across a district, the Tolsta Chaolais monument was funded by the community and erected in 1921 for villagers who lost their lives in the First and Second World Wars.

Moreover, it is the only monument in the islands that recognises the contribution of a woman along with the men. Catherine Macleod died in the First World War and is honoured alongside the 17 men from the village who lost their lives. Catherine left the rural crofting community to work in a munitions factory on the mainland where she was exposed to the influenza that took her life.

Wildly scenic Loch Carloway provides shelter for creel fishing boats and safe anchorage for yachts. Surrounding hills host traces of traditional stone-built homes and cultivation where the crofting community banked up earth to grow arable crops in long rows known in Gaelic as *feannagan*. The intensive labour required to nourish these mounds with seaweed and manure makes a mockery of the English term for them, lazy beds.

Dun Carloway broch rises from the landscape, looking, I must confess, like a half-eaten giant Walnut Whip. The extraordinary Iron Age tower, a powerful symbol of local identity, appears on the community flag. From the lofty ruin, which originally stood some nine metres high, the elevated view across outlying islands confirms the strategic importance of the defensive site, built around 2,000 BC.

There's an unexpected horticultural treat at nearby Leathad Ard, which means 'Steep Hill' in Gaelic. Created from the rough slopes of Upper Carloway, a domestic garden with views over Loch Roag warmly welcomes visitors.

The Pentland Road arrives in Carloway and Breasclete to connect small fishing communities with Stornoway, the epicentre of Lord Leverhulme's fisheries revolution. The route, which was more of an unsurfaced track until the 1980s, is named after John Sinclair, known as Lord Pentland, Secretary for Scotland. His support secured funding for the highway project.

Throughout the Hebrides, former stone-built homes, known as *taigh-dubh* in Gaelic, or blackhouses, where families entered by the same door as their animals and lived under the same roof, are collapsed in heaps overgrown by juniper and heather. At Gearrannan a seashore village of restored blackhouses is infused with modern amenities, including self-catering accommodation, a hostel, café and souvenir shop. For intrepid hikers, the nearby Aird Liamisiadair headland is a spectacular coastal adventure. Allow around four hours for the five-mile circuit in the company of seabirds and perhaps golden eagles too.

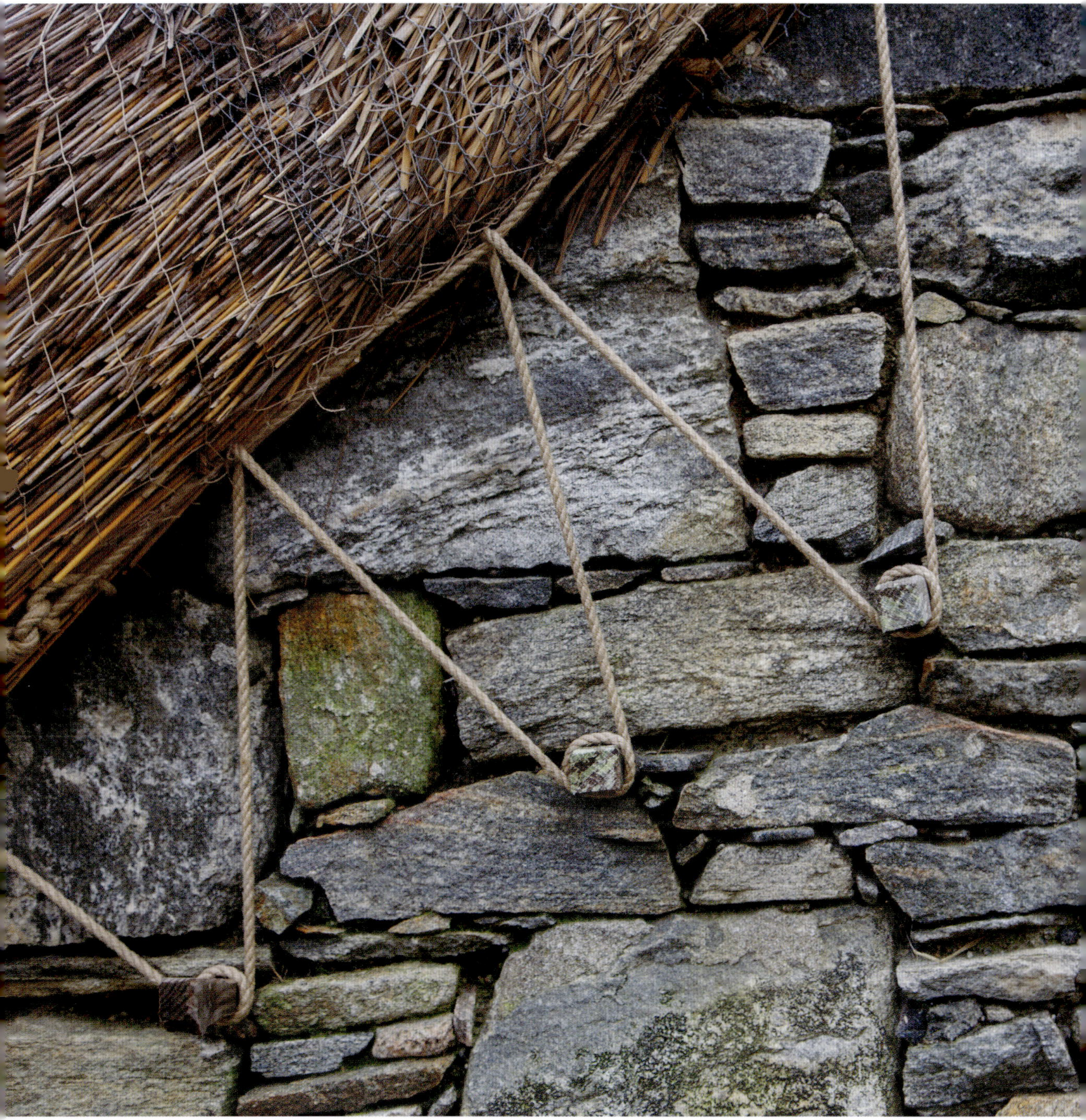

HEBRIDEAN JOURNEY

Beauty Spot

Twin beaches beyond Gearrannan invite a simple Gaelic lesson in size. Traigh Dail Mhor is a large beach of thundering rollers and surfers. Traigh Dail Beag is smaller and more secluded. Both are magical at sunset when the cliffs and sea stacks are beautifully illuminated. A favourite story tells of the Tea Field near Dail Beag. When a cargo of shipwrecked tea washed up around the coast, local crofters put it to good use as fertiliser.

The community of Shawbost is in three parts, north Shawbost, south Shawbost and new Shawbost. A central horseshoe-shaped sandy beach offers safe swimming. From the small car park by Loch Raoinavat, a path leads over the hill to a beautifully renovated Norse mill beside a pretty burn that provided power for the workings. Here barley grain was processed into meal up until the 1930s. The companion oval-shaped kiln is impressively simple: grain was spread evenly across a raised stone floor above a fire that provided heat for the drying process.

Clò-mòr is the Gaelic name for the 'big cloth' known as Harris Tweed and produced exclusively in the Outer Hebrides. In mills at Carloway and Shawbost, pure virgin wool is fibre dyed, carded, spun and warped to create threads from which independent weavers produce one of the world's most famous fabrics.

In keeping with tradition, the skilled artisans work at home on single- and double-width treadle looms. Every length of the prestigious cloth, protected under the 1993 Harris Tweed Act of Parliament, is inspected for quality by the independent Harris Tweed Authority to guarantee that only genuine handwoven Harris Tweed is stamped with the distinctive orb mark. Discover the fascinating story of tweed making at Shawbost Museum within Shawbost community centre, formerly the district school.

The track beyond Shawbost water treatment plant leads to a popular route up the modest slopes of Ben Bragar for great views to the Flannan Isles. On approach to Bragar a sorry heap of stones at Loch an Duna, close by the road, is all that remains of an Iron Age broch tower.

Towards the village, the unmissable arch made from the jawbone of an 80-foot-long blue whale in the 1920s heralds Lakefield, the former home of postmaster Murdo Morrison. When the stricken creature first drifted into view off the coast of Bragar, some mistook it for an upturned boat, others for a supernatural island. Fishers rowed out in two small boats to discover a botched kill. The lethal harpoon lodged in the doomed leviathan's back was still attached to a trailing rope severed hastily when the creature's thrashing agony threatened to capsize the whale hunters' ship. Villagers hauled the whale to the shore to extract as much oil and blubber as possible, chucking intestines into the sea and local lochs. Murdo Morrison raised the jawbone arch, complete with gruesome harpoon at the apex, to commemorate the extraordinary event. The postmaster declined to sell the trophy to his landlord, Leverhulme.

Bragar Bay is the haunt of surfers who refuel on homebaking at the wonderful Grinneabhat community café, exhibition space and laundrette in the former primary school. Guest accommodation is also available. At Arnol, the opportunity to visit an authentic *taigh-dubh*, or blackhouse, complete with original furniture and fabrics, is unmissable. The long low dwelling, owned and managed by Historic Environment Scotland, reveals how crofters built homes of drystone walls with rounded corners to reduce wind resistance. Thatch was weighted with stones hanging on woven heather or straw ropes to deter gales from snatching the roof. For cooking and heating, the fire in the central hearth was managed skilfully to ensure that it never went out. Without chimney or windows to evacuate peat smoke, the fug percolated endlessly into the rafters. Resourceful islanders renewing a roof repurposed sooty old thatch as fertiliser.

The fascinating Arnol site also demonstrates authentically the difference between the blackhouse dwellings and the later development of *taigh-geal*, or whitehouses with pitched roofs, partition walls, chimneys and windows.

Beyond the dwellings, a track leads to the RSPB nature reserve at Loch na Muilne. Here the colourful females of the rare, red-necked

Curiosity

Up until the mid 20th century, it was not unusual for courting islanders to sleep discreetly alongside each other, fully clothed, in the communal room surrounded by the young woman's extended family. This tradition known as *caithris na h-oidhche* means 'watching by night' in Gaelic. The woman's legs were tied together in a stocking hence the alternative name, bundling.

phalarope species reverse traditional roles, performing most of the courtship and leaving the males to incubate eggs and rear the chicks. The prize-winning Highland cattle of the Bru Highlanders Fold graze the township shore. Individual animals are given evocative Gaelic names: Canach is Bog Cotton, Fiochag is the Little Angry One, Lal is a Gleam of Sunshine, Cuag is Giddy, and Laochag the Little Heroine.

At Tom Mor Urrahag an inspired reconstruction of a shieling depicts life on summer pastures beyond the village. In early spring, islanders visited the family shieling to repair winter damage prior to the women, children and cattle installing themselves from May to September. This transhumance tradition permitted grazing land around the village to regrow in time for winter. The experience of the community decamping is remembered fondly as a time of great freedom and simple pleasures. Children monitored the cattle feeding on lush new growth and delivered the flavoursome fresh milk to their fathers who remained at home, occupied with fishing, making repairs and tending the crops.

This time-travelling route loop returns to Stornoway, across Barvas Moor, passing the Clach Aonghais Greum, a white-painted boulder with a plaque confirming that west-side strongman Angus Graham lifted the great weight in 1850. Apparently, Angus came upon labourers unable to make progress because the obstacle, weighing around a ton, was in their path. He kindly lifted it out of the way and so it sits on the moor. Stone lifting was a traditional rite of passage for young men in the country and though they may be long gone, the mighty boulders remain here and there. Many are painted and identified with plaques bearing witness to the physical prowess of local champions.

The Eye Peninsula

The worst peacetime loss of a British ship in British waters occurred within sight of harbour lights at Stornoway in the early hours of New Year's Eve, 1919. As island families celebrated the first Hogmanay after the end of the First World War with expectant joy at imminent return of their men from service in the Royal Navy Reserve, the ship bringing them home was sinking in darkness, agonisingly close to the shore.

The naval yacht HMY *Iolaire* broke up with the loss of 174 men from Lewis, 5 men from Harris, 2 men from Berneray, 2 men from the *Iolaire* base and 18 crew members. The trauma, sorrow and long-term consequences resonate profoundly through the islands.

Even before the disaster, the Outer Hebrides had suffered the loss of a higher proportion of servicemen than most other areas of Britain. Grasping the enormity of the loss of the men aboard the *Iolaire* is an insight into any experience of the islands.

A chilling yet important way to connect with the tragedy is to visit the coastal memorial where the vessel foundered. The site is a couple of hours' walk from the centre of Stornoway on the Point and Sandwick Trail; alternatively take the bus, cycle or drive to an unassuming lane on the quiet Sandwick shore.

A footpath leads through information panels recounting the heart-break and heroism of that appalling Hogmanay night. The wreck site, within reach of dry land, is unforgettable. How is it possible that hundreds of lives could be lost so heart-breakingly close to home? The question hangs in the sea air. When the iron-hulled *Iolaire*, which means 'eagle' in Gaelic, changed course in stormy seas on approach to Stornoway harbour, she struck the Beasts of Holm rocks at full speed. Surging walls of water pushed the yacht back and forth violently and as she scraped, rolled and disintegrated hundreds of men were washed overboard. Bodies and kit bags were strewn around the coast; one third of the men who perished were never recovered.

Investigations revealed that the vessel was not only overloaded but also without enough life jackets, lifeboats or even seats for the exhausted servicemen homeward bound from war. According to survivor reports, the shortfall of crew members was compounded by a catastrophic failure of leadership.

Somehow serviceman and boatbuilder John Finlay Macleod from the Port of Ness found the strength, belief and courage to swim ashore through turbulent water with a long heaving line. His comrades followed along, holding it taut for others as they reached safety. Though 40 men grappled their way successfully, many were ripped away by the storm. The public inquiry into the *Iolaire* disaster, widely regarded as utterly inadequate, lasted just two days.

From Sandwick, the A866 skims the runway of Stornoway Airport and tracks the sweep of the Braighe isthmus to reach An Rubha, known also as the Eye peninsula though most locals call it Point. In severe weather the seashore causeway is closed. Check the live camera video stream on the Comhairle website if in doubt. From a small car park at the end of the Braighe, a footpath leads to the towering Aignish Raiders cairn honouring the courage of impoverished local families who fought in 1888 to reclaim farmland taken from them by estate owners. Police and marines intervened in the so-called Crofters' War but ultimately, the goal of land reform was delivered.

Across the field from the monument, Ui Church clings to the eroding shore of Broad Bay. The site dedicated to St Columba is a melting pot of buildings and extensions dating from the 14th century and the burial place of at least 18 Clan Macleod chiefs. Grave markers around the chapel range from decorous marble with inscriptions to simple anonymous stones, often from the deceased's home, simply marking a burial

Curiosity

Discover sustainable fashion at the Old Shop in Bayble township where inspired lecturer Rebecca Smith instigated a project to slow down the environmental impact of collective consumer habits. Estimates suggest that globally 80 per cent of discarded textiles go for incineration or landfill where they may decompose for over 200 years, emitting methane gas that contributes to climate warming. Just 20 per cent of textiles are reused or recycled.

To make a positive difference, the Bayble Exchange supports local sewing skills to repair clothing and restyle fabrics and garments into something useful and new. *Cruinn*, meaning 'circular' in Gaelic, is the name of the visionary eco fashion brand at the Exchange.

Beauty Spot

Portnaguran enjoys a big bay view beyond the white-painted sea wall. The pier is neat, the picnic area prettily planted and a decorative clinker-built boat laden with creels makes a thoughtful finishing touch.

place. The war grave of Norman Mackenzie is especially poignant; the 18-year-old deckhand from Garrabost perished in the sinking of HMY *Iolaire*. Uplifting coastal walks explore local footpaths and Café Roo in the Old School at Knock is a great place to refuel. The adjacent community shop sells hand-dived scallops, herrings, kippers, and lobsters in season.

The Broad Bay coast from Garrabost to Portnaguran offers rugged walking on the Point and Sandwick Trail. For sea swimmers there's the thrill of steep steps to the briny, with a reassuring handrail, at Goedha nan Eathraichean, or 'Boats' Gully' at Shulishader.

Sea fishers follow lanes to the shore to cast from the rocks at Portvoller. At the northern tip of the township Tiumpan Head lighthouse occupies dramatic cliffs with spectacular views of marine life. Deep waters around the Eye peninsula are a nursery for Risso's dolphins feasting on squid, their favourite food. Take binoculars and scan the sea on a clear calm day; orca, fin whales, bottlenose dolphins, white-beaked dolphins, common dolphins and porpoise may also be seen. Little wonder the briny Minch is known in Gaelic as Cuan nan Orc, the 'Ocean of the Whales'. Views to snow-capped mainland mountains and the lighthouse at Stoer Head are fantastic. The aurora borealis, or Northern Lights, seen from here is magnificent.

At lovely Sheshader great plumes of pampas grass sway on the breeze. A signpost indicates the beach down a lane that dwindles to a track and a steep slipway overlooked by a beautifully situated seashore bench. This poignant itinerary began with the *Iolaire* disaster and concludes in a small village profoundly impacted by it. The close-knit families of Sheshader lost ten of their men in the homecoming tragedy; some were never found.

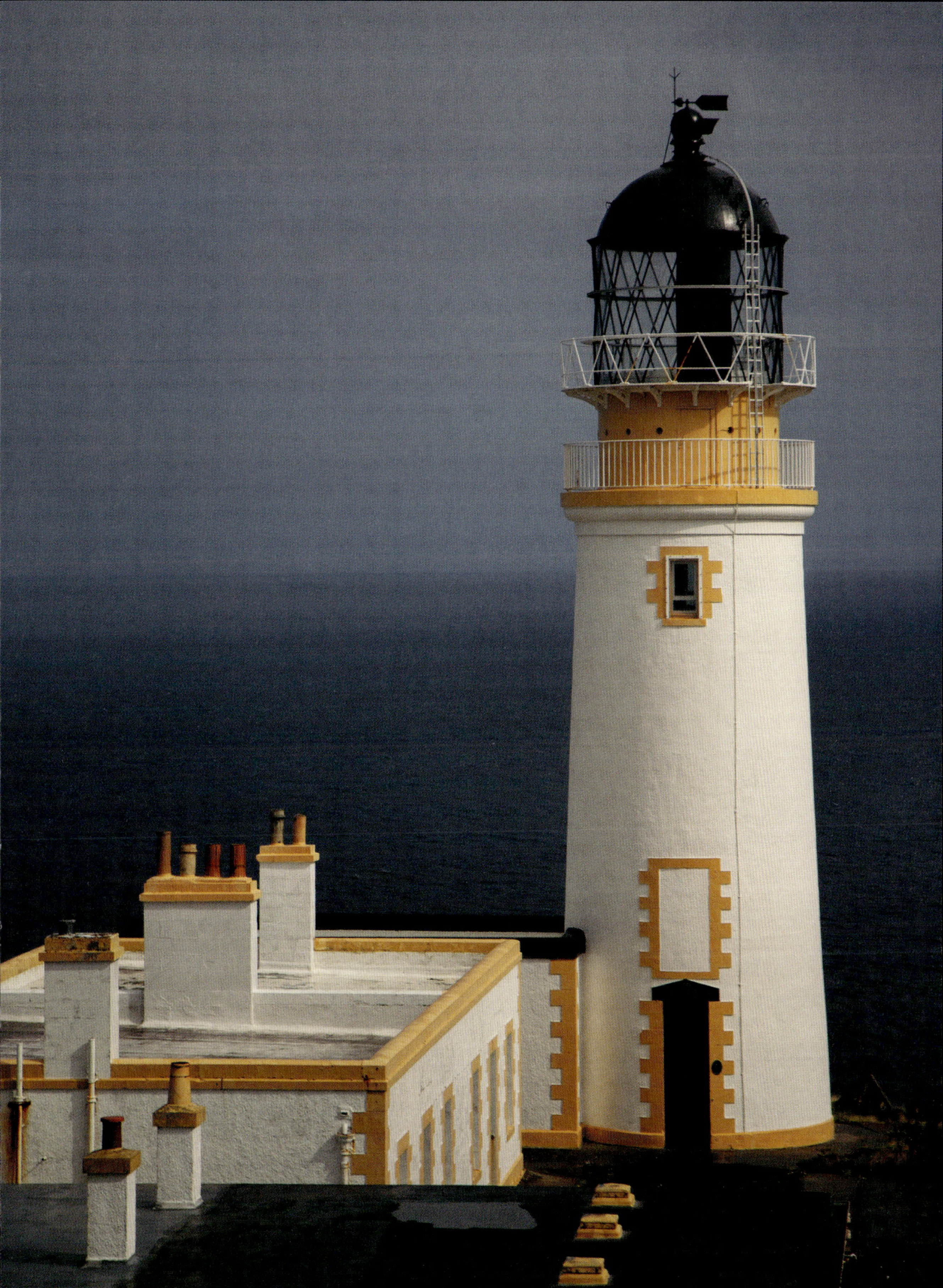

n
0
5 km
0
5 miles
Little Bernera
Bosta
Croir
Loch Riosaigh
Tobson
Gallan Head
Aird Uig
Valtos
Pabbay Mor
Valasay
Breaclete
Loch Roag
Siaram Mor
Great Bernera
Kirkibost
Miavaig
Reef
Timsgarry
Callanish
Vuia Beg
Uig Bay
Vig
Glen Valtos
Carishader
Eilean Chearstaidh
Mangersta
Ardroil
Geshader
Suainebhal
B8059
Ungeshader
Einacleit
Islibhig
Scaliscro
B8011
Breinis
Mealasta
Lewis

Over the Atlantic to Great Bernera

North Atlantic tides rise and fall around more than a dozen islands in Loch Roag, but only Great Bernera is connected by two bridges to the shore. In response to fears of depopulation, the first crossing constructed in 1953 stitched Great Bernera, known locally as Bernera, into the fabric of Lewis, or, as the *Stornoway Gazette* noted: 'On that day Bernera ceased to be an island and became part of Lewis. Or perhaps it would be more accurate to say Lewis ceased to be an island and became part of Bernera.'

The crossing was the first prestressed concrete bridge in Europe, constructed in the UK, with breakthrough technology developed in Belgium in response to the post-war steel shortage. A model was exhibited at the 1951 Festival of Britain, a showcase intended as a tonic for the post-war nation. The short single carriageway served islanders on both sides well until a survey in February 2020 confirmed it had deteriorated to such an extent that it was necessary to implement a weight restriction with immediate effect; fuel supply tankers and the usual refuse collection vehicles were denied access. Possible solutions included hiring a ferry to transport lorries to the island. Happily, a modular steel span bridge without piers resolved the crisis and opened in 2021, alongside its vintage neighbour.

I'm fond of the unpretentious working pier at Kirkibost, where stacked creels, coils of rope, unruly mounds of net and hauled-out craft share the quayside with the helipad, a lifeline for island emergencies. Boat trips depart for the heavenly blue lagoon on Pabbay Mor and other destinations too. Booking is essential.

The Great Bernera Trail circuit walk of 11 miles begins in Breaclete, the island's sweetly modest capital. The community centre comprising museum, café and garden is a main attraction, though the shiny stand-alone 24-hour fuel pumps of Bernera Community Association filling station on the shore of Loch Geal are quite something to behold and

Curiosity

Megalithic standing stones on the hill above the Great Bernera bridges are in the orbit of the henge at Callanish. A track to the west of the stones, known as Callanish VIII, or Tursachan, is a coastal shortcut to Hacklete, a small community with views of uninhabited islands in Loch Roag. The road route to this south-west corner rolls up and down hill and sways around the shore of Loch Bharabhat, where a stone causeway from the shore connects with an Iron Age dun on an islet. To visit, take the path signposted a mile along the road from the Bernera bridge towards Breaclete.

invaluable to locals and visitors alike. Electric car charging points are available at the community centre.

The wonderful island circuit walk explores the coast and boggy moor and requires at least four hours to savour views of Loch Roag's ocean-washed islands and the distant Uig hills looming large over the immense golden swathe of Reef beach. Encounters with otters, birds of prey, grazing red deer and brightly daubed sheep in purple heather are very likely.

The road and the walking trail travel west together to Valasay where an elegant footbridge carries pedestrians across the tidal rapids of Tob Valasay. There are many tobs in the islands, the term refers to places deriving their name from the Gaelic *ob*, meaning 'a site where the briny sea washes over freshwater at high tide'. At lovely Valasay this flowing fusion promotes the growth of rare seaweeds in a Special Area of Conservation.

A monument situated at the centre of Great Bernera honours the heroes of the 1874 Bernera Riot who challenged the intention of island owner James Matheson to increase his sporting estate by clearing livestock from summer grazing on the moor. Resistance was met with threats of eviction and rent rises. The ensuing court case supported the community and paved the way for land reform in Scotland.

In 1962 Count Robin Mirrlees bought the islands of Great Bernera, Little Bernera and Eilean Chearstaidh sight unseen. The aristocrat lived happily in a whitewashed croft house without a telephone and was popular with the community. Following his death in 2012, the community voted to negotiate a buyout of their island home, a hope that remains, as yet, unresolved.

On the north-west coast, rocky knolls and patches of land nourished with seaweed surround island homes at Tobson. Fresh algae carried to the shore by winter storms is spread across agricultural land to decompose before digging in as fertiliser. The addition of seaweed produces more stable and fertile sandy soil to grow crops for families and livestock. Generous spring equinox high tides also land mounds of seaweed on island beaches and rocky ledges.

In 1993 an exceptionally fierce winter storm shifted the dunes of Bosta beach and exposed the remains of a village built in the sixth to ninth centuries, known as the Iron Age or Pictish period. The settlement, built upon dwellings from even earlier periods, was, in turn, built upon by Viking settlers who named the area Bostadh, meaning 'farm' in Old Norse. A faithful reconstruction of a turf-roofed Iron Age dwelling house, just like those revealed by the storm, is tucked into a deep hollow on the shore. A curving stairway reaches the below-ground sheltered door. Inside, the welcome is warm, the peat fire aglow. The fascinating visit by candlelight is a spine-tingling time slip.

The paradise white shell sands of Bosta are frequented by Highland cattle with a taste for seaweed. On a small skerry, a tide bell with a wave catcher sounds the ebb and flow of the ocean. The magical installation created by Marcus Vergette is one of 12 specially cast bronze bells erected around the coast of Britain. The seashore project was inspired by the ringing of bells in Vergette's Devon village to mark the

Curiosity

Count Robin Mirrlees inspired a fictional James Bond character in Ian Fleming's novel *On His Majesty's Secret Service*. Educated at the English School of Cairo and later in Paris before attending Merton College, Oxford, the dashing count became a captain in the Royal Artillery, serving in India during the Second World War. In 1952 he entered the College of Arms as researcher Rouge Dragon Pursuivant of Arms in Ordinary and shared insights with author Ian Fleming who was on a research mission to ensure his genealogist character Sir Hilary Bray had correct credentials. Among the foreign knighthoods and titles bestowed upon him, Count Robin was crowned Prince of Incoronata; the Adriatic island archipelago was gifted to him by his pal, exiled King Peter II of Yugoslavia. In *Who's Who*, widely considered to be a dubiously selective reference book, the Buddhist fox-hunting aristocrat and laird listed 'mystic philosophy' among his recreations.

Beauty Spot

On the shore beside the small sandy bay of Camas Sanndig at Tobson, a picnic bench within a drystone wall enclosure is a dreamy place to dine al fresco with fine views to the hills of Uig.

end of the 2001 outbreak of bovine foot-and-mouth disease.

The small community of Croir overlooks the Kyles of Little Bernera. While staying at Tigh a' Chaolais, or the 'house on the channel', author William Black wrote his acclaimed gothic romance, *The Princess of Thule*, published in 1875. The tale tells of island girl Sheila enchanting Frank, a visiting artist. Friendship blooms into romance and marriage but choices about how and where the couple will live impact them both deeply. William Black's heroine was inspired by Isabella Macdonald of Croir. Isabella is buried in a scenic cemetery beside a small chapel on the shore of Little Bernera. When people were cleared from Little Bernera a new cemetery was built on the Bosta shore. Here, too, the deceased repose with glorious sea views.

A faint and sometimes-squelchy rough path to the shore of Loch Riosaigh reaches another of Bernera's atmospheric time slips. A humble drystone building under a thatched roof is a partly restored corn mill that functioned until the First World War. Simple Norse technology harnessed running water to power the millstones. The lonely historic mill would have been previously at the heart of island life. The bustle of deliveries, the rhythmic sound of the workings and lively conversations are all gone now.

On the rocky shore beyond the mill hosts an extraordinary sea water lobster pond built by Murdo Morrison in the 1860s. Bernera fishers supplied prime lobsters to the London market, where agents paid the best prices, only if the lobsters were alive and healthy upon delivery. Sadly many died in transit delays.

Ingenious Murdo envisaged a solution. Marking out a proposed lobster pond, he left Bernera and worked his passage to Wooloomooloo on the fast-developing shore of Sydney, Australia. After two years, he returned with enough funds to employ island men to build the seawater catchment, designed cleverly with an interflow of water at the rise and fall of the tide. Enterprising Murdo bought lobsters from local fishers and released them in his pond, holding them safe until the weather was suitable for them to arrive at market alive and in their prime. The beautifully built catchment served the fishing community until the 1960s when air freight from Stornoway replaced the longer transit by sea to the mainland. Discover Murdo's story, marked with a personal tragedy too, at the intimate Bernera Museum in Breaclete.

Uig and the Western Shore

The glorious coast of Uig extends from sheltered Scaliscro on the eastern shore of Little Loch Roag to exposed Mealasta on the North Atlantic coast. Within these rugged bounds, thrills, treasures and stupendous beaches await.

The longest B-road on Lewis is surely the slickest too. The B8011, a former single-track carriageway, was widened and realigned to create a swifter and more streamlined connection between the communities of Uig and the rest of Lewis and Harris. Where once the route panted and crawled around lochs and hills, it now glides with consummate ease.

The road improvement scheme bypassed thinly populated Einacleit, lending an air of discovery to the village telephone box. The hideaway hillside booth features a rare double door to permit safe exit in a blasting Atlantic gale. Ungeshader and Geshader are a pair of treasures on my happy list of Outer Hebrides Places with Spellbinding Names. Geshader is the larger of the diminutive duo and, though hardly Venice, the community certainly appreciated the benefits of a canal: here, the artificial inlet from West Loch Roag served to float rafts of mounded seaweed, used as a soil improver, closer to the cultivated land. Sadly, the ingenious waterway is no more.

The Congested Districts Board promoted a variety of schemes between 1898 and 1912 to assist vulnerable communities impacted by potato blight, including the loan of prize bulls, rams and stallions to improve the quality of stock. Most families had at least one cow to provide milk, butter and soft-churned cheese known as crowdie. The transhumance tradition of women and children relocating with the cattle to summer grazing at the family *àirigh*, or shieling, supported the regeneration of pastures closer to home. On return to the village in early autumn, the cows discovered the ready and waiting prize bull on loan. Ungeshader cattle were herded to Geshader for their turn in his company.

Keeping the bull from the cows through winter was no mean feat. Uninhabited islands offshore were a convenient solution, though much depended on the safety of the terrain and the size of boats available to make any transfer. Most bulls were forced to swim behind small boats, lashed by a rope around the horns.

The Geshader bull was taken to Cliatsay from Gob Scrith headland, a relatively short but nonetheless traumatic swim for the poor creature. Sadly, a bull drowned when making the return trip in spring. Wary of visitors after lonely winter months on the island, he suffered the indignity of having his horns lashed with rope before being taken out to sea to swim behind the boat back to the village. Tossing his head in wild panic, the thrashing bull risked holing the small craft. Reluctantly the crew cut him free in the vain hope he might be able to swim to safety.

Island communities have a knack of making excellent use of items washed onto the shore. In 1898 the Carishader village stores installed the bell from the shipwrecked *Esra* to announce customers' arrival. The remains of the three-masted vessel lie beneath shifting sands on Cliff beach. Happily, the entire Norwegian crew was

Curiosity

My dear friend Cubby kindly shared boyhood memories of persuading Uist bulls into boats. Recognising his intuitive relationship with animals, the men of the village appointed him to sweeten the beasts for the daunting transfer. Leading a bull gently to the water's edge near the waiting boat, Cubby combed its long thick coat, a traditional way of bonding and building trust with Highland cattle. Whispering soothing assurances in Gaelic, he promised the bull all would be well and sang soft low lullabies to further relax the fellow. When he sensed his charge was in a delicious trance and ready to lie down, Cubby signalled men to the rear. The moment the bull bent a front leg to settle down, the men all shoved at once. With Cubby's help, and without any fuss, the village bull found himself stepping safely aboard the boat.

saved. Carishader is the start of a rewarding walk to Suainebhal, the whaleback mountain with panoramic views of golden Uig Bay and the dramatic summits of Harris.

Boat trips around the islands sail from Miavaig slipway, owned by Bhaltos Community Trust which comprises five settlements known as Bhaltos/Valtos, Cnip/Kneep, Riof/Reef, Ùigean/Uigen and Clibhe/ Cliff. A scenic coastal road discovers them all, with plenty of walking opportunities too. My preference is to travel the loop anticlockwise because I especially enjoy the elevated view of white-crested Atlantic breakers surging onto Cliff beach before following the road down to the shore. One of my favourite public artworks anywhere is to be found a top a

Beauty Spot

The term *An Suileachan* creatively suggests the intention of seeing the past and the future which is appropriate for the fantastic elevated monument at Reef, honouring the 19th-century Lewis land clearances and the 20th-century land claims by raiders at Reef farm, and celebrating the creation of the Bhaltos Community Trust.

A short hillside path climbs to a platform of two large stone circles bounded by handsome drystone walls made from the ruins of local blackhouses. Paving at the centre of the eastern circle bears the names of the Reef raiders. A walkway connects to the western circle under a triumphal arch made with stones from the uninhabited island of Vuia Beg, cleared of its people in 1827. The focus of the western circle is a large iron brazier, made of defunct graveyard railings from Stornoway. The brazier stands on an old millstone. A circular bench around the fireplace is made from windblown island trees. *An Suileachan* rises in celebration above community-owned land, overlooking lush islands in Loch Roag, sheep and lambs and common grazing, and the astonishing white sands of Reef beach, a dazzling swathe backed by dunes and summer wildflowers on the grassy machair. Unforgettable.

rocky knoll at Reef. Magnificent *An Suileachan* is a striking celebration of Scottish land reform.

The dreamy mile-long arc of white shell sands at Reef is especially luminous under seal-grey skies. Snaking around windblown dunes the narrow coast road climbs the hill to Kneep, a modest sandy bay in comparison with the showstopping supersize local competition, yet delightful all the same. Archaeological excavations revealed the grave of a high-status Viking woman buried on the headland with her brooches and glass beads. A sophisticated Iron Age wheelhouse lies hidden in the sands; these subterranean buildings with partitions like spokes of a wheel are found only in northern Scotland.

A smattering of whitewashed cottages cascade from the green slopes of Valtos to the shore, a picturesque island scene. From the sands, kayakers paddle easily to the island of Siaram Mor, formerly the lonely winter residence of the Valtos community bull. Beyond, the island of Pabbay Mor hosts a turquoise lagoon, secret caverns and a natural stone arch sculpted by the sea. Remains of an early Christian church suggest the island was a sanctuary for hermit monks who prayed for the spiritual well-being of the community. Valtos crofters send their sheep and lambs to the island for lush summer grazing with heavenly views.

Curiosity

I have a very soft spot for the iconic concrete bus shelters of Lewis. The brutalist Four Winds design offers protection from island gales and horizontal rain blasting from any direction. On dark winter mornings, they offer refuge to shivering students awaiting school buses. At Glen Valtos, the Carry bus shelter sports a large collage by artist Janie Nicoll. Get close to appreciate more fully the Saltire design made of local maps and newspaper cuttings.

It seems to me that sombre Glen Valtos is the yin to the luminous yang of Uig's white sand beaches. The dark passageway shaped by glacial meltwater connects the Valtos peninsula with far-west Gallan Head and mystical shores to the south. The glen may be gloomy now, yet previously it hosted hundreds of people attending open-air religious meetings and encampments of seasonal visitors offering welcome skills to the local community. The itinerant indigenous Gaelic-speaking Scots, known as the summer walkers, were renowned tinsmiths especially. Ceilidh nights were lively, the visitors and locals mingled for joyous music and dancing. Much-loved summer walker James Drummond famously played the pipes and melodeon and left his mark, shaping 'JD' in rocks that are still visible. When travelling west, they can be seen on the right-hand side of the glen, after a steep zigzag path.

The coast road arrives at picnic benches situated high above Cliff beach; breezy al fresco dining comes with spectacular views of surfers far below. The Atlantic Ocean serves thrilling, reliable swell, thundering winter waves are immense, but rip tides are strong. Beware.

The far-west promontories of Aird Uig and Gallan Head are steeped in drama. Traditional stories tell of the fearsome Gallan whale, a dreadful creature that sank fishing boats and gobbled up the crew. In the political climate of fear following the Second World War, the Ministry of Defence established a Cold War surveillance station at Gallan Head to monitor Soviet aircraft and submarines. When the facility closed the local community acquired the site for more wholesome pursuits. Visitors are invited to experience natural thrills, not least starry dark skies, and the aurora borealis. However, the Trust does have plans for surveillance; a hydrophone will relay the sound of passing whales.

The curvaceous shore of Uig Bay is a ginormous stage of dazzling white sands washed by aquamarine waves and the effect, to put it bluntly, is gobsmacking. Low tide best reveals the enormity of the mesmerising desert fringed by wildflower machair and scattered crofting communities. Gentle Crowlista occupies a sleepy bay on the north side. The road looping around Timsgarry visits the site of the school, community centre, seasonal café and small museum guarded by a towering wooden sculpture of a buck-toothed warrior with sword and shield. The quirky doorman is a large-scale replica chess piece, but more of that soon. A favourite island pit stop is the brilliantly stocked Uig

Community Shop complete with fuel station, laundrette and post office.

Sparkling white beaches around Uig have the highest shell content of any shore in Scotland, hence the extraordinary luminosity. Uig Lodge enjoys panoramic coastal views, though fly-fishing guests visit mostly for the rivers and lochs of the Fhorsa System and the Bruton Stream, regarded as the most exciting and unique salmon fly water in the British Isles.

Now about that warrior chess piece: in the small community of Ardroil, nestled between the Fhorsa river and the Abhainn Dearg, or 'Red River', a hoard of medieval gaming pieces emerged from windblown sand dunes. The exact circumstances of the discovery are vague, but the treasure trove of 93 kings, queens, bishops, knights, warders and pawns made of elaborately worked walrus ivory and whales' teeth was displayed in Edinburgh in 1881 by Mr Rirrie of Stornoway and broken up for sale soon after.

Each brilliantly characterful piece has a distinctive expression. My favourite is the seated queen, clasping her long glum face in one hand and a horn in the other. The poor woman looks like she is having the most atrocious fortnight of Hebridean weather. Many experts believe the collection was made in Norway, around 1150–1200, when the islands of the Outer Hebrides were part of that kingdom. Another theory suggests they are the work of Margaret the Adroit, the finest ivory carver in Iceland. A traditional saga tells how her patron, Bishop Pall, commissioned exquisite gifts for international friends. The National Museum of Scotland has 11 pieces on permanent display, the British Museum has 67 pieces, and a showcase of 6 pieces on loan is a star attraction at the Stornoway museum. My favourite grimaces among them. Uig has a pair of giant wooden replicas: the eight-foot-tall berserker guarding the community centre and a commanding king on the Ardroil machair.

Abhainn Dearg craft distillery produces single malt. For every barrel used in the process, two trees, either oak or Douglas fir, are planted locally. At the south end of Uig Bay, headland walks around Carnish discover secret sandy beaches. Pounding Atlantic waves sculpt and smash the exhilarating coast around Mangersta. A superbly camouflaged bothy in the cliffs offers basic shelter. Overnight stays may be booked, and donations made to The Linda Norgrove Foundation. Environmental expert Dr Linda Norgrove was kidnapped in Afghanistan in 2010. American forces located her but tragically Linda was killed in the rescue attempt. Her grieving parents, builders of the bothy, established The Linda Norgrove Foundation to support women and children in Afghanistan.

On a clear day, the island archipelago of Hirta, Boreray, Soay, Dun and Levenish, known collectively in English as St Kilda, is visible from the Mangersta headland, some 40 miles away. A scheme to create a three-stage St Kilda trail through Lewis, South Harris and North Uist is underway. Remote-access visitor centres will share the experience and history of the volcanic islands where a hardy community survived for more than 5,000 years. In 1930 a practical and emotional decision was made to abandon the outpost which had become an ever-greater tourist attraction. For generations prior the people of St Kilda posed for troupes of early photographers in hot pursuit of wild landscapes.

Beyond Mangersta, high sea cliffs front the sparsely populated edge of Europe. The narrow coast road teeters along the tops. Fearsome Atlantic gales thrash the land, restless waves erode deep caverns and jagged stacks. Scant traces remain of the Islibhig Chain Home Low Radar Station that provided support to Atlantic convoys of merchant ships relaying essential supplies throughout the Second World War. Playful lambs prance around the transmitter building while their mothers rub up against the crumbling air-raid shelter. In bright sunshine the entire flock snoozes on the toasty warm concrete bases of dismantled Nissen huts that hosted a far-west wartime bar and cinema.

At Breinis the road slopes to the remains of fish curing and drying houses. Sunshine illuminates the distant white lighthouse atop the Eilean Mor, the largest of the seven Flannan Isles. Scuttling onward the skinny thread of tarmac reaches a modern magic circle of rocks, each indicating the direction and distance of faraway places. My favourite is the North Pole, 4,026 miles hence. I expect it gives Father Christmas a warm glow on his busy Christmas Eve.

On approach to the road end, the shore dips to a series of sheltered golden bays, lovely swimming spots in gentle weather. Traditional stories tell of a medieval nunnery, Tigh nan Cailleachan Dubha or 'House of the old Black Women' on the machair where crofters grow seashore potatoes. The tarmac stops abruptly at Mealasta slipway. Here a rusting winch services a handful of small local boats. The community was cleared by the laird in 1837. With hopes of a brighter future, the islanders sailed to Canada on immigrant ships and settled in Bury, Eastern Quebec. The trauma of such losses and the outmigration of young people who want the choice to remain in the islands is felt keenly throughout the Outer Hebrides. Affordable homes and secure employment are priorities for the well-being of the islands.

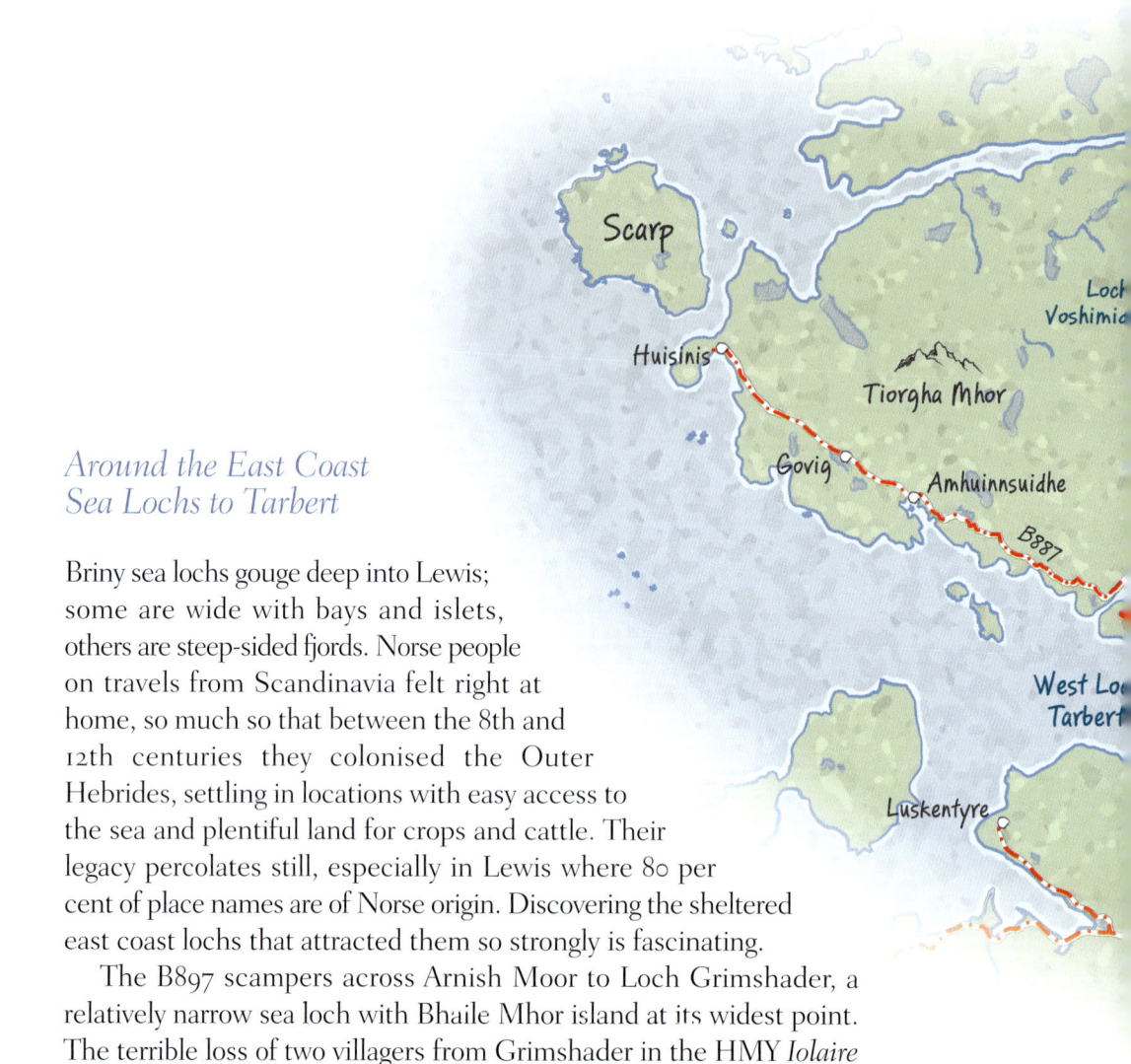

Around the East Coast
Sea Lochs to Tarbert

Briny sea lochs gouge deep into Lewis; some are wide with bays and islets, others are steep-sided fjords. Norse people on travels from Scandinavia felt right at home, so much so that between the 8th and 12th centuries they colonised the Outer Hebrides, settling in locations with easy access to the sea and plentiful land for crops and cattle. Their legacy percolates still, especially in Lewis where 80 per cent of place names are of Norse origin. Discovering the sheltered east coast lochs that attracted them so strongly is fascinating.

The B897 scampers across Arnish Moor to Loch Grimshader, a relatively narrow sea loch with Bhaile Mhor island at its widest point. The terrible loss of two villagers from Grimshader in the HMY *Iolaire* homecoming disaster of 1919 is a hellish irony. Having survived the horrors of the First World War, the only servicemen from the clachan lost their lives in familiar waters when the ship returning them to Lewis sank just yards from the island shore.

A skinny thread of tarmac connects the Grimshader community to

B897
Loch Grimshader
Leurbost
Loch Leurbost
Ranish
Crosbost
North Lochs
Laxay
Keose
Eilean Chaluim Cille
Balallan
Crobeg
Cromore
Loch Erisort
Garyvard
Kershader
B8060
Marvig/Marbhig
Arivruach
South Lochs
Calbost
A859
Gravir
Loch Odhairn
North Harris
Lewis
Orinsay
Eishken
Lemreway
Ardvourlie
Loch Shell
Eilean Liubhaird
An Cliseam
Maraig
Loch Seaforth
Gleann Lacasdail
Bunavoneader
Loch Claidh
Loch Bhrolluim
Ardhasaig
Rhenigidale
Molinginish
Tarbert
Urgha Beag
Leac Easgadail
Scalpay
East Loch Tarbert
Eilean Glas
to Uig, Skye
n
0
5 km
0
5 miles

Curiosity

In the Weaving Shed in Crosbost, Miriam Hamilton produces tweed cloth on a vintage cast-iron Hattersley loom, made in Keighley, Yorkshire by the oldest firm of loom makers in the world. Hattersley looms were introduced to the islands at the end of the First World War to support ex-servicemen to make a living.

In 1834 the company's original power loom design was smashed by Luddite hand weavers who intercepted its delivery to a customer in Bradford. Inspired by textile worker and activist Ned Ludd, the group feared the loss of their livelihood with the introduction of powered looms. They were proved right. How they would marvel at the looms of Hebridean handweavers still going strong.

Ranish and settlements around the headland. Crosbost occupies the north shore of Loch Leurbost. Scenic views to Na h-Eileanan Baircln, the Barkin Isles, are especially lovely from the rocky knoll beyond the road end. A distinctive Outer Hebridean trio meets at the water's edge: the war memorial, honouring the dead of North Lochs; the pier; and the church. When the first Lochs Church was built in 1845, many of the Gaelic-speaking throng arrived by boat from surrounding coastal communities; now a huge car park awaits the congregation. Several factors caused the regular Gaelic services to cease in 2016, the English alternative was better attended, the number of fluent Gaelic speakers in the congregation was dwindling, and so was the supply of Gaelic-speaking ministers.

The sea loch community of Leurbost forms the main settlement of the North Lochs district. Here the players of Lochs Football Club, founded in 1934, wear a kit with a sailing ship emblem. When James Matheson acquired Lewis, he aspired to build a castle at Keose, but church authorities thwarted his plans, refusing to release a historic hold on farmland. Today the Keose Glebe estate, including seven small islands, is in community ownership following a land buyout.

The long-distance Hebridean Way Cycling route joins the A859 around the shore of Loch Erisort. During the Second World War, top-secret activities took place in the eight-mile-long tidal waters. A landing stage on the site of the Keose seaweed plant was known simply as Port D. Here men from the Royal Navy and Royal Marines trained to operate midget submarines with the capacity to cut through anti-torpedo and anti-submarine nets and attach warheads to enemy vessels. The midget submarines, or X-craft, were towed to the area of operations by a full-size submarine.

Laxay village is between two renowned salmon rivers, Abhainn Laca-saidh to the west and Abhainn Eallaidh to the east. A favourite island tale recounts an extraordinary night in December 1926 when the village cats went bonkers. Under cover of darkness, a spectacular shoal of silver herrings swam into Loch Erisort forming a mighty wall so deep and wide that it banked up in the narrows, splurging flipping fish around delirious cats on the shore. The rare shoal was so vast that for days large boats sailed into Laxay from other parts of Lewis to share the abundant spoils.

Balallan, the longest village in Lewis, gets a mention in one of the witty tracks by cult island band Peat and Diesel. The lyrics of 'Calum Dan's Transit Van' suggest the eponymous driver speeds through the four-mile-long village at 106 miles an hour. Most people go a fair bit slower, but not all.

At the head of Loch Erisort, the B8060 rounds the muddy shore to discover coastal villages off the fast road. In Kershader a community-owned hostel in the former school complex adjoins a community shop, museum, laundrette and café. Delicious homebaking comes with lovely views across Loch Erisort. Fuel is available from community-owned self-service pumps operating 24 hours.

The Pairc Historical Society curates the Kershader museum with loving care. Discover inviting room sets, whaling-ship souvenirs, a portable folded pulpit for open-air religious gatherings, and the Angus 'Ease' Macleod archive, a collection of writings offering precious insight

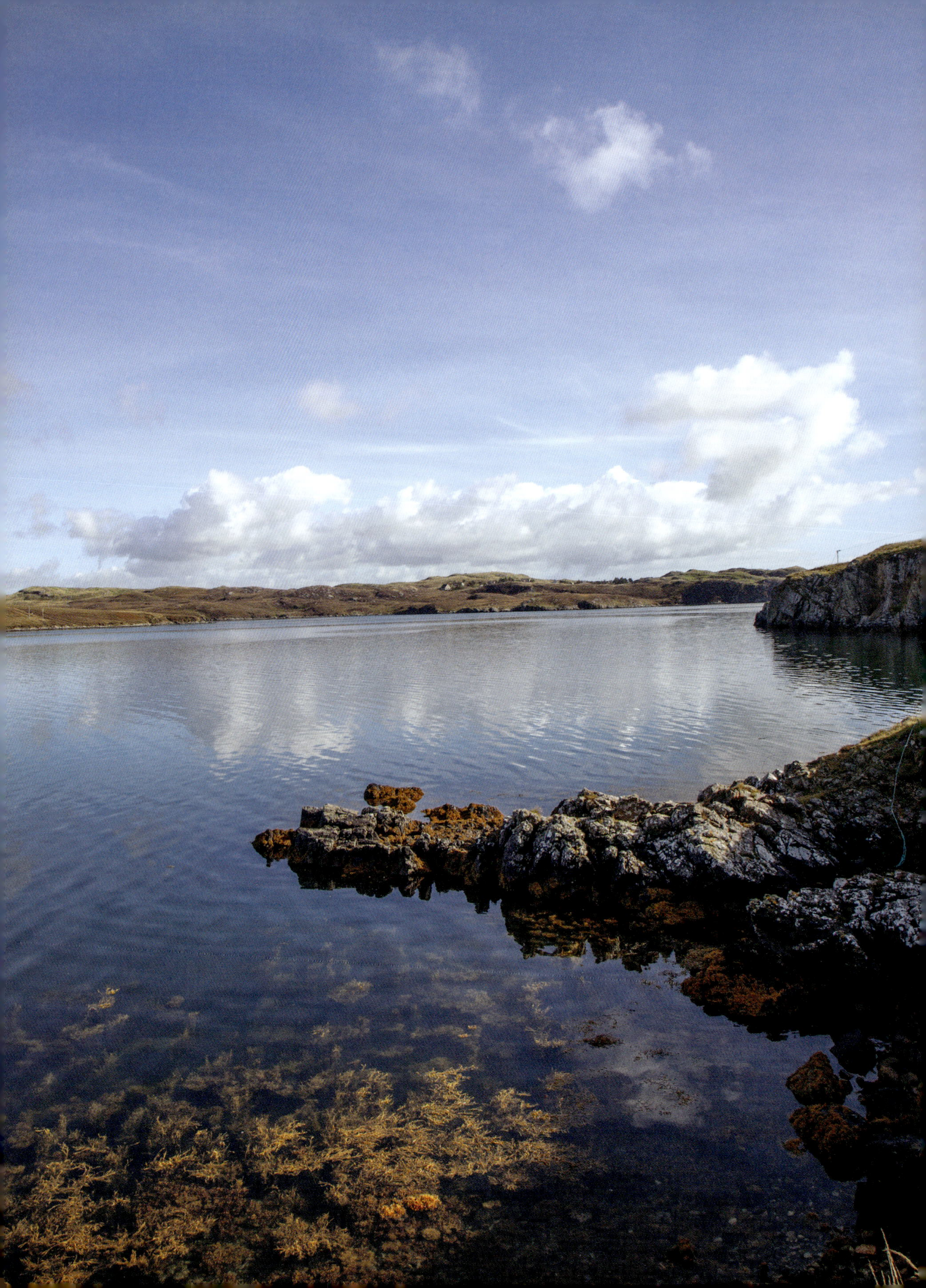

into historical land struggles and the passing of the old clan system.

The former school complex is also the headquarters of the Pairc Trust, formed in 2003 to care for 11 crofting townships on land purchased by the community in 2015. The long-term mission is to reverse a century of population decline in the beautiful South Lochs district, a wonderfully scenic and peaceful area. The lochside settlement of Garyvard is peaceful now but in the past a lively community of herring fishers communicated with neighbours in Keose on the opposite shore of Loch Erisort by shouting across the water.

A waymarked circular walk through the hills of Cromore explores wonderful coastal scenery. Parts of the four-mile route cross boggy ground and wellies are advised. Allow around three hours to break away from it all in the company of golden eagles, otters and seals. Marvig provides sheltered anchorage for visiting yachts and the charming settlement is a paradise for freshwater and saltwater fishers. The stony shore at Calbost served the fishing community faithfully. In sunshine and wind, they spread the catch across the rocks to dry fast and clean.

A young man from this quiet fishing community, Malcolm Morrison, became an extraordinary wartime hero. In 1939 a German U-boat torpedoed and sank the British merchant ship ss *Arlington Court* as she crossed the Atlantic from Brazil to Hull with a cargo of grain. Survivors scrambled to lifeboats, but few had the ability to pilot them. Stepping into the breech, 18-year-old deck boy Malcolm demonstrated exceptional skill and courage to steer, sail and navigate the small open boat hundreds of miles across heavy seas for six days until rescued by a Norwegian tanker off the coast of Britain. The young islander was awarded the Gold Medal of the Shipwrecked Fishermen and Mariners Royal Benevolent Society, bearing the inscription, 'Presented for heroic exertions in saving life from drowning'.

At Gravir the fishing community settled on both sides of steep and narrow Loch Odhairn. The pier remains in use by small boats and fish farm vessels. At the Glen Gravir road end fishers with rods, nets and

Beauty Spot

The road to Crobeg visits a farming settlement with heavenly views of Eilean Chaluim Cille, a holy island close by the shore. Here followers of St Columba, who was born in Ireland in AD 512 and died in Iona in 597, created a religious community around a church, granary, market garden and orchard. Though the buildings are ruined, the atmosphere of the island sanctuary is very special. Be sure to check tide times before walking the tidal causeway from Crobeg shore.

wellies tramp happily to the moor in pursuit of prize brown trout. The isolated freshwater lochs are said to be the haunt of supernatural water horses.

Delightful Lemreway and Orinsay have a distinctly serene end-of-the-line feeling. When family boats were more commonplace, and the sea was the main highway, both settlements on the shore of Loch Shell were within easy reach of communities around the coast. Bonnie Prince Charlie crept quietly to this shore in May 1746. The royal fugitive, with a £30,000 bounty on his head, hid on Eilean Liubhaird, a staging post on his successful flight through the Outer Hebrides to evade capture after defeat of his Jacobite army at the Battle of Culloden on 16 April 1746.

Sunshine-yellow flag iris and fluffy willow grow thickly around the trickling burn by Lemreway pier. Islanders valued the iris as a natural dye to colour their homespun cloth; they planted it liberally around their homes and villages to create hues of bright green from the leaves, yellow from the petals and black from the root. With willow they shaped creels to catch crab and lobster, and sturdy baskets to carry freshly landed fish. In large deep baskets tied to their backs, they transported mounds of seaweed from the shore and dried peats from the moor.

A waymarked Heritage Path crosses rough and boggy moorland to reach the evocative empty village of Steimreway, cleared by landowners in 1857. Part of the route traces the path taken by children attending the local school in Lemreway. On a clear day, views to the enigmatic Shiant Islands and the lonely landscape of Eishken are breathtaking. Eishken is identified by Scottish Natural Heritage as one of only four areas in Scotland more than five miles away from any road. Allow around three hours for the spectacular four-mile return walk, strenuous in parts over rough ground, but the beautiful encouragement of white-tailed sea eagles and golden eagles is sure to spur you on.

Back on the A859, the imposing roadside Pairc Raiders Monument honours courageous families who resisted the laird's plans to extend his sporting estate by evicting the community in 1887. The monument is built with the stones

Curiosity

Much of the open land across the Outer Hebrides is treeless, yet traces of prehistoric woodlands exist in deep layers of peat. The lonely hills of the privately owned Eishken estate host a rare clutch of native trees with undiluted genetic material, an extraordinary natural treasure requiring significant protection.

of ruined homes. An observation platform surveys the battleground.

A stone monument at Arivruach recalls the 1746 manhunt for Bonnie Prince Charlie. The inscription affirms: 'It is to the eternal honour of all Hebrideans that regardless of their loyalties he was not betrayed to the authorities.'

Aline Community Woodland comes as a surprise in a landscape where trees are few. Discover leafy walks and picnic benches. The playground is a great place for children to let off steam.

The transition from Lewis to Harris and vice versa around the shore of Loch Seaforth is almost imperceptible, without fanfare or hullabaloo. An easily missed road sign is about the sum of it, however don't let that put you off. There is plenty of drama ahead, but first to Ardvourlie.

In Ardvourlie Woodland car park at Bogha Glas, a plaque honours the momentous day in March 2003 when the people of North Harris achieved a community buyout and became owners of the surrounding land. From this celebratory spot, a stony hill path climbs 11 miles across high hills to Miabhaig. A woodland observatory along the way offers elevated views over Loch Seaforth into the Harris hills, the heart of the highest golden eagle density in Europe. The likelihood of seeing them is strong, especially from the dedicated observatory in Gleann Miabhaig, part of the Bird of Prey Trail through the islands.

As if not to be outdone by eagles, the A859 from Bogha Glas soars up the slopes of An Cliseam, or the Clisham, the highest summit in Harris. The direct walkers' route from the road to the hill is demanding but pales in comparison with the nine-hour Clisham Horseshoe Walk, a Hebridean classic that starts low and rises high. The dizzying swirl of the smooth, fast road climbing upwards is thrilling in clear weather. Dense low cloud blots out views and increases anxiety. A single-track offshoot threads precariously to Maraig and Rhenigidale, the last place in Britain to be connected by road. Electricity arrived in 1918, tarmac in 1990.

From Maraig a walking route through Gleann Lacasdail reaches Urgha Beag to connect with the road to Tarbert and the Postman's Path. Braw mailmen ran this flabbergasting route three times a week, in all weathers, to ensure that post, medication and news got through to isolated families. Larger supplies arrived by boat from Tarbert. A spur off the Path leads to Molinginish, a small settlement on a hushed bay. Without a safe harbour the community was especially isolated. In the 1960s they abandoned their homes. Pressure mounted to bring the road to Rhenigidale lest the same depopulation happen there.

From the Clisham's heights, the helter-skelter A859 arrives on the shore of West Loch Tarbert. At Ardhasaig casks of whisky from the community-owned Isle of Harris Distillery mature quietly in a seashore warehouse. The popular gin is already flowing. Tarbert derives its name from the narrow neck of land that served as a crossing place for boats hauled out of water. The overland shortcut gained swift access to the waters of East Loch Tarbert and West Loch Tarbert.

Regular ferry crossings on the triangle route between Uig in Skye, Tarbert in Harris and Lochmaddy in North Uist have promoted economic growth. In recent years the Tarbert shore has been redeveloped to create a new pier at the ferry terminal and a marina with excellent facilities adjacent to the distillery. Every day a peat fire burns at the distillery hearth, symbolic of the warm welcome extended by the people of Harris to visitors. One of my favourite island buildings is the timber-built Tarbert Stores. The wood arrived as ballast in a ship from Sweden that departed with a cargo of fish.

Beauty Spot

The trail through Gleann Lacasdail combines with the Postman's Path to Rhenigidale to make a thrilling and challenging circular walk with spectacular views to Skye and the Shiants. Allow around six hours for the 12-mile route. Mountain bikers are requested to ride the loop in a clockwise direction from Urgha Beag; this kindness reduces damaging erosion. A Rhenigidale croft house became the first of a small group of youth hostels established by Herbert Gatliff in 1962. Facilities are basic yet cosy.

Curiosity

The Harris Hotel was built in 1865 as a sporting retreat for anglers. Treasured guest books record the visits of J.M. Barrie, author of *Peter Pan*. After the death of his friends Arthur and Sylvia Llewelyn Davies, in 1907 and 1910 respectively, Barrie adopted the couple's five boys. In July 1912, he took them all on a fishing holiday to Harris. Before returning home, he etched his initials in a dining-room windowpane.

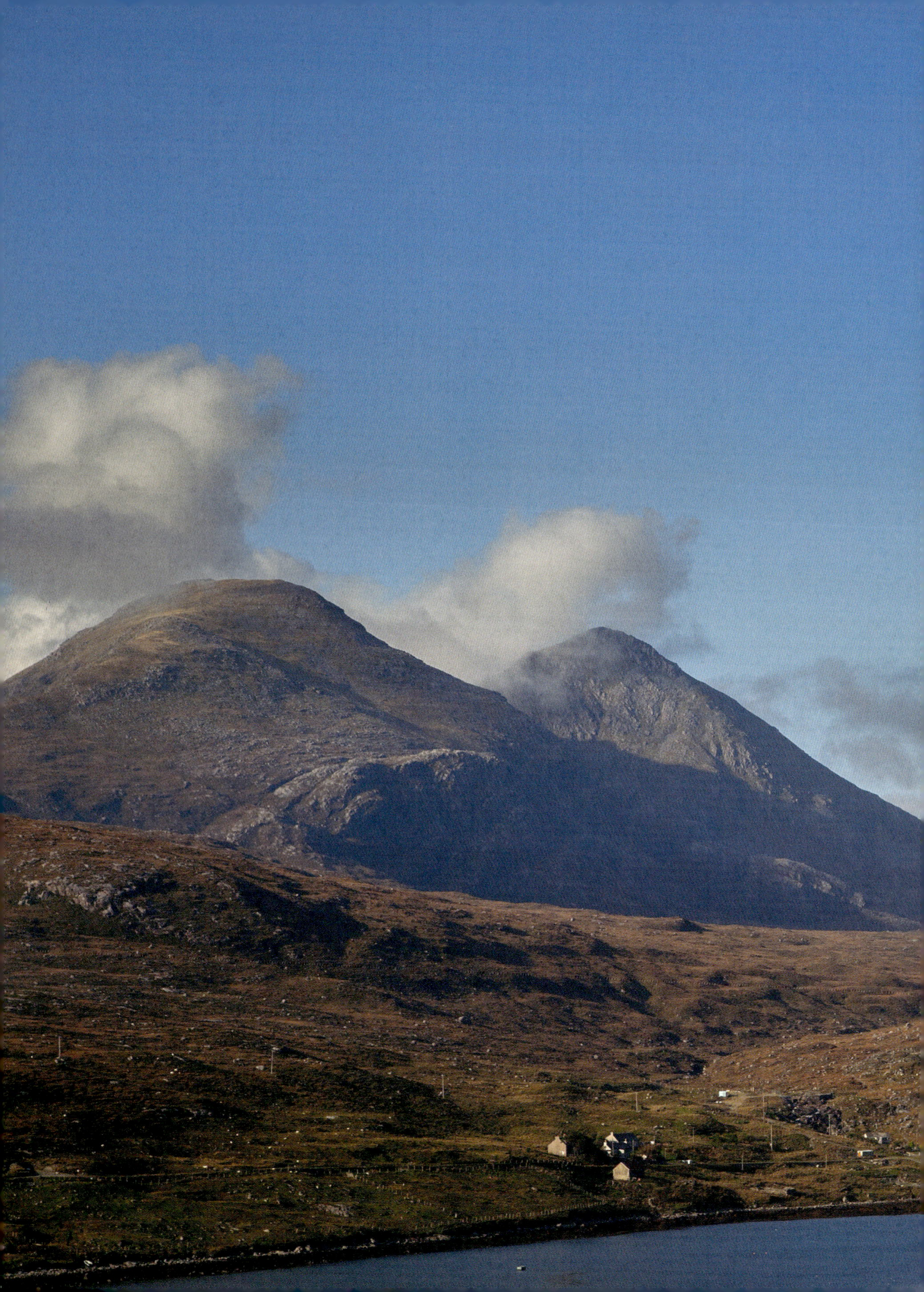

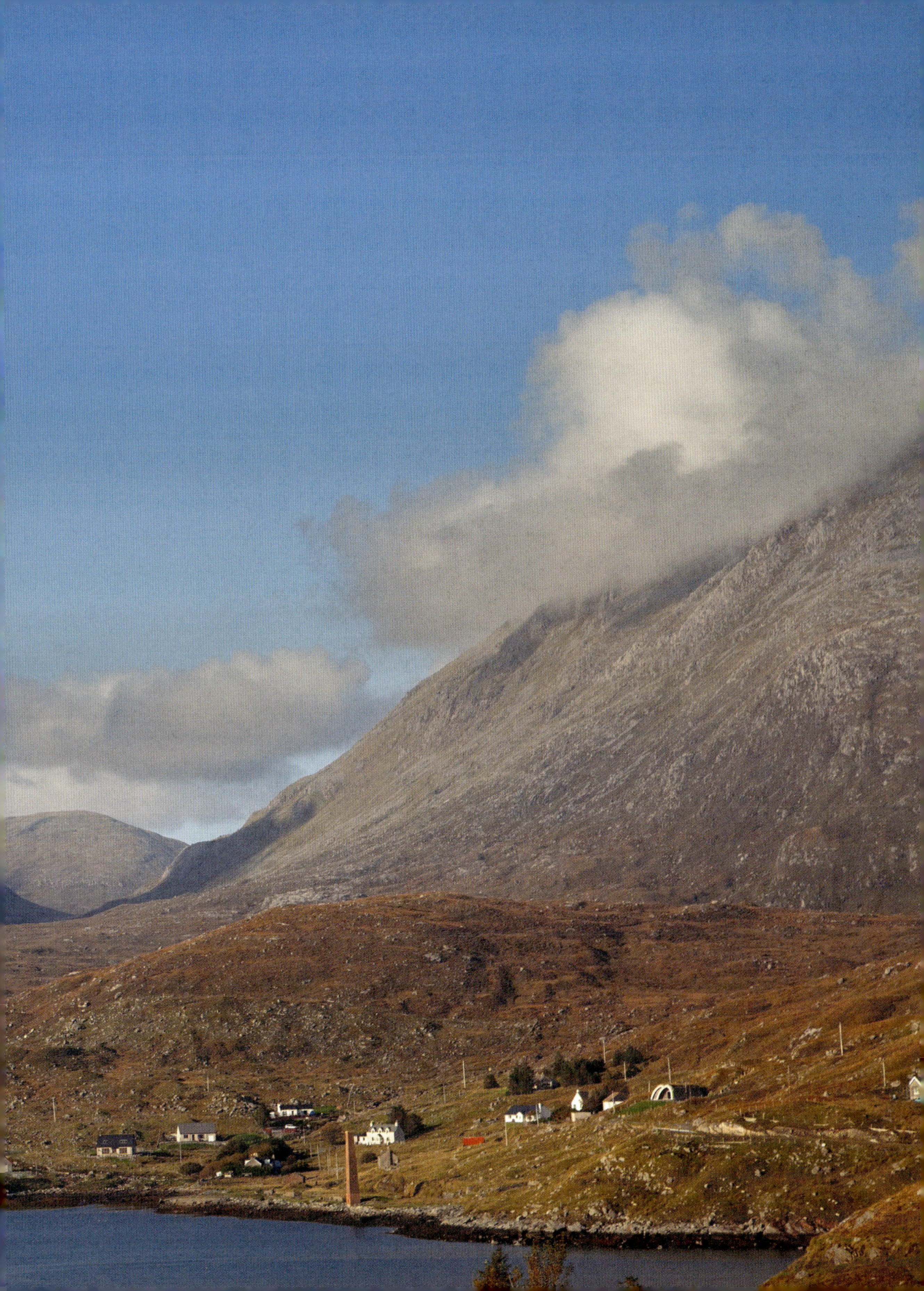

HEBRIDEAN JOURNEY

To Scalpay

A favourite route scampers along the South Harris coast, from Tarbert to intriguing Scalpay island. The expedition begins on the fabulously short A868. The shrimpy A-road began life as the even shrimpier B868. Promotion to major classified road status came in the 1920s, for all 0.2 miles of it.

From Tarbert the little road soon arrives in Oban, a small cluster of crofts, quite different to its mainland namesake. The Loomshed Brewery graces the hillside overlooking the waters of East Loch Tarbert towards the Isle of Skye. The brewery team crafts beers named in celebration of traditional Hebridean life: The Crofter is a pale ale; Iasgair, which is Gaelic for 'fisherman', is a lager; and The Poacher is an altogether darker brew with tasty hints of peat.

At Urgha Beag the A-road signs off, passing the baton to an unclassified thread of tarmac that sallies steeply uphill to Scalpay. Urgha Beag is a lonely but significant junction. The country bus from Tarbert to Scalpay halts at a small car park to deliver gleeful walkers to the start of the classic Urgha and Maraig circuit walk of 12 miles deep into thrilling Harris hills, and along the lovely shore of Loch Lacasdale towards the historic Postman's Path, which delivers outstanding rugged and hilly coastal scenery all the way to Rhenigidale.

An optional spur visits the deserted village of Molinginish, secluded and snug on the sheltered shore of Loch Trollamarig, a heavenly spot. Allow around six hours for the spectacular adventure and prepare well. It is essential to take appropriate kit, including maps, clothing, food, and drink; remember, the weather can change quickly and dramatically here. It is good practice to always let someone know you are going deep into the hills and remote places, even if you only leave a note at your lodgings. Should anything untoward occur and you fail to return in due course, the information will make all the difference to the coastguard and heroic volunteers of the mountain rescue teams finding you swiftly.

In my experience, people in remote communities notice when someone appears to be lost, or perhaps has not returned to their car for a long while. Their caring and generous spirit is a most precious thing.

Beyond the Urgha Beag walkers' car park, the road crosses Loch

Lacasdale, passing a lane to the quiet shore. Shorter walks around the loch are especially popular with local people, and the rich waters attract anglers in pursuit of salmon and brown trout. Onward towards Scalpay, the road zips steeply uphill to reach a roadside picnic bench with delicious views over scattered islands in East Loch Tarbert. Floating rings pattern the surface of the seawater, evidence of farmed salmon in cages below.

Scampering along the shore of the hill coast, the road reveals first glimpses of sleek Scalpay bridge. A striking and sparing design that reminds me of an expertly measured dining table wedged exactingly, with great aplomb, in the gap between two high steep hills. I love it.

The distinctive road and footbridge opened in 1997 replacing the ferry from the Kyle of Scalpay slipway, a crossing of just five minutes to the island. Now island moggies rule the slipway, scouring the heaped creels for any juicy titbits of crab and lobster left behind by the fishers. On closer approach to the bridge, a favourite roadside sign announces unusual traffic: Otters Crossing.

Scalpay native Christina Morrison, aged 110, was among the first people invited across the bridge. In celebratory mood she reflected on historic changes in the Hebrides through her lifetime and attributed her longevity to island life and a diet rich in herring and potatoes. There is a warm welcome in Scalpay; the island community treasures what they have and supports low-impact tourism. Visitors are encouraged to experience the island, just 2.5 miles long, on a waymarked circular walk. Allow around three hours for the loop of approximately seven miles. Some sections cross heathery moorland; stout waterproof boots are advised.

Scalpay's muddy creeks, rocky knolls, whitewashed cottages, moorland spaces and clear views to the enchanted Sound of Shiant are spellbinding. Tottering sheep wander island lanes and otters patrol the seashore. Scarlet hedges of wild fuchsia and blazing clumps of fiery orange crocosmia set the island aglow in late summer, an especially lovely time to visit.

The island circuit visits Loch an Duin, where a causeway connects from the shore to a fortified island, from here the walk climbs the gentle slopes of Beinn Scorabhaig, just 341 feet high and dwarfed by lofty Leac Easgadail across the straits. On a crisp clear day, Beinn Scorabhaig offers an astounding panoramic spectacle of Harris hills, island shores in Lewis, Benbecula, Barra, and, across the sparkling sea, the distinct summits of Skye and mainland Wester Ross and Sutherland too. Scalpay's lovely lighthouse tower at Eilean Glas, dressed in the red and white of a barber's pole, is another highlight of the walk.

When Harris lairds cleared tenants from their land in the 1840s, fragmented communities faced hard choices. Some evicted families summoned hope for a fresh start far away. They emigrated to the Americas or Cape Breton. Others remained in the Hebrides or moved to the mainland. Scalpay received a wave of homeless people, and the compact island was soon congested. Without croft land for everyone, new ways of making a living were a priority.

The island is blessed with two large natural harbours that offered the possibility of harvesting the sea commercially and so the men of Scalpay became herring fishers, and teams of island women sized, gutted and salted the catch at curing stations around the shore. As the fleet grew, Scalpay crews became renowned as immensely skilful seafarers. Fishing brought prosperity to the island; in the 1960s Scalpay enjoyed the highest income per capita of any community in Britain. The island fleet is now much reduced: only North Harbour remains a commercial fisheries pier.

The historic island hub, known simply as The Village, gathers around a grassy green between the harbours. North Harbour Bistro, just a few creels away from the slipway, serves mouth-watering, freshly landed seafood dishes. From the delightfully named Outend Road at Kennavay, where a clutch of crofts cling to a fertile hillside, a rough hardcore track snakes across the heathery moor to reach the lighthouse on Eilean Glas. Allow around 30 minutes to walk to the magical spot.

The teasing tip of the red-and-white striped tower and lantern appears in the distance long before the full reveal. A magnificent drystone wall necklace elegantly encircles the beacon and surrounding plots of rough land where keepers and their families housed livestock and tended vegetables. Stepping through an imposing pillared gateway in the moorland boundary wall feels like entering a magic kingdom.

Exploration reveals not one but two lighthouses. The main tower, completed in 1824, superseded a much smaller tower built in 1789. The taller of the pair remains in service and closed to visitors who are welcome to discover other parts of the intriguing complex. I am always taken by the stylish flourishes around the doorway of the keepers' cottages, exotic details in a wildly rugged location. This is

Curiosity

The tower of Eilean Glas lighthouse is striped red and white to distinguish it as a navigational day mark. The first keeper was Alexander Reid, a former sailor from Fraserburgh who arrived with his family in 1789 and stayed for 35 years. Reid attended faithfully to the light that supported safe passage of shipping from Norway, Sweden, Lapland, Prussia and Russia with cargoes of timber, tallow, tar and flax. When Reid met civil engineer and lighthouse builder Robert Stevenson, he advanced his brother John as the ideal candidate to keep vigil on Bell Rock, also known as Inchcape. The Bell Rock lighthouse was completed in 1811 and John Reid became the first keeper.

Curiosity

A simply beautiful poem by Norman MacCaig remembers boyhood visits to Scalpay where his Aunt Julia, a glorious force of island nature, spoke her native Gaelic mother tongue at him loudly and fast, with a distinct *blas*, or twang. He remembers the angst of not being able to understand her any more than he could answer her, much as he might have wished to do both. Yet he felt safe and secure in her domain where things that might otherwise have unsettled him seemed comforting. Unable to converse with his aunt, he observed her closely and sensitively, noting the seabird tenor of her voice, the black garments of widowhood, her dark peat-stained feet, one grown stronger than the other by working hard at the treadle of her whirring spinning wheel. His evocative tribute to Aunt Julia reflects on the precious bonds we have with each other and at her graveside in the seashore burial ground of Luskentyre on mainland Harris, he regrets he did not have command of her Gaelic language sooner.

repeated at Ardnamurchan, another of my lighthouse favourites. The mighty Eilean Glas foghorn was installed in 1907 and decommissioned in 1987.

Eilean Glas is an important shorewatch site on the Hebridean Whale Trail, frequented in summer by minke whales, Risso's dolphins and basking sharks. Happily, the beacon is no longer lit by whale oil. Views from the lighthouse terrace to the nearest neighbours, the Shiants, known in Gaelic as 'the Enchanted Islands', are serene on a clear day and eerie in brooding weather. The enigmatic group is empty of people now, but census records reveal the population peaked in 1901 when a community of 16 people inhabited the islands. Among the last people to leave for a new life in mainland Harris was a young woman of 21 years old who had never previously left the Shiant shores.

The Huisinis Road

It is a long rocky road to far-away Huisinis, a dreamy bay with an Old Norse name that means 'House on the Headland'. Befitting a mythical quest, the approach to this magical shore is not for the faint-hearted or anyone uncomfortable with the prospect of managing their vehicle with supreme dexterity along a 14-mile-long roller-coaster single-track road that is an essential lifeline to the local community. Seriously.

The skinny vertiginous route to Huisinis is entirely unsuitable for anyone who does not feel confident about reversing their vehicle deftly and sometimes urgently around precipitous bends and up steep hills. The remote coastal highway is of vital importance to local people going about their everyday lives. The importance of slower-moving drivers, unfamiliar with the road, understanding how to use passing places correctly and permitting local traffic to overtake cannot be overemphasised. This consideration and kindness is hugely appreciated by islanders on single-track roads throughout the Outer Hebrides.

The journey begins deceptively gently on the northern shore of West Loch Tarbert. Ceann an Ora is a bay with a bloody past to which the landmark red-brick chimney bears witness. Bunavoneader is the best-preserved example of a shore-based whaling station in the UK, founded in 1904 by Norwegian Karl Herlofsen. Much of the site has been cleared but the carcass slipway remains. The grim but important ruins became a Scheduled Ancient Monument in 1992.

Hebridean whale pursuit ships sailed to hunt leviathans in waters far beyond Bunavoneader. To make each mission cost-effective, they paid rent to anchor their haul of harpooned whales in Village Bay on

Curiosity

The business of hunting whales for processing at Bunavoneader contributed to a critically reduced population of many species, not least the local extinction of the tragically named right whale, or *Eubalaena glacialis*. The wonderfully acrobatic yet hefty creatures, once widespread, are among the world's most endangered large species. Only a few hundred right whales survive due to human threats. Their common name hints at the reason for their especially desperate demise. Moving slowly at the surface, gentle right whales were perfectly easy targets for the hunters' harpoons. Whales and Dolphin Conservation, the leading charity working to protect whales and dolphins around the world and the conservation of the habitat in which they live, depends on public support and awareness to make a difference to their future.

Hirta, the largest island in the St Kilda archipelago, before returning to hunt for more. As days passed, the decomposing corpses of Village Bay rose from the sea. Breezes carried the deathly stench ashore, but the St Kilda community tolerated the stomach-churning fetor in return for precious steady income. When sufficient whales had been killed, the hunters hitched up to six of them to the pursuit ship and returned to Bunavoneader. Occasionally St Kilda folk travelled with them, to visit their distant island neighbours for business and pleasure.

On the shore of Ceann an Ora the magnificent whales were hauled up the slipway and hoisted aloft to be butchered and flensed. Nothing was wasted. The ocean giants were processed into oil, fertiliser, bonemeal, cattle food, and dried and salted meat. Bunavoneader closed during the First World War, but Lord Leverhulme acquired the business to sell whale meat to Africa in the 1920s. After almost a decade the shore station closed again with a brief resurgence in the 1950s. The ruinous Bunavoneader complex is an especially significant location on the Hebridean Whale Trail and in this unsettling place I am always touched by the granite monument near the shore, dedicated to Sam, the faithful sea dog of Norwegian Captain Jesperson.

Through whaleback rounded hills, the coast road to Huisinis travels onward, passing salmon farm cages in the sea loch where the tragic cavalcades were towed ashore. To come upon the jarring sight of a pristine green tennis court and small wooden clubhouse in a sea of peat, rock and heather is wonderfully surreal and mind boggling. Beautifully remote and perfectly flat, Bunavoneader tennis court, built in 1988, is available to hire, along with racquets and balls, an awesome testament to the determination of local people who raised funds to change up from traffic-dodging games on the bumpy highway, bouncing balls over fishing nets.

The road reaches a car park for walkers entering the realm of golden eagles. The Gleann Miabhaig observatory offers the opportunity to survey the resident birds though the seasons. Allow half an hour for the two-kilometre walk along a rough track. Beyond the observatory, Loch Voshimid is a renowned fishing spot and the inspiration for J.M. Barrie's 1920 play *Mary Rose*.

The dreamy and eerie piece introduces Mary Rose as a spirited young woman who loves to go sketching on a favourite uninhabited Outer Hebridean island 'that likes to be visited'. When Mary disappears without trace for 20 days, everyone fears the worst. The joy of her re-appearance is marred by something deeply disturbing about her. To reveal any more would spoil the haunting plot.

A further surreal experience awaits at Amhuinnsuidhe where the road prances straight through the manicured grounds of a baronial castle with splendid canons on the lochside lawn. The wonderful weirdness of the stately pile is in keeping with the incongruous red-brick whaling station chimney and the emerald tennis court. In Gaelic, Amhuinnsuidhe means 'sitting by the river' and, sure enough, the castle lounges on a riverbank where migrating Atlantic salmon leap through white water cascades to reach upstream spawning beds.

The grand abode was built in the 1860s for the 20-year-old Charles Adolphus Murray, seventh Earl of Dunmore. His grandfather purchased Harris in 1834, and by 1839 his father, the sixth Earl, was enlisting the support of police from Glasgow and armed soldiers to evict tenant crofters from the estate. Charles sold the castle to his bankers. Subsequent proprietors included aviator and aircraft manufacturer Sir Tommy Sopwith. The North Harris Estate was purchased in 2003 in a joint bid by the residents of North Harris and businessman Ian Scarr-Hall, who acquired the castle with attendant shooting and fishing rights.

Beauty Spot

From the hidden Huisinis north shore, local crofters transfer sheep to summer grazing on the uninhabited island of Scarp, another lost Hebridean community. Scarp reached a population peak of 213 inhabitants in 1881. A rough path from the north-shore jetty scrambles to white shell sands at Traigh Mheilein, haunting and extraordinarily luminous on the greyest day.

A track to the east of Amhuinnsuidhe discovers rugged lonely hills, the haunt of red deer and golden eagles. The summit of Tiorgha Mhor rises above the hydro dam at Loch Chliostair; views of surrounding uplands and islands are fabulous. The stalker's path into Gleann Uladail guides climbers to the imposing mass of Sron Uladail, the largest overhanging cliff in the United Kingdom.

Departing Amhuinnsuidhe under a triumphal arch, the road passes the stone jetty where visitors and fish are landed. The only side road along the entire journey slips to Govig, a clutch of crofts between a freshwater loch and the sea. A yomp across the moor from here reaches a tidal wild swimming pool at Rubha Buic. The long road pushes on and Huisinis hoves into view, a handful of cottages on a deep arc of white sands backed by grassy machair. In summer, the green is awash with wildflowers. The community-managed Huisinis Gateway facility welcomes visitors. Five motorhome parking spaces are available on a first-come, first-served basis.

The fishers of Scarp sent live lobsters to Billingsgate fish market in London and received payment only for those that survived the tortuous journey, a reflection of the challenging economic and social circumstances of island life.

When Scarp islander Christy Maclennan became unwell after giving birth to her baby girl, Mary, in January 1934, the new mum was transported urgently by boat to the Huisinis shore and bus from Harris to Stornoway in Lewis for medical attention. There she gave birth to another girl, Jessie. The twins were known affectionately as Miss Harris and Miss Lewis.

Possibly inspired by the plight of Christy and her daughters, German rocket scientist Gerhard Zucker suggested that the Scarp community would benefit hugely from the delivery of mail and medicine loaded into a canister attached to a rocket fired from Amhuinnsuidhe. His ambitious plan failed after a few disastrous explosive attempts in July 1934. Through the following years, the Scarp community dwindled. In 1967 the primary school closed; the post office closed in 1968. When Mr and Mrs MacInnes and their two sons departed in December 1971, aboard a small boat stacked with furniture and their two cows swimming behind, Scarp was no longer the most westerly inhabited island in Scotland.

The Golden Road to the East

This journey discovers fascinating fragmented shores at the eastern edge of Harris, from Tarbert to Rodel, and a stretch of highway that proved so costly to build it became known as the Golden Road.

Just a short distance from Tarbert, the Diracleit headland is a favourite vantage point, a happy place to observe the CalMac ferry steaming through islands and islets in East Loch Roag. The road around Loch

Ceann Dibig offers sweeping views of Scotosay, a privately owned island that hosted a community of 20 people at its peak in 1911.

The road to the gold coast of west Harris swerves inland through the hills, leaving a splendid spur to loop around the sea lochs of the eastern shore. At Miabhaig a handsome building beside the burn reveals how community needs changed in the wake of estate clearances that drove evicted farming families to resettle on less fertile land here, to nourish the spiritual needs of the rapidly growing community; the former corn mill became a Free Presbyterian prayer and meeting house.

The ribbon of Golden Road gilds the shores of lochs and lochans between Plocrapol and Scadabay and it is easy to imagine the delight of the first car drivers tooting horns in celebration of the new highway connecting communities previously reached by the sea. A bracing moorland path from the north end of Loch Plocrapol to Greosabhagh forms part of the Harris Walkway, much of which features on the long-distance Hebridean Way for hikers. The Hebridean Way for cyclists follows a different route in parts.

Beauty Spot

A picnic bench opposite the red painted gate of the Old Post Office at Drinishader enjoys views of islets and ferries in East Loch Tarbert. Discover a colourful celebration of Harris Tweed through generations of weavers at the Clò-Mòr exhibition in the Old School. Nearby, Drinishader Hostel offers budget accommodation in an attractive stone cottage with an open fire.

Thin windswept soil around the east coast bays is unsuitable for planting and so hard-working communities grew staple crops of oats, potatoes and barley in labour-intensive ridges of mounded earth, known as *feannagan* or, entirely inappropriately, lazy beds, nourished with manure, seaweed and straw. The bare-knuckle terrain of this landscape feels so much a world apart that Stanley Kubrick chose it to represent planet Jupiter in his 1968 sci-fi movie *2001: A Space Odyssey*. The local rock, known as anorthosite, is used for road building; it is also found on the moon.

From Greosabhagh the road rises and falls through the hills to visit Collam, Cluther and Kyles Stockinish where an offshoot sweeps to the working pier. The North Harris Free Presbyterian Church of Scotland

Curiosity

An historic footpath from Aird Mighe at the head of Loch Stockinish follows the Bealach Eorbabhat pass through the hills to Seilebost on the western shore of Harris. Mourners from the rocky east coast travelled this nine-mile coffin route to bury their dead safely in the deeper soil of the west. The pass was used also by people from the west delivering wool to Geocrab mill where a cast-iron pipe aqueduct at Geocrab, and still in service, supplied a hydro-powered wool spinning and carding mill built in 1923 by Lord Leverhulme. The building is now a fish hatchery.

Allow around five hours for the coast-to-coast adventure.

is an elevated landmark beside freshwater Loch a' Chaolais, thick with waxy white lilies in summer.

Children from Lacklee trekked to school in Kyles Stockinish with a slab of dry peat for the classroom fire. To protect the youngsters from getting mired in the bog along the way, the community built a solid level track on an embankment, extending it to Greosabhagh when a new school was opened. Allow around two hours to walk The Scholar's Path, an extraordinary school run with spectacular sea and mountain views.

Here, an array of spur roads discover wonderful hideaway shores. The team at Lickisto campsite liken the landscape to Middle Earth, the fantasy continent imagined by author J.R.R. Tolkien. When the aurora borealis swirls in the vast night sky, the comparison grows stronger.

A hill path to the rear of the wonderfully vibrant Skoon Art Café in Geocrab reaches the ruins of a small community at Struparsaig. Children from this sheltered outpost tramped to school at Manish. To reach the nearest shop, they rowed around the coast to Stockinish. Decorated stones and plaques on old walls remember with love people who lived in this gentle place. The atmospheric walk and serene experience of Struparsaig makes for a magical couple of hours.

The road curls to Beacravik where an undersea cable makes landfall, connecting Lewis and Harris to the national electricity grid. Ardslave is an extension of the little township. Blissful Manish is a high point with views to the imperious mountains of the north-west mainland. Headland cairns, possibly constructed by Norse settlers, continue to serve as navigational landmarks. A side road drops to a blackhouse with a fun window made of jam jars and sauce bottles set in rough cement. Nothing is wasted on an island. Donald's novelty window is celebrated in a traditional song 'An Uinneag a Rinn Domhnall'. Manish was home to Gaelic-speaking Anna Eoghainn, or Annie MacDonald, who emigrated to the United States and landed the highly regarded role of housekeeper at the White House. An extraordinary transit.

While the snaking narrow roads through the Bays district make for joyous cycling, treasure islets and secret coves enchant sea kayakers. Encounters with otters and seals are frequent. For fishers, there are wild brown trout in freshwater lochs and herring, mackerel, crab and lobster offshore. The Finsbay Fishings comprise about 50 lochs on Finsbay, 35 on Flodabay, and 17 on Stockinish.

From Flodabay the winding road negotiates the extraordinary Braigh nam Bagh, pool upon pool of dark peaty water illuminated by waxy white lilies in summer. A branch road jaunts to the cape of Quidinish which stares into the dramatic Cuillin mountain range on the Isle of

Skye, some 18 miles distant across the Minch. At Ardvey a fork in the road presents the opportunity to visit Leverburgh or Rodel. We visit Leverburgh in the next section so let's take the road to Rodel.

The Mission House Studio at Finsbay is an oasis of art founded by photographer Beka Globe and ceramic artist Nickolai Globe. Also at Finsbay is a public phone box which, for a brief magical interlude in the 1990s, allowed callers to connect anywhere in the world for just ten pence. Folk still talk about the magnificent glitch. Over the hill, Borsham is a small, attractive inlet on Loch Finsbay.

The surrounds of Lingarabay remain largely unscathed after moves to build a super quarry were seen off by islanders and environmental campaigners. The proposal to extract millions of tonnes of anorthosite from the belly of Roineabhal, which means 'rough hill' in Old Norse, resulted in protracted legal dealings between 1991 and 2004. Summit views from Roineabhal scope the Minch, the Atlantic Ocean, and the extraordinary Sound of Harris, awash with reefs, skerries and islets.

Bayhead gardens brim with pink and blue hydrangeas and swaying golden spires of pampas grass. From here the C79 road makes its final wiggling approach to Rodel, the spiritual capital of Harris.

St Clement's Church is one the finest pre-Reformation buildings in the Outer Hebrides. The religious site occupies a rocky rise above Roll an Tighnhail, a natural harbour in the shelter of three small islands. The haven permitted Alasdair Crotach Macleod, eighth chief of the Macleods of Harris and Dunvegan,

> # Curiosity
>
> A short film made in 1938 captures aspects of summer crofting life in Flodabay. *They Are Forsaken* is just 20 minutes long and free to watch on BFI Player. Geography teacher and amateur film-maker Henry George shows a crofter using traditional natural plant dyes for her Harris Tweed palette, a father and son making nets and frames for their wooden lobster creels and the postie walking his rugged coastal round to deliver important news.

> # Curiosity
>
> Celtic tradition recognises that the balance of female and male energies creates harmony. Women enjoyed equal status to men with the possibility of moving through society to become leaders, warriors, inventors, teachers and artists. This changed when the Romans and Christianity came to Britain. People from the Celtic tribes were made slaves. Under Roman law, women were not equal to men, they were assigned to men as chattels. Sculptures on the tower at Rodel celebrate the Celtic tradition. A graphic figure of a crouching woman with splayed legs hints at the energy and fertility of womanhood. She is a Sheela-na-gig, one of many in religious buildings across Scotland including the refectory at Iona nunnery and St Magnus Cathedral in Kirkwall, Orkney. On the south side of the Rodel tower a counterpart sculpted man is depicted holding something in both hands that has been removed. He is known as Seumas a' Bhuid, or 'James of the Willy'. According to local tradition, the Countess of Dunmore, who owned Harris and restored the church in 1873, requested that his penis be shot off.

to approach the church he founded and dedicated to Pope Clement I, patron saint of mariners, from the sea. The clan chief commissioned ambitiously decorative carvings around the church and supervised the design of his own table tomb two decades before his death in 1528. In choosing Rodel as his burial place, he broke with tradition; his forebears are buried in Iona.

A handsome historic mansion house at Rodel harbour was originally

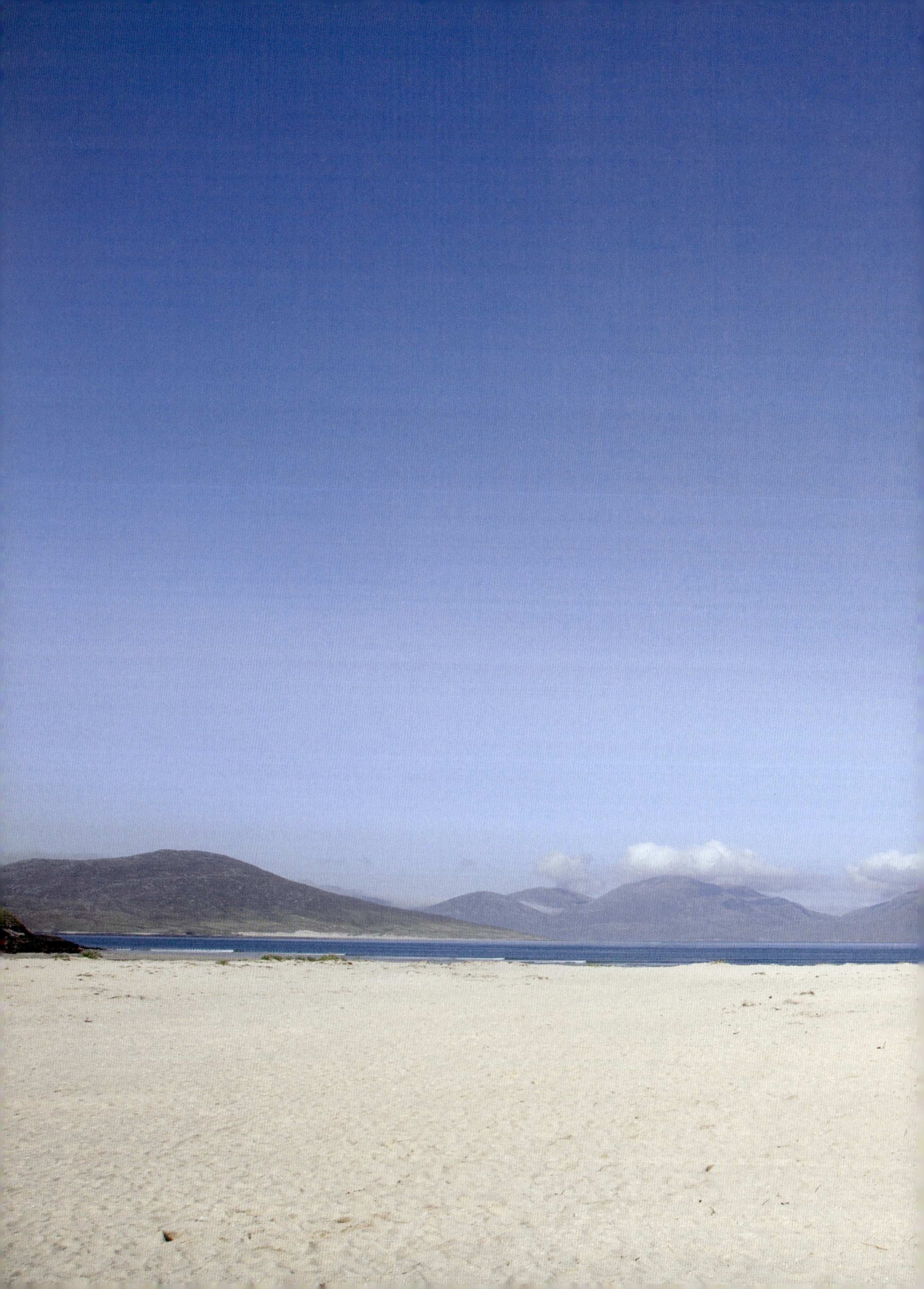

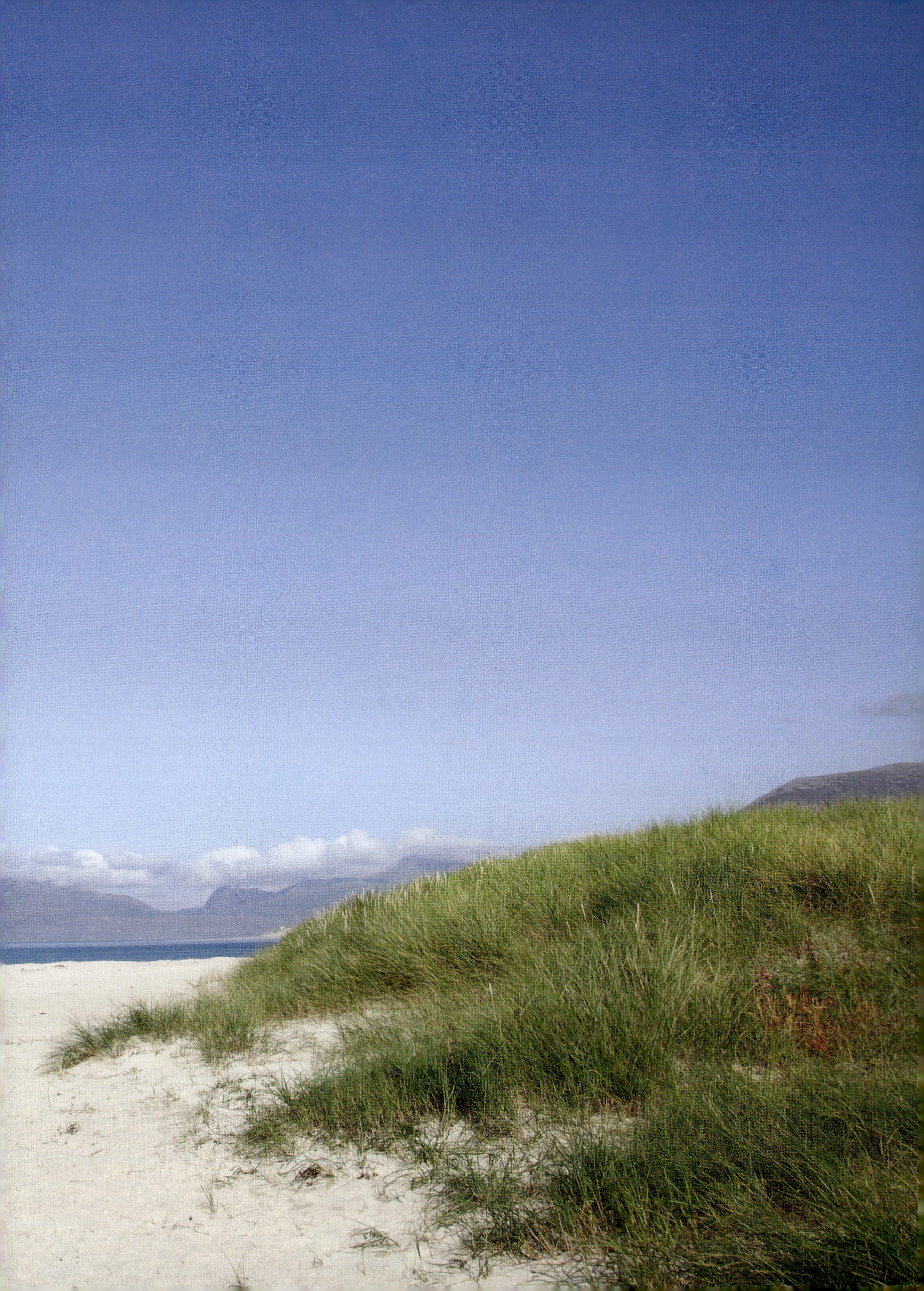

the home of Captain Alexander Macleod who bought Harris in 1779. The laird's pile graces the quays he developed to provide a solid landing place for deep-sea fishers, the ferry service connecting with the Isle of Skye, mailboats, cargo ships and harvests of kelp. A distinctive sloping ramp ensured the safe transport of livestock at all states of the tide. On surrounding land, the laird built a corn mill and a mill to spin wool for tweed and linen, and twine for herring nets.

The mansion house later became the Rodel Hotel and enjoyed a reputation for faraway quirkiness. When Northern Irish poet Louis MacNeice wrote 'I Crossed the Minch' in 1938, he was struck by the sensation that the former Rodel Hotel is 'at the end of everything'. In the 1950s the hotel bar served rarely available Royal Household whisky to the cognoscenti; the blend was created for the royals by James Buchanan in 1900. Rodel features in a famously tangled real-life island love story from 1850 which happens to involve unrelated characters by the name of Macdonald.

Jessie Macdonald of Balranald House, North Uist, was the sweetheart of Donald Macdonald, a native of Skye. Her beau worked as estate factor to the laird of North Uist but his lenience towards the crofters caused him to be dismissed. Deeming jobless Donald unworthy, Jessie's ambitious father forced his daughter towards Patrick Cooper, Commissioner to the Macdonald Estate and instigator of the North Uist evictions at Sollas. Big mistake.

Spirited Jessie determined to have her man. Declining Cooper's advances, the 21-year-old woman plotted successfully to escape her father's plans and quit North Uist under cover of darkness with Donald. The lovers set sail for the Isle of Skye, but pesky Hebridean winds blew them to Tarbert in Harris where news of the elopement was widespread. Jessie was captured and taken to a room in her uncle's house at Rodel where her aunt kept close guard.

Donald sailed to Skye and raised a posse of pals who helped him release Jessie from confinement. The couple fled to Edinburgh where they married. Donald was charged with assault and breaking into Rodel House. His acquittal, on the grounds that Jessie was being held against her will, was celebrated throughout the islands. Jessie and Donald emigrated to Melbourne, Australia, in 1852. The couple had 12 children; tragically only six survived their parents.

The Remarkable Sound of Harris

The Sound of Harris is a remarkable channel between the waters of the Minch and Little Minch to the east and the Atlantic Ocean to the west. The perilous shallow waters, thick with reefs, skerries and islets, are the hunting ground of white-tailed sea eagles. Exploring this fascinating shore is a wonderful adventure.

Upon purchasing the South Harris estate in 1919, Lord Leverhulme proposed a revolutionary modernising scheme to exploit overlooked coastal assets and set his sights upon the quiet fishing village of An t-Ob. The Sound of Harris sea passage offers access to the lucrative fishing grounds of the North Atlantic and this proved irresistible to the businessman. With extraordinary chutzpah, the laird renamed the community of An t-Ob in his honour, enjoying the consent of local people, most of whom were his tenants, and so from 1920 the settlement became known as Leverburgh.

The industrialist had form in this regard; much of his wealth came from his detergent factories beside an inlet of the River Mersey. He named that site, and the attractive Wirral village he built for his workers, Port Sunlight, to celebrate the runaway success of Sunlight soap, the world's first packaged and branded household soap for general use, launched in 1884.

Much as Captain Macleod's improvements provided employment at Rodel, Leverhulme envisaged islanders landing and processing fresh fish for distribution through his newly acquired chain of more than 400 fish shops known as MacFisheries. He wasted no time recruiting 300 construction workers to transform Leverburgh with a new pier for deep-sea trawlers, warehouses, stores, smokehouses, workers' accommodation, coffee house and school. By 1924 the stage was set, and fishing began in earnest. Herring drifters from Great Yarmouth landed a catch so enormous that extra labour was drafted in to process the bounty. But after a trip to Africa in 1925, the laird developed pneumonia and upon his demise the great MacFisheries project ended too.

After the whirlwind, Leverburgh readjusted. The lovely shore, thrown so extraordinarily into the spotlight, is without pretensions or airs and graces. Much evidence of the great fisheries project is gone. The community-managed store, An Clachan, is a treasure trove of essential foodstuffs

HEBRIDEAN JOURNEY

and exotic treats. Don't miss the Harris Millennium Tapestry in the gallery upstairs, beautifully observed vignettes of island life and history stitched by local people. The former school is a further community hub comprising a laundrette, museum and thrift shop, democratically named Aosd' is Ùr by public vote. The English translation is 'Old and New'.

Leverburgh harbour and ferry terminal are hard-working neighbours, separated by mounds of fishing gear, waste oil drums, pallets, industrial scrap, the lifeboat station hut and the iconic black Butty Bus, a former on-location film and TV catering unit decked out with bunting and hanging baskets. The Butty Bus is an island institution, serving friendly wit and sustenance to visitors and locals alike. Beside the ferry slipway the bustling Anchorage restaurant offers freshly landed seafood and local craft beer with appetising views of islands in the Sound of Harris. Reservations are always advised.

The narrow coast road that slips quietly away from Leverburgh towards the Carminish Islands is a delight. On sunny days the shimmering sea, speckled with islands near and far, is a sight to behold. At Strond, a small cairn honours two sisters whose weaving prowess is credited with igniting the fashionable spark of Harris Tweed.

In 1846 the Countess of Dunmore, owner of the North Harris Estate, commissioned sisters Catherine and Marion Macleod from the island of Pabbay, in the Sound of Harris, to refine their weaving skills in the mills of Paisley. When the women returned their patron encouraged them to produce high-quality island cloth for promotion to her affluent friends with country estates. The venture was a success and growing demand for the warm and durable fabric appropriate for furnishings and outdoor attire secured the future of the fledgling industry.

The Harris Tweed orb, in the design of a Maltese cross studded with 13 jewels, is the UK's oldest design trademark, registered in 1910 by the Harris Tweed Association Ltd. An Act of Parliament, passed in 1993, asserts only cloth dyed, spun, and woven by islanders in the Outer Hebrides may receive the orb seal. Inspectors assess every metre of fabric for quality before the heat-pressed beeswax seal is bestowed upon the reverse of the cloth.

The tarmac thread beyond the memorial cairn travels through shoreline crofts at Borrisdale and Port Eisgen before coming to an end beside whitewashed garden walls studded with seashells. From here a walk into the rugged coastal scenery of Renish Point is exhilarating. Allow around an hour to reach the most southerly headland in Harris. On clear days the Isle of Skye beckons. In mizzle and dreich it clears off. A shorter walk to Rodel, just 20 minutes away, also departs from the

Curiosity

In most island harbours, I might be inclined to wait patiently for otters and seals. At Leverburgh, it is cats I am after. A troupe of feral Harris moggies provide a rodent elimination service around the pier and in return for sterling work, the grateful fishing community cares for their well-being. The salty cats are so at ease around boats that one of the gang became an accidental stowaway in 2016, leaving Leverburgh on a yacht bound for mainland Oban some 200 nautical miles away. His adventure made the local news and, happily, repatriation efforts were successful.

road end. Encounters with golden eagles are distinctly likely.

Leaving Leverburgh behind, the smooth A859 sprints to the junction at Northton, a significant place of pilgrimage for visitors seeking information about their Western Isles family history. Co Leis Thu? is an important genealogy research centre within the Seallam! visitor centre established by Bill Lawson. The name recalls a traditional Gaelic proverb, *Cuimhnich cò leis a tha thu*, or 'Remember who you belong to'.

Temple bakery and deli takes its name from a medieval chapel on the shore of Toe Head. The enterprise occupies a quirky building that would happily befit an Outer Hebrides Hobbit. Freshly baked machair buns, infused with meadowsweet, are a taste sensation, especially with a morning coffee on the sandy shore of Traigh na Cleabhaig. Temple founder Amanda Saurin works further botanical magic to produce high-end skincare products and Wild Eve, a supreme, sunset-red, non-alcoholic drink like no other.

The Sound of Harris channel is littered with natural dangers, not least fast-flowing tides, submerged rocks and reefs. In 1858 HMS *Porcupine*, a three-gun wooden paddle steamer that had seen active service during the Crimean War, was commissioned to conduct a hydrographic survey to assist the safe passage of mariners. Under the command of the delightfully named Captain Otter (if ever there was a man for the job), HMS *Porcupine* examined 155 miles of coastline to deliver astonishingly detailed nautical charts revealing what islanders already knew: the Sound of Harris is passable only with extreme care. The chart identified exacting channels including The Grey Horse, The Gunwale, and the McNeil, and graphically named rocks, among them the Drowning Rock and the Cabbage group, apparently named in memory of an incident when a cargo of cabbages washed ashore.

The considerable achievements of the good captain are celebrated in many stories, yet my favourite concerns his wife and a pregnant woman on Hirta, the main island in the St Kilda

Beauty Spot

From Northton, a favourite walk explores Toe Head and the slopes of Ceapabhal. Elevated coastal views are sublime; in hues of emerald, azure, sapphire and aquamarine, the Atlantic Ocean washes dazzling beaches that extend for miles along the coast from Scarista to Luskentyre. The ruined Temple chapel on Rubh an Teampuill overlooks islands in the Sound of Harris from where the congregation came by boat. On Pabbay, Ensay, Killegray and Shillay only a handful of habitable houses remain and are visited occasionally. The islands are seabird stations now. Pabbay's loss is especially stark; the island supported a community of 338 people in 1841 before it was cleared by the laird. Families left for Australia and Canada and some of the men became shepherds in Patagonia and the Falkland Islands. By 1962 just two people lived on the island.

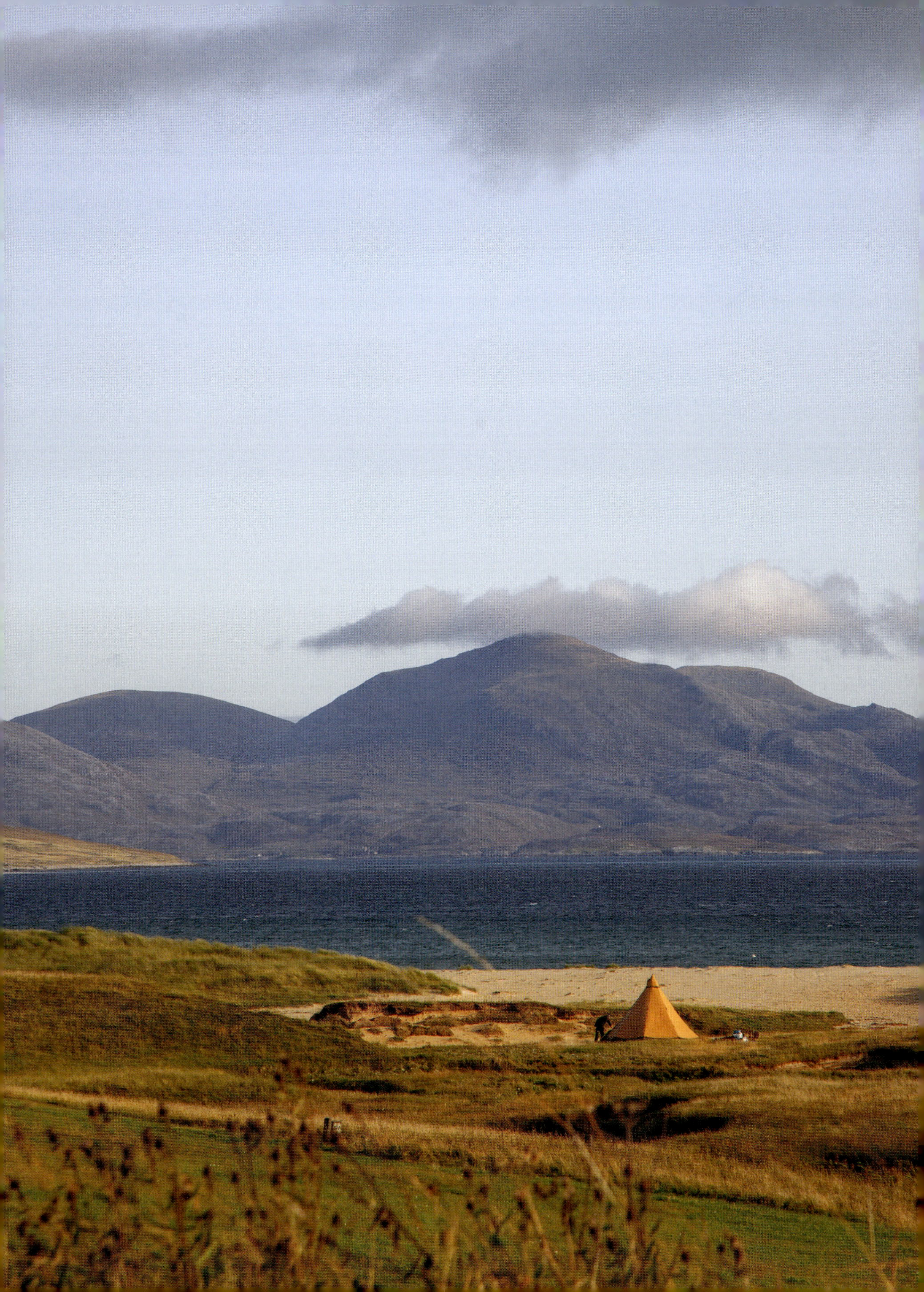

archipelago. When Mary Jemima Otter disembarked HMS *Porcupine* in Hirta in 1860, she discovered Anne Gillies suffering the agonies of a difficult childbirth. Neonatal mortality in the isolated islands was notoriously high and Mary anxiously offered support. Happily, Anne was delivered of a healthy baby girl, named in appreciation of her visitor's kindness, Mary Jemima Otter Porcupine Gillies.

In considering the tragic loss of so many St Kilda babies to neonatal tetanus, modern science suggests the grim possibility that the community may have taken the same knives to cut an umbilical cord as those used to make horsehair ropes, without sterilising them sufficiently in a flame.

Wondrous West Coast Harris Beaches

Stupendous sands gild the west coast of Harris. Fantasy swathes washed by crystal-clear waters of sapphire blue, emerald green and everything in between. Backed by moody mountains and wildly scenic islands the whole experience is unforgettable, sometimes unbelievable, and certainly unmissable.

West coast Harris beaches feature regularly on those dubious lists that claim to know exactly which sands are the Best in the World, as if some ace squad of egalitarian beach inspectors has tramped every shore on the planet with a trusty clipboard leaving no grain of sand unturned.

There is no denying that the west coast beaches are truly spectacular, but the well-worn tag, 'Just like the Caribbean' tends to bemuse islanders. Heaven help anyone who arrives in anticipation of sexy tropical heat, fresh coconut sundowners and bathwater seas. Forget that. No, the thrill of this fabulous sandy fringe is a decidedly Outer Hebrides experience and anyone who lives by the motto that bigger is better is going to feel right at home. Just wrap up warm.

From Northton the low-lying road hugs tidal saltings grazed by sheep before reaching a small roadside parking place and gateway to

Curiosity

Naturally, different states of the tide create different experiences of the coast. Low water exposes the spectacular fullness of the Harris sands. When the tide is high, some are completely submerged. Furious storms at high water are exhilarating. Unbridled North Atlantic rollers rise in white-crested force and wind-whipped spray fills the highly charged air. The experience is sensational and extremely dangerous. Resist all temptation to venture close to the action; powerful rogue waves may reach further up the shore at any moment.

the immense wide-open space of Scarista strand. Scarista Beag sands merge seamlessly into Scarista Mhor at the edge of a thinly strung-out township, neatly parcelled crofts exposed to the Atlantic Ocean. In high winds the weighty red door of the telephone beside the former post office was held firmly closed by a large rock.

Few nine-hole golf courses enjoy such a staggeringly scenic wind blasted location as Scarista's headland links. In fiercely gusting wind, I have encountered gleeful golfers of all ages struggling to stand straight, absolutely relishing the battle to direct a small white ball through wildly churning air. They cannot get those clubs out of the car boot quick enough.

Scarista's former manse is a cosy luxury hotel with romantic sunset

Beauty Spot

West Harris Trust extends a warm welcome to visitors. Discover a clutch of dedicated pitches for caravans, motorhomes and camper vans at Talla na Mara; excellent facilities and views to the island of Taransay are a neat combination. Smaller designated camping spots are also available around the West Harris estate. Islanders appreciate visitors choosing to support this initiative to protect precious and fragile community land against erosion. Booking ahead is strongly advised.

The West Harris Trust website carries important information about the legal use of drones and metal detectors on private and community land. Local people witness the increasing distress and disturbance caused to wildlife by intrusive and unnecessary drones. Research finds that animals' heart rates spike steeply in the vicinity of drones, especially among adults with young. Drones are widely available, and amateur operators may be unaware of the unseen impact of the sound and motion on wildlife and livestock. Increasing concern resonates throughout the islands, especially for nesting birds, golden eagles, sea eagles, red deer herds, seals and otters, and crofters' cattle, sheep, calves, lambs and sheepdogs.

---

views. Elegant and whitewashed, the classically Georgian building seems confidently at ease in the company of striking modern architectural designs further along the road.

On approach to Borve, the coast is indented with deep narrow chasms and wide sweeping bays. The sea behaves differently here, and local safety advice is to monitor the reach of waves rolling in for at least ten minutes before approaching the shore. A lonesome ancient monolith rises above Bagh Steinigidh. Fallen and buried companion stones nearby suggest that this headland site, with impressive views to the Isle of Taransay and the hills of North Harris, was a Neolithic complex for ritual and celebration in association with the movement of the sun.

In Borve village a grassy waymarked path leads to Loch Duin and the remains of Dun Bhuirg, a fortified Bronze Age dwelling atop a hill. Stories tell of fairy people in this enchanted place. Tracking the shore closely, with barely any places to stop, the road brushes the edge of tantalising bays and deep dark gullies before reaching a lay-by parking place where folk spill excitedly out of their vehicles to admire the panorama. A little further beyond, the hillside hub of Pairc Niseabost is a welcome stop for refreshment. Talla Na Mara means 'Centre by the Sea'; here you will find the work of local artists and makers. The huge glass walls of An Traigh café bar offer yet more elevated views across the magnificent Sound of Taransay. One can never have too many.

On the Aird Niseabost headland, a standing stone makes an imposing territorial marker. Clach Mhicleod is known also as the Macleod stone. The monument has witnessed dramatic change since it was erected some 5,000 years ago by people who farmed fertile and wooded land; now trees are few and coastal features have moved through erosion.

In the dunes of Horgabost, a simple campsite offers the possibility of moonlit strolls along white sands under a dark sky full of stars, the stuff of dreams. The seashore road weaves onward to the dunes at Seilebost where the former primary school is the headquarters of the West Harris Trust.

A remarkable scene awaits at the next turn. Low tide reveals a huge arena of luminous sands where the shores of Seilebost and Luskentyre merge and swirling channels of aquamarine flow into deep tidal pools. The extraordinary radiance is a natural phenomenon caused by high white shell content and in the gloom of heavy weather the wondrous effect is yet more beguiling. Historic paths from this magic shore lead through the glen to reach sea lochs of the east.

While the A859 commences a hill climb toward Tarbert, a turning to Luskentyre slips around Loch Fincastle, separated from the sea at high tide by a dam wall. The shallow

Curiosity

A tin loom shed on Luskentyre shore is an extraordinary global gateway. Independent home weaver Donald John Mackay MBE produces an average of 27 yards of Harris Tweed per day, beautiful cloth commissioned by clients around the world. Donald designed the tweed used by Nike for a limited edition 2004 update of the Terminator trainer basketball shoe from the 1980s. When the sports brand placed an early order for 10,000 yards, Donald rallied the support of weavers around the island. The commission was fulfilled, and further orders followed. Nike's fashion-statement trainers revitalised the profile of the versatile and durable unique island cloth. The potential global reach of the Outer Hebrides cannot be underestimated.

pool on Borve Lodge Estate attracts anglers fishing for sea trout and grilse.

 Passing picnic benches with idyllic views to the heather hills and shining beaches of Taransay, the little coast road reaches the ten crofts of Luskentyre.

Thin shallow soil and exposed rocky terrain in the east coast of Harris made it impossible for communities to bury their dead without the prospect of the grave being disturbed. Funeral parties walked a coffin path through the glen to the western shore, taking turns at carrying the deceased on a stretcher and stopping to rest for refreshment at marker cairns along the way. The seashore burial ground at Luskentyre was journey's end. Here lies Aunt Julia, famously celebrated by Norman MacCaig, her nephew, and one of Scotland's finest poets.

Aunt Julia by Norman MacCaig

*Aunt Julia spoke Gaelic
very loud and very fast.
I could not answer her –
I could not understand her.*

*She wore men's boots
when she wore any.
– I can see her strong foot,
stained with peat,
paddling with the treadle of the spinningwheel
while her right hand drew yarn
marvellously out of the air.*

*Hers was the only house
where I've lain at night
in the absolute darkness
of a box bed, listening to
crickets being friendly.*

*She was buckets
and water flouncing into them.
She was winds pouring wetly
round house-ends.
She was brown eggs, black skirts
and a keeper of threepennybits
in a teapot.*

*Aunt Julia spoke Gaelic
very loud and very fast.
By the time I had learned
a little, she lay
silenced in the absolute black
of a sandy grave
at Luskentyre. But I hear her still, welcoming me
with a seagull's voice
across a hundred yards
of peatscrapes and lazybeds
and getting angry, getting angry
with so many questions
unanswered.*

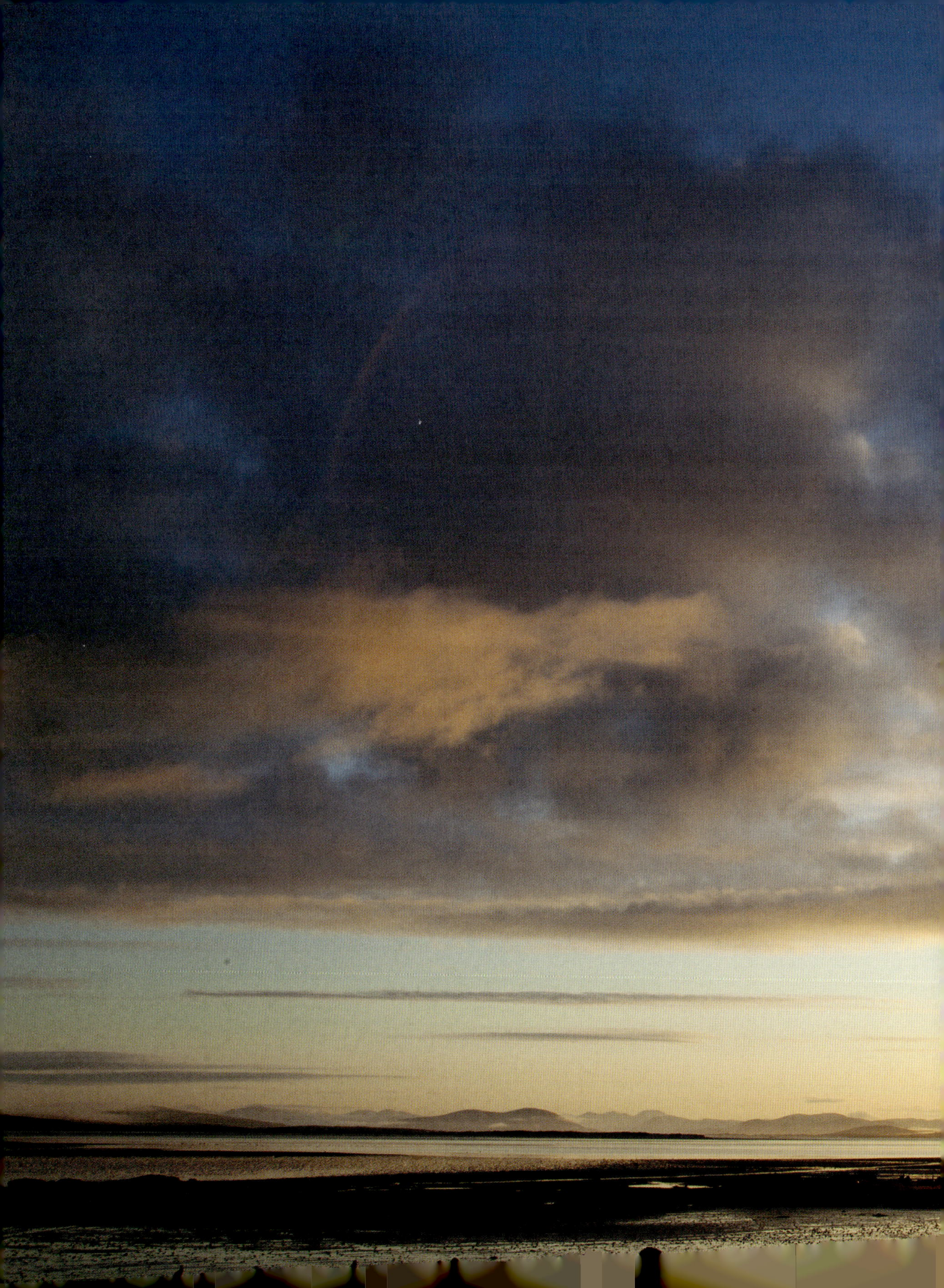

PART TWO
Berneray and North Uist

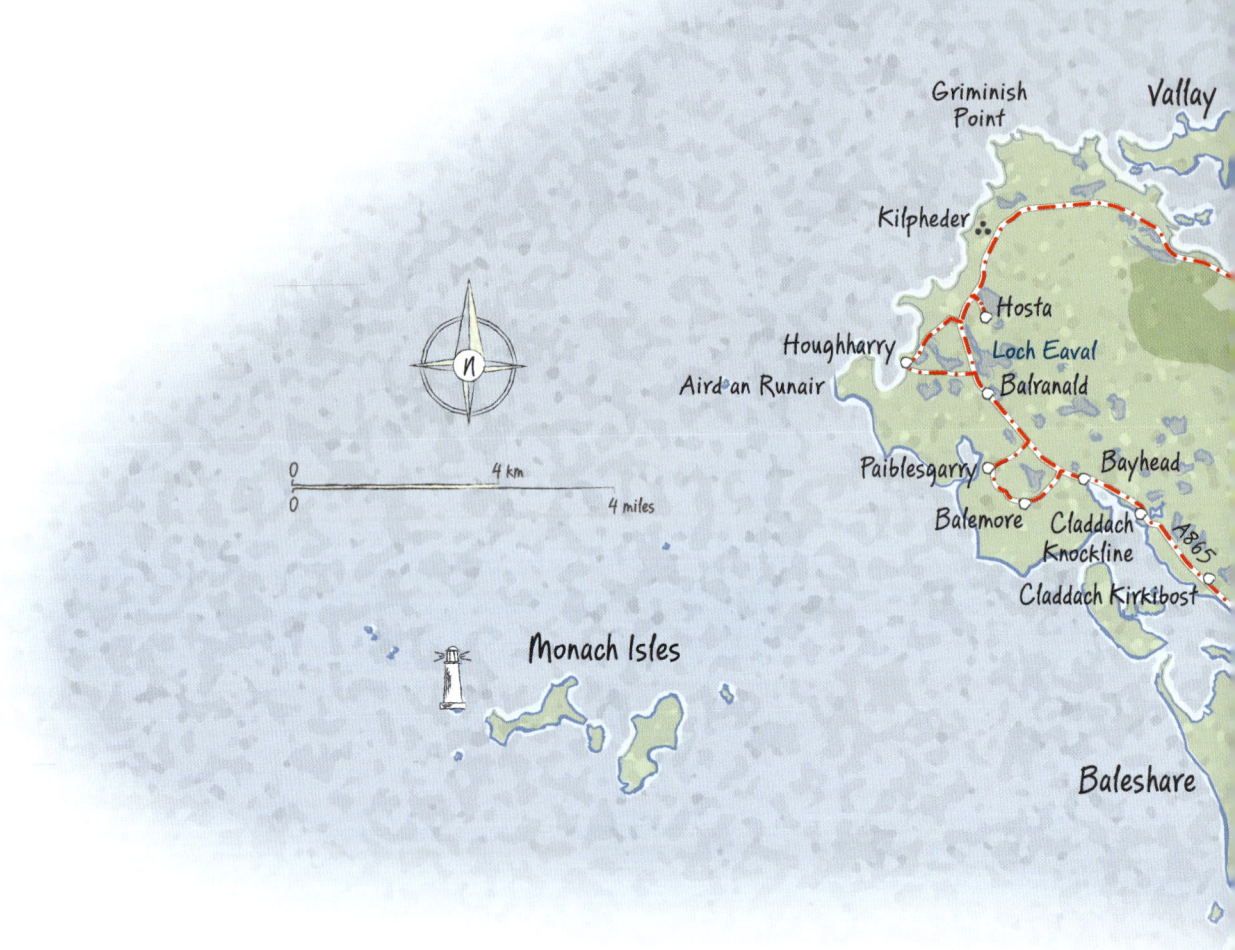

The Seals, Sands and Stones of Berneray

The Caledonian MacBrayne ferry bound for Berneray dances an exacting jig. Safe passage from Leverburgh is a cautious route through the confusion of reefs, skerries, sandy shallows, islets and submerged rocks in the extraordinary Sound of Harris. As the seal swims, the distance shore to shore is just eight nautical miles, yet the doughty vessel requires an hour to sail with care, guided by bright beacons and buoys.

The sea passage lies between the Atlantic Ocean and the Little Minch. Tidal conditions in the perilous channel change swiftly, and the weather likewise. The Marine and Coastguard Agency requires the ferry to proceed only if the next two buoys are visible. Sailing cancellations and delays triggered by changing tides and weather can be frustrating, I know from experience, and yet this raw, true relationship with the sea and maritime climate is an integral part of island life. This remarkable sea crossing remains, without doubt, among my favourites and I recom-

119

mend travelling on deck to appreciate the ubiquitous natural obstacles and the skill of the crew navigating 22 exacting changes of direction to the sound of seasick car alarms.

As the CalMac ferry steams through the Sound of Harris it is poignant to consider that Berneray is the last populated island in the stream. Uprooted crofting communities on surrounding isles are long gone.

Low-lying Berneray is roughly at the midway point of the Outer Hebrides chain, a position that seems to have afforded the island a powerful role as a significant meeting place. That sense of connection continues. The CalMac ferry lands close by the causeway that connects Berneray directly to North Uist. The pier is relatively tranquil, disturbed only by the ferry and vehicles rumbling across the cattle grid that denies free-roaming livestock the opportunity of tottering across to North Uist. Fishing boats work from the harbour further around the coast.

The ferry terminal waiting room is the lone

Beauty Spot

Rare white-tailed sea eagles fish the shallow Sound of Harris. The magnificent raptors are the United Kingdom's largest bird of prey, with a massive wingspan of around two metres. They are seen easily from the shore and from the ferry; keep a look out. It is astonishing to witness the spectacle of a powerful sea eagle swoop low and pause for just a fraction of a second before thrusting forth golden talons to snatch hopeless prey clear from the water with pinpoint precision. These majestic creatures with a beady pale stare are named romantically in Gaelic as *iolair sùil na grèine* – 'the bird with the sunlit eye'. Sea eagles are inclined to be relatively comfortable around human activity and this ease led to their downfall in Britain where they were persecuted, shot for sport, and driven to extinction in 1918. Cautious reintroduction of birds from Norway, to establish a breeding programme, has proved a slow, steady success, although a wet, cold spring threatens a growing chick's chances of survival.

building at the pier, a place of refuge when Hebridean wind and rain are in action. I have much fondness for these snugs. I especially appreciate the way each reflects the character of the surrounding local community. Island news and visitor information is posted on noticeboards. There may be a stash of second-hand books for sale by donation to charity, and exhibitions of local culture, heritage and art. Some waiting rooms have showers, picnic benches, outdoor sculptures and coffee; all have toilets.

Diminutive Berneray lends itself perfectly to a day spent walking the coast; the island is just two miles wide by three miles long. Elevated western views extend across islands in the Sound of Pabbay to the St Kilda archipelago, and to the east rise the majestic mainland summits of Wester Ross. Allow around six hours for the Berneray Explorer circuit of around eight miles in fabulous coastal scenery. The South Berneray Circular is a shorter walk of three miles, requiring just a couple of hours.

The Explorer route starts and finishes at the community hall. The hike climbs gentle island summits for panoramic views of the island chain. On Beinn a' Claidh, known also as the 'Hill of Burial', the ancient Cladh Maolrithe strikes a pose, the last stone standing in a group of recumbent monoliths. Across the hillside rough turf has overgrown archaeological remains from different eras, lending the impression that this vantage point on the midway island in the Outer Hebrides chain has a long history of significance.

The South Berneray Circular walk is a curtailed version of the Berneray Explorer. The isolated memorial to a real-life gentle giant is among the highlights. Angus MacAskill was born in Berneray in 1825. Along with many others from the community, Angus and his family emigrated to Cape Breton Island in Nova Scotia province. They settled in the fishing port of Englishtown on St Ann's Bay. Through his teenage years Angus experienced an extraordinary growth spurt that halted only when he measured seven feet and nine inches tall. For fun, the young man lifted boats, barrels and anchors with ease. News of his stature and physical prowess spread fast. Showbusiness soon beckoned and Angus joined P.T. Barnum's Circus, touring with General Tom Thumb who measured three feet tall. Angus died of brain fever at his home in St Ann's in 1863. In 1981 he was named the world's largest true giant, without growth abnormalities, by the *Guinness Book of World Records*. Berneray remembers the island son with pride.

The main activity of island life unfolds on the eastern shore and the island road departs the ferry terminal to discover the friendly stores adjacent to Berneray Bistro where freshly landed seafood is served at outdoor tables with views over the Sound of Harris. Around the bay of Roll an Oir disintegrating boats let themselves go in that artful devil-may-care way. A turning off the main road connects with inland crofts, the community hall and hilltop burial ground beyond.

The coast road reaches the neatly organised harbour built in 1989. The colourful Coral Box store occupies a gentle rise with views over the attractive company of fishing boats and yachts. Visit the store's website for scenes of Bays Loch live streamed around the world; otters put in frequent appearances.

The cottage previously provided for the island nurse has become a visitor centre where knowledgeable volunteers from Berneray Historical Society ably assist visitors in search of their island forebears. Backhill is a small hub of church, post office and red granite war memorial inscribed with 22 names. The island school at Ludag, built in 1877, was a place of learning for almost 130 years. Due to falling student numbers the seashore classrooms closed in 2005. Now Berneray children attend lessons in North Uist.

I have enjoyed great entertainment at Seal Bay where Berneray's boisterous colony of common and Atlantic seals gather on a falling tide, an unruly crew jostling for position on favourite drying rocks. Without enough ledges to go round, competitive efforts to stake a blubbery claim are often hilarious and sometimes vicious. Hauling out with shiny slapping flops, the adult seals roll and wiggle to reach exact favourite spots, nothing less will do. Once in position, they may indulge in enthusiastic flipper scratching before settling for a snooze. This is the cue for wide-eyed pups to peep from the deep, cautiously assessing their chances of unseating the snoring elders with whiffling whiskers. Invariably clumsy attempts are met by seriously grumpy growls. Admonished youngsters return to the sea, hanging about until distracted by something tasty underwater. On full throttle, their streamlined torpedo pursuit is sublime.

The shore road arrives at Baile, where a distinctive 16th-century building served as Sir Norman Macleod's armoury. The knight, loyal to King Charles II, fought Cromwell's army at Stornoway, Worcester and Loch Garry. He died in 1709 and is buried in the graveyard of St Clement's Church at Rodel on the Isle of Harris.

The pretty Gatliff Trust youth hostel at Berneray comprises two traditional blackhouse cottages slap bang on the seashore. Snug thatched roofs are weighted down with stones. Small windows in thick white-

Curiosity

In rough turf at Sgalabraig a strangely seat-shaped block of stone with a high back is surrounded by a group of further stones, some overgrown. The mysterious Chair Stone may have been the focal point of a Viking court or meeting place. Another significant Berneray stone is known as Leac an Righ, or the 'Flat Stone of the King'. A foot shape cut into the rock suggests the slab served in the ritual initiation of new leaders following, quite literally, in the footsteps of others.

Perhaps Prince Charles checked it out when he stayed incognito on the island in 1987. Working on an arable croft, the heir to the throne planted and lifted potatoes, cut peat, helped dip sheep and planted trees. The prince returned in 1999 to perform the official opening of the 900-metre-long causeway connecting Berneray to North Uist.

washed walls keep watch over the beach. Facilities are simple and the welcome is warm. John's Bunkhouse on the west coast is another great place to stay on a budget. There is no official campsite or overnight parking on Berneray, however bed and breakfast and self-catering accommodation is available.

From the doorstep of the Gatliff Trust hostel the seashore curves to the lovely sands and wildflower machair of Traigh Bheasdaire which derives its name from the Norse, meaning 'a place where cattle are housed'. Views across islands in the Sound of Harris are glorious; a walk at the water's edge, in the company of oystercatchers, curlews and turnstones, is a joy.

And so, to the west coast of Berneray where a wondrous runway of dazzling white sand extends uninterrupted for three fabulous miles. Across the transparent turquoise green sea beckon the empty islands of Boreray and Pabbay. Spectacular West Beach is often deserted. Time it right and you may have this earthly paradise to yourself although the chances of meeting seaweed-munching Highland cattle are high. Their deep ambling hoof prints and freshly dumped cowpats pattern the strand. Otters fish this ocean edge, especially on an incoming tide. Telltale webbed feet leave playful scampering tracks into the high dunes and marram grass.

Across the Causeway to Lochmaddy

A group of Outer Hebrides islands is known by the collective name Uist; they are Berneray, North Uist, South Uist, Grimsay, Benbecula, Eriskay and the Monach Isles, home to the second-largest grey seal colony in the world. To avoid any confusion, the islands of team Uist are identified by their individual names throughout this journey.

North Uist, Benbecula and South Uist emerged from a single land mass that that succumbed to coastal erosion. Spectacular North Uist hosts a rare, drowned landscape. To the east, countless pools and tidal inlets are contained within the weak grasp of sodden land and the effect of a vast mirror in smithereens is visually astounding. Wet shards far and wide conjure fragments of swift-moving clouds and smooth rocky hills.

Rising sea levels are of critical concern and the Outer Hebrides Climate Change Group works towards improving understanding of climate change and developing actions to adapt for the benefit of the community, the economy and the natural environment.

The causeway connecting the islands of Berneray and North Uist across the Sound of Berneray opened in 1999. The crossing, just under one kilometre long, is punctuated by underwater culverts to permit the safe passage of otters, fish, and cetaceans especially.

On the far north shore, the discovery of human bones and iron rivets at Otternish suggested the ritual funeral burning of a Norse man and his boat sometime before the 11th century. Port nan Long takes its Gaelic name from the 'Port of the Ships'; tradition records the wreck of a ship from the Spanish Armada. Archaeological surveys suggest the shore was used also for Bronze Age burials.

Iron Age causeways extend into the peaty waters of Loch an Sticir to reach the tumbled

Curiosity

Fascinating archaeological sites are a feature of North Uist and they come thick and fast. I recommend highly the *Uist Unearthed* app to experience these atmospheric places in situ in wonderful, augmented reality.

remains of Dun an Sticir, which translates from Gaelic to 'Fort of the Sulker', and a further islet known grimly as Eilean na Mi-Chomhairle, the 'Island of Bad Council'. Walking out to the stronghold at low tide is an extraordinary time-travelling experience.

The North Uist loop road traces a rough heart shape around the island. Before reaching Lochmaddy an unassuming junction explores a favourite road through a maze of pools that shimmy in the Hebridean breeze. It is a fantasy land for fishers. Islets and islands are plenty, people and buildings are few. The quiet spaciousness is exceptional. Passing by Loch Portain the road ends at Cheese Bay, speckled with islands said to be the resting place of herring fishers who became involved in a dreadful fight between crews of fleets from around the coast of Britain.

Back on the road to Lochmaddy, Asco seaweed processing works occupies the hollowed-out former site of Crogarry Beag

Beauty Spot

The elegantly walled burial ground on a grassy knoll at Clachan Sands contains croft stones, simple grave markers made with rocks from the walls of the deceased's home. Without decoration or inscription, the quiet anonymity of these tributes is very special. Beyond the cemetery a rough, bumpy track invites discovery of a breathtaking shore. At low tide the immense strands of Hornais and Lingeigh merge, a gigantic apron of sand under the huge Hebridean sky. Rolling clouds ride Atlantic winds and inviting tidal islands call. Splashing through shallow lagoons to reach the gentle summit of uninhabited Lingeigh is a favourite adventure. The panorama of Harris hills, North Uist sands and the nearby islands of Boreray and Berneray is unforgettable.

quarry. The company derives its name from *Ascophyllum nodosum*, known also as egg wrack and knotted wrack. The clarity of Hebridean water encourages seaweed to grow to great depths and throughout history and prehistory, island people have used seaware for food, fodder and fertiliser.

A branch road to Sponish reaches a narrow spit of land where a tall building surveys the sea. Sponish House was built in 1803 as a sporting lodge. In 1955 it became a seaweed factory. The unusual conversion transformed the top floor into the manager's residence, the ground floor into office space and the walled garden into the factory processing site. A small pier was built for coasters loading seaweed and puffers landing coal to fuel the drying furnaces.

An intriguing turf-roofed cell on the rocky shore echoes the smooth shape of islands offshore. *Both nam Faileas*, the 'Hut of the Shadow', is the work of artist Chris Drury. His magical hideaway connects inner and outer worlds using a pinhole camera to project a blurry image of the loch onto a large white stone deep inside. Commissioned by Taigh Chearsabhagh Museum and Arts Centre, the hut is one of seven artworks on the Uist Sculpture Trail.

Lochmaddy is the main port of entry to North Uist and the largest settlement on the island. The sea loch containing a profusion of islets, islands, reefs, basins and skerries is the most diverse saline lagoon system in the United Kingdom. The Gaelic name Loch nam Madadh is inspired by two fierce-looking islets that guard the shore. The translation means 'Loch of the Hounds', or '—Wolves'. I like the sound of the sea wolves best. The wild pair is joined in these western reaches of the Minch by a dense otter population and six resident marine mammal species, harbour porpoises, white-beaked dolphins, Risso's dolphins, killer whales, minke whales and common seals.

The bustle of Lochmaddy ebbs and flows with the coming and going of Caledonian MacBrayne ferries on the triangular route connecting North Uist with the ports of Uig on the Isle of Skye and Tarbert on the Isle of Harris. Beside the pier a gleaming dolphin leaps from a plinth to greet passengers disembarking from the ferry; the polished steel sculpture was commissioned by the local volunteers of Comann na Mara, the Society of the Sea.

The Caledonian MacBrayne ticket office at Lochmaddy is a delight.

Huge glass walls overlook the pier inscribed with song lyrics of 'Flower of the West' by cult Scottish folk band Runrig. Evocative Gaelic and English words float around the airy space. A colourful parade of maritime flags traces the history of island ferries. Display cases brim with associated curiosities, including vintage table linen and crockery emblazoned with Caledonian MacBrayne logos. And in the far corner is something I can never resist. The Traveller Book Exchange is piled high with second-hand books available for a donation. Funds raised support the work of the Comann na Mara charity.

    The Lochmaddy Hotel, built in 1864, traditionally hosted auctioneers attending livestock sales and anglers on island fishing trips. Island livestock sales continue in quayside pens though they are smaller events now. Animals arrive by truck and trailer; previously they were hoofed from far and wide. Crofters from offshore islands first transported their beasts to nearby shores in small craft. Less fortunate animals had to swim across narrow straits.

    Once ashore the livestock crowd was guided to the market stance,

HEBRIDEAN JOURNEY

travelling across sandy beaches, through rocky hills and over peaty moors with diligent working dogs alert to the possibility of disorientated creatures making a bid for freedom.

Following the sale, animals bound for the mainland were herded onward to island harbours. Gathered in rudimentary pens beside the sea, and daubed in rainbow colours signifying their destination, they awaited cattle boats to cross the Minch on the next stage of their epic journey. At mainland ports many were transported further south by rail. Despite all the skill and care of the crofters and drovers, the fear, stress and fatigue of the Hebridean menagerie must have been immense.

Waterside Taigh Chearsabhagh hosts a museum, arts centre, post office and café. Fascinating collections and exhibitions celebrate Gaelic language, culture and heritage including the Runrig archive of artefacts from 1973 to 2018. The café offers an outdoor seating area with views across Loch Maddy's lagoons to the distant hills of Harris.

The handsome Gothic architecture of the sheriff court built in 1875 encompasses former jail cells and an exercise yard. There's much more fun to be had on the rough turf of Lochmaddy FC. Grazing sheep are often in goal. A lane leads from the pitch to fishing gear and creels stacked on the old wee pier, as it is known locally. The opportunity to order freshly landed Lochmaddy Bay prawns for collection direct from the fishers is a treat.

On the edge of Lochmaddy, the former village primary school has been given a new lease of life as a community hub for health and well-being, economic development, education and conservation. A dedicated environment centre will showcase unique natural aspects of Uist and Barra under the banner 'Our Island, Our Environment, Our Future'.

> # Curiosity
>
> The Taigh Chearsabhagh centre cannot develop further buildings on the Lochmaddy shore due to predicted storm-surge sea levels. To illustrate this aspect of the climate crisis artists Pekka Niittyvirta and Timo Aho created an extraordinary light installation activated by the incoming tide. The artwork known as *Lines* wraps around the former dairy building and reaches almost to the top of a full-height door. This powerful visual presentation of climate crisis, based on factual storm-surge heights and the possible future sea-level rise within the next century, is inspired and thought-provoking.

Lochmaddy to Baleshare

A smooth fast road from the harbour village of Lochmaddy connects with the North Uist crossroads of Clachan. This journey discovers favourite public artworks and intriguing stories along the way, tales of fantasy giants, real-life bears, wartime swans, and travels to low-lying Baleshare island.

The A867 carves a swift path through matted peat bog and clumped heather in the open landscape beyond Lochmaddy. A quartet of hills dominates the scene, North and South Lee rising shoulder to shoulder while small, fierce Burrival cosies up to Eaval, the highest hill on the island.

The waterworld of North Uist, strewn with lochans and fingers of sea loch reaching inland, makes it almost impossible to walk a steady straight line across the remarkable landscape. It is spectacularly easy to go wrong in this maze. Stick to reliable routes, even if they seem occasionally counter-intuitive; this rare landscape often requires some circumnavigation to where you might want to be.

Some ten minutes' drive out of Lochmaddy, a small yellow sign beside the road indicates the start of an adventure that begins on sheep tracks and reaches the modest heights of North Lee where golden eagles patrol rocky ridges. Clear-day views from the hill are staggering at every turn. The full extent of Loch Maddy, the second-largest fjardic sea loch in Europe, is seen in all her briny glory, a stupendous mosaic of shallow basins, lagoons, islands and tidal rapids. In the Sound of Harris beyond, the chaos of scattered islets and islands is backed by mountains that rise above streaks of white shell sand. Hills in Benbecula, South Uist, Eriskay and Barra crowd views to the south. In supremely clear weather the St Kilda archipelago floats into view. Allow around five hours for the ten-mile return trip; take a detailed map and refreshments, and prepare well for fast-changing Hebridean weather.

Scooting onward, the streamlined road reaches a rare sight to behold; a dense stand of trees shouts out in a landscape largely bereft of them. Barpa Langass Community Wood is a novelty with an extraordinary twist. The opportunity to go on a bear hunt is very real here. Track the paw-print trail through woodland paths and glades to reach a life-size sculpture of a bear standing upright. He announces the burial place of Hercules, a brown grizzly who went on an awfully big Hebridean adventure.

Wrestler Andy Robin and his wife Maggie acquired Hercules as a cub from Highland Wildlife Park in Kingussie for £50 in 1975. The trio lived a showbiz whirl for 25 years and so it is perhaps no surprise that when filming a toilet roll commercial on the lovely island of Benbecula in the summer of 1980, Hercules fancied a taste of Hebridean freedom. The grizzly took his chances successfully and was at large for over three weeks until a crofter spotted him swimming in the sea. Upon capture it was evident that Hercules had lost a huge amount of weight; raw food had never been part of his diet though he was famously

Curiosity

Emerging from the deep cover of sika spruce and lodgepole pines at Barpa Langass into the wide-open terrain of treeless peatland is a weird sensation. While North Uist has no remaining native wood, and other islands in the chain have only scant patches where animals and fire have not damaged the stock, pollen records reveal the Outer Hebrides had a naturally wooded landscape up until 8,000 years ago. Burning and grazing took their toll. Peat became the main source of fuel and buildings were constructed with stone. Across the islands new woodlands projects are designed and nurtured with immense care.

partial to ice cream. His rescuers were at pains to reiterate that no livestock were injured in his escapade. Hercules and Andy are both buried in the cool and peaceful shady wood.

The fast moorland road soon reaches another extraordinary resting place. A steep path climbs from a large car park to the burial chamber of an early Neolithic warrior deep within a lonely mound of grey stones. The atmospheric site with far reaching views is a short walk from an oval ring of weathered standing stones on the southerly slopes of Ben Langass known as Pobull Fhinn or 'Finn's People'. According to folklore, this is where the heroic giant Fionn mac Cumhaill set a fire under his equally giant cooking pot of deer. He certainly enjoyed a fine view with his dinner; the interlocked waters of Loch Langass and Loch Euphort reach to the pyramid hill of Eaval, enough to whet anyone's appetite.

Alternatively, the stones may relate to the faintly visible conical hill of Glamaig, the northernmost of the Red Hills in the Isle of Skye. The alignment of both sites possibly served as a Neolithic solar calendar. From the ancient stone circle, it is a short walk to Langass Lodge hotel, a former shooting retreat with views over lochs, islets and pools spread at the foot of Eaval. The comfortable lodge renowned for seasonal local food and fine dining welcomes non-residents, however booking is essential.

From the east coast the long reach of Loch Euphort pierces so deep into the interior of North Uist that it almost breaks through to the west. The sea loch shore is explored on the B894, among my favourite island roads. The journey through a sparsely populated and strange realm of peat, stone, heather and water is remarkable. The landmark hills of Eaval and Burrival rise above sleepy bays and small harbours and it is no surprise that this atmospheric landscape inspires a community of artists.

At Shoreline Stoneware Louise Cook employs natural materials to create sculptures inspired by island life and the Atlantic coastline. The display in her bright airy gallery also features work by other artists. At the far-flung road end, a strikingly graceful bronze sculpture by Roddy Mathieson is a beautiful find. His piece *Sanctuary* is part of the Uist Sculpture Trail. Overlooking the sea loch and mirror pools reflecting sky and hills, the evocative artwork suggests the energy of white whooper swans in flight and hints at the strong ribs of a wooden fishing boat; both inhabit this waterworld.

Beyond the turning for Loch Euphort, the main road reaches the North Uist war memorial and the Clachan na Luib hillside where islanders converging for rural livestock sales mixed business with pleasure. The unveiling of the war memorial cairn was attended in August 1923 by crowds of people from across the island and smaller islands in the parish, many of which are now uninhabited. At the ceremony, Colonel Cameron of Lochiel described the men who had fallen in the Great War as 'the pick and the flowers of the islands'. Their loss drained the lifeblood of countless crofting communities, especially because so many islanders joined the war early.

Clachan junction presents a choice. Turning south begins the approach to Benbecula across the North Ford causeway and visits the crofting community of Carinish rich in history, not least the 2008 conversion of the local pub to a church. The A865 shows little respect to the village's ancient stone circle, charging straight through in its hurry to reach

Benbecula. However, the notorious Ditch of Blood remains intact. The gruesome trench relates to a grisly battle in 1601 when villagers saw off raiders from Harris. Much blood was spilled by both sides. A visit to Carinish Temple is far more soothing. Surrounded by wild yellow flag iris and grazing sheep the intimate ruins of Carinish Temple enjoy views extending across the sandy Oitir Mhor between North Uist and Benbecula. The early medieval centre of religious training is regarded as the oldest university in Scotland.

Before completing the remaining section of the North Uist loop, a turning off the A865 invites discovery of Baleshare, known as Baile Sear in Gaelic, meaning 'East Island'. This suggests an island to the west of it most likely succumbed to storms and coastal erosion. The disappearance of an island is one thing, the loss of an island population is quite another; the narrow causeway that has linked Baleshare to mainland North Uist since 1962 is a further example of the importance of keeping island communities connected to reduce the risk of depopulation.

Curiosity

Many islanders who joined the Great War were leaving the Outer Hebrides for the first time. The horrors that awaited them are described in the Gaelic-language love song '*An Eala Bhàn*', or 'The White Swan', composed by Dòmhnall Ruadh Chorùna, or Red Donald of Corunna, a tiny settlement on the road to the North Ford.

Auburn-haired Donald was a stonemason and war poet who composed in the oral tradition. The bard did not learn to read or write in his native Gaelic because only English was taught at his village school under the 1872 Education Act. Donald composed the heart-rending 'An Eala Bhàn' for his sweetheart Magaidh while wounded in the trenches at the Battle of the Somme. He tells of exploding shells and roaring cannon around him and fears he may not survive. Happily, he was proved wrong.

Donald returned to North Uist and did not marry Magaidh; tradition suggests her father did not support their union. Annie became his love and wife. Donald died in 1967 and is buried in Kilmuir cemetery with a headstone depicting a white swan and words from the second verse of 'An Eala Bhàn' which is among the most celebrated Gaelic language love songs. Versions by Karen Matheson and Julie Fowlis are especially beautiful.

Low-lying Baleshare is perfect for cycle rides through lush farmland and picnics on the shore where artist Andy Goldsworthy created ephemeral works transformed by wind and tides in 2008. Discover another artwork on the Uist Sculpture Trail at Claddach Baleshare. The piece, known as *Reflections* and by artist Colin Mackenzie, sits among crofts, cattle and tractors, beside the muddy tidal channel where islanders crossed to reach the North Uist mainland prior to the construction of the causeway. Homemade signage guiding seekers to sculpture delights me almost as much as the artwork. *Reflections* is a low stone bench that curves elegantly over and around a group of boulders. Tiled in smooth and rippled island colours of sea, sand and sky, this lovely seat is indeed a special place to rest and reflect.

Changing Times, Shifting Sands:
the Coast Road from Clachan to Udal

The rural junction at Clachan is no longer a significant staging post for travellers, drovers and livestock crossing the great North Ford sands on foot, hoof, horseback, or cart, and by boat at high tide. The opening of the causeway to the islands of Benbecula and Grimsay in 1960 brought much change. The hub where so many people had gathered for the ferry or with their livestock for sales fell quiet and after 140 years of faithful service the Clachan Stores closed in 2015.

New island enterprises have emerged. Parcels of fragrant peat-smoked salmon, trout and scallops from The Hebridean Smokehouse at Clachan are sent to destinations afar via Benbecula Airport, situated across the causeway at Balivanich.

A cairn by the roadside at Clachan na Luib overlooks the strand where a fledgling air ambulance pioneered by Doctor Alex Macleod landed to transport seriously ill islanders to mainland hospitals for urgent specialist care. The memorial celebrates his contribution to the well-being of islanders over 40 years and reflects on the extraordinary dedication of island doctors and nurses who often made distant house calls in all weathers on foot and horseback, by bicycle and boat. The surgery was a room in their house and impoverished patients often paid in kind, perhaps with services and livestock.

At Claddach Kirkibost shore, the former village school has become a community centre and airy café with views to low-lying islands. Student numbers peaked at 79 in 1890 and declined until 1975 when the school closed permanently. The Westford Inn, a dandy 1872 building with a steep slate roof, is described often as a vintage tea caddy. The handsome premises were converted from doctor's surgery to public house in 1896. With a sailing ship over the doorway and lattice-glazed windows believed to have come from Kilmory Castle in Argyll, the friendly inn is the most westerly pub in the Campaign for Real Ale's listings. Fishing permits for island lochs are available at the bar, although, in accordance with respect for Sabbath solemnity, the North Uist community does not offer fishing on Sundays.

The Bayhead stores sits quietly behind two fuel pumps on a large forecourt. Inside, not one speck of shelf space is wasted. Serried ranks of brightly packaged goods are a technicolour whirl. Fresh meat and fish, art brushes, stationery, Stornoway black pudding, island gins, Macleans bakery fancies, midge nets and repellent, seed potatoes for machair plots, car-care items, birthday cards and a post office counter are all to be found somewhere in the superbly organised den.

The purple wall of Sgoil Uibhist a Tuath catches the eye from a distance. The school on Bayhead shore is a focal point providing community activities and childcare, early years, and primary education to the youngest people on the islands of North Uist and Berneray. Built on elevated terraces, the building is sensitive to the threat of flooding on the low-lying island. The distinctive U-shape design is inspired by the historic courtyard of Nunton Steading farm buildings in Benbecula.

The small settlement at Claddach Knockline is known in Gaelic as Cnoc a' Lin, meaning 'Hill of the Flax'. A tidal crossing

Curiosity

Beyond the Bayhead stores, a shortcut to Malaclete through peat banks where crofters dig for fuel is known as the Committee Road with reference to the committee who commissioned it as a public relief project during the 1846 famine caused by the potato crop failure. The surrounding moorland is the favoured hunting ground of hen harriers, golden eagles, short-eared owls, peregrines and merlin. The small car park on the Outer Hebrides Bird of Prey trail is an excellent vantage point.

connects to fertile fields where flax was grown to make linen. On a prominent rocky knoll at Balemore, a large rock known as Craig Hasten is said to be the dwelling place of fairies. The resident sprites are blessed with beguiling views to surrounding hills and islands on the Atlantic horizon.

Heisker is a quintet of uninhabited islands four miles off the west coast of North Uist. The low-lying group, known also as the Monach Isles, is identified easily by the stalky red-brick tower of the 1864 lighthouse on Shillay. The light was extinguished in wartime and remained mothballed until 1948 when it was deemed unnecessary. But the Braer disaster of 1993, when a tanker foundered off the Shetland Isles spilling almost 85,000 tonnes of crude oil into the sea, prompted the installation of a small new beacon on Shillay in 1997. The range proved inadequate and so, in July 2008, a new light with a wider reach was installed in the old red-brick tower.

A trio of islands in the group, Ceann Ear, Ceann Iar and Sibhinis, supported a community linked by exposed sands at low tide. But scouring Atlantic winds depleted thin soil too poor for crops and grazing; unable to sustain themselves, the islanders were forced to abandon their beautiful outpost. The deserted isles remain a traditional fishing ground for the North Uist fleet; the old schoolhouse provides shelter in bad weather.

Undisturbed by grazing livestock, the machair regenerated and the islands became a National Nature Reserve in 1966, home to one of the world's largest breeding colonies of grey seals and at least 100 bird species, including herons who nest in abandoned buildings. Beach memorials bear witness to wartime tragedy. In March 1918 the bodies of Otto Schatt and two unidentified crew men washed ashore after British destroyers sank their U-boat off the coast of Northern Ireland. Lonely cairns at the Atlantic edge honour the young men. A further plaque honours William McNeill who died in the 1917 sinking of RMS *Laurentic*, the luxury White Star Line vessel, commissioned as an armed cruiser. Sailing from Liverpool for Halifax, Nova Scotia, she was struck by two mines at the mouth of Lough Swilly in County Donegal.

In spring, roadside verges aglow with daffodils recall the North Uist Bulb Project, a 1960s scheme to trial bulb-growing on the machair at Balemore, Kyles Paible and Knockline at a time when the Dutch bulb industry was struggling with disease and shortage of space. Dutch consultants were appointed to assess the prospect of reclaiming 1,600 acres of Vallay tidal strand for a bulb field. The trials went well, however the reclamation scheme was abandoned.

An enclosed garden beside the road at Paiblesgarry contains a monolith monument honouring 12 First World War veterans who organised direct action in 1921 because they felt cheated by the hollow promise of a plot of land on return from service. Led by piper Donald Ewen MacDonald, the men raided the laird's estate land at Balranald. Some were jailed in Inverness before the government came forth with the promised crofts.

The striking Gothic design of Kilmuir parish church makes a bold statement. The ecclesiastical building with battlemented parapet and pyramid spire occupies the Loch nam Magarlan shore alongside boats used by anglers fishing for brown trout, but not on Sundays. A turning to the seashore discovers the heavenly bay and RSPB reserve at Balranald, a key site in the UK corncrake recovery programme. Sandy paths through the reserve reach Aird an Runair, westernmost point of North Uist. The coastal scenery and views to the Monach Isles are thrilling. The seasonal Dunes Cabin beside the family-run campsite offers freshly landed seafood, local smoked salmon, and delicious homebaking.

On a grassy hillock overlooking the RSPB reserve, Cille Mhoire, or the 'Church of Virgin Mary', is in a ruinous state. In 1703 explorer Martin Martin wrote of an enigmatic stone opposite the church which served to procure rain. In times of drought, local people stood it upright; after the deluge they laid it back down again. The exact location of this obliging stone is no longer known though it may be on the headland.

The pretty seashore crofting community of Houghharry features in a traditional song. *'Bodaich Odhar Hoghaigearraidh'*, which translates from the Gaelic to 'The Dun-Coloured Men of Houghharry'. Renowned local singer Julie Fowlis performs this North Uist tune worldwide. The narrow ribbon of coastal highway passes alongside Loch Eaval where heaped stones on an island are the last of a fortified dun tower.

The road climbs inland through fertile fields leaving the rocky headland; here a deep chasm formed by storm-force Atlantic waves is known as Slochd a' Choire or the 'Spouting Kettle'.

Powerful waves attract experienced surfers to Hosta. The north-west-facing shore is wide open to almighty Atlantic rollers and though this sloping bay is exhilarating, it is also extremely dangerous. Tragically, there have been fatalities. A lonely stone cross on the Kilpheder hillside was re-erected around 1830 after lying undiscovered for centuries on a grassy plateau to the south. The monument surfaced during the ploughing of a field thought to hold the remains of a burial ground and chapel dedicated to St Peter. A striking octagonal tower occupies the shore of Loch Scolpaig; the folly commissioned in the 1830s provided local employment for famine relief. The Georgian monument to hunger stands on the site of an Iron Age dun.

Coastal scenery around Griminish Point is wildly spectacular, especially at sunset, however dangerous deep chasms lurk in the clifftops and it is essential to keep children and dogs under close control. At Foshigarry a mysterious mound in the machair revealed the remains of a large Iron Age settlement alongside more recent ruins of a crofting township cleared of tenants in the 1820s.

A ruinous mansion house on an uninhabited tidal island surrounded by golden sands sounds like the setting of an atmospheric movie and the story of the island of Vallay does not disappoint. Wealthy industrialist Erskine Beveridge luxuriated in the fortune accumulated by the family business producing damask linen in Dunfermline. While the company furnished polite society around the world with fine cloth and tableware,

Beauty Spot

The St Kilda viewpoint on the slopes of South Clettraval is a surreal experience. Information panels around an enclosure of drystone walls identify distant landmarks in a spectacular panoramic view that scopes the Monach Isles, Kirkibost, Benbecula, South Uist and Barra, and St Kilda, the most remote part of Britain some 50 miles west on the horizon. A little further up the hill an active radar station tracks missiles from the Royal Artillery Range linked to Rueval on Benbecula. The massive white golf balls of the listening post are a North Uist landmark.

Beveridge indulged in outdoor passions. The keen naturalist, archaeologist and landscape photographer acquired Vallay in 1901 and commissioned his architect to design an imposing summer retreat, undeterred by the challenge of building on a schedule dictated by the tides. The construction of the baronial mansion known as Taigh Mor, or the big house, took three years. No expense was spared, pipes were laid to carry fresh water to the island, huge fireplaces warmed the chill of ocean winds, and a grand staircase with a pineapple finial swept glamorously up to the collector's museum where Beveridge displayed rare birds' eggs and prehistoric artefacts unearthed on his amateur archaeology missions. He was renowned for presenting the rare and precious finds to guests who appreciated them. While in residence, he ignored British Summer Time, living instead by solar time which governs the tides.

When Beveridge died in 1920, his son George inherited the island estate. Upon his engagement to Eva Flora MacDonald of Balranald, her father refused their marriage. Tragically neither of the heartbroken sweethearts went on to marry anyone else. George let the mansion out to occasional guests and Scottish novelist Naomi Mitchison was among those who took a dreamy summer lease. On a November night in 1944, after visiting crofter friends across the bay, George returned to Vallay by boat. When local people noticed the next day that there was no sign of smoke from the chimneys, they raised the alarm. George was found drowned on the shore. Since then, Taigh Mor has declined desperately; shattered dreams hang heavy in the air. Seabirds nest in rooms where

Curiosity

A large and significant early medieval cross from Vallay was uplifted sometime prior to 1901 and taken to the rockery garden of Kilmuir Castle in Lochgilphead, owned by the Orde family who also owned the island as part of their North Uist estate. The cross has since been relocated to St Margaret's Church in Lochgilphead. Might it ever return home?

once their stolen eggs were displayed.

Crossing the strand to Vallay is an unforgettable adventure. Plan with care, be sure to know the exact route, take a detailed map, know the tide times, and prepare for sudden changes of weather. Allow 30 minutes for the walk from Aird Glas, across mudflats and seawater channels. Aim for the mansion house gateway and bear in mind that once on the beguiling island, it is incredibly easy to lose yourself in the thrall of baronial ruins, coastal scenery and archaeological remains. A modest hilltop cairn erected for George Beveridge surveys the scene of his father's dreams. Allow plenty of time for the return journey through a clutch of islets in the vast sandy arena. The sheer wonder of it all can be disorientating; take care.

The coast road sweeps around Vallay Strand passing dwellings of grand and traditional design. Squat stone cottages under snug thatch keep happy company with timber eco houses. The Co-op at Sollas is a favourite island store. The wonderfully warm team recognises the social role of the little supermarket, especially in winter when older residents brave the expedition less frequently. I am in awe of caring staff in island stores who manage such friendly chats with customers while still getting on with their tasks.

The community remembers the Battle of Sollas in 1849 when impoverished men, women and children resisted eviction by employees of the landowner Lord MacDonald. The laird's response was to secure police reinforcements from the mainland. Houses were burned and hundreds of people left the district, many against their will. Some moved elsewhere in the islands, others emigrated. Around 50 years later, the district was at last resettled as crofting townships. Michael Grey of Ontario, Canada won the composing contest marking the 170th anniversary of the battle in 2019. His winning bagpipe composition is a four-part march.

Udal is a spectacular tombolo peninsula, connected to mainland North Uist by a long arm of sand. Allow at least three hours to discover it on a magnificent seven-mile walk from a small car park with picnic benches on the Grenitote shore that served as an airfield for pioneering air ambulances. Northern & Scottish Airways inaugurated services here in February 1936. A bench overlooking the sandy runway honours John Angus Macleod, founder of the more recent Sollas Fly-In.

The peninsula walk explores towering dunes and paradise sands with views to the mountains of Harris and Atlantic islands near and far. Boreray island, just offshore, is a profoundly spiritual place. The burial ground contains the graves of monks and possibly St Donnan, a contemporary of St Columba, who was killed along with over 50 companions in the destruction of his monastery on the island of Eigg in AD 619. The island is uninhabited now yet previously it supported a crofting community that swam their cattle to Udal and walked them on to sales at Clachan.

Udal is uninhabited now, yet remnants of early occupation reveal Viking and Bronze Age communities lived here. Two tragic skeletons found in the dunes witness the climate crisis experienced by our ancestors. Tests revealed death by starvation. Their homes were subject to catastrophic sand blows, erosion by the sea and floods that claimed land and livestock.

The low-lying islands of Uist remain critically vulnerable to climate change. Much of the terrain is below sea level during tidal cycles. In each severe storm event islanders might lose up to five metres of land to gouging waves. Livestock fences are moved ever further inland. Rising levels of winter rainfall trigger flooding on land and across the causeways.

Before returning to the loop road, anyone with a stationery habit should call by Sollas Bookbinding in Grenitote where Corinna Krause handcrafts exquisite journals with artisan papers. The island circuit rolls on past Oronsay island towards the Berneray causeway and Lochmaddy; alternatively take the Committee Road towards the North Ford causeway and the next island on this Outer Hebrides journey, Grimsay.

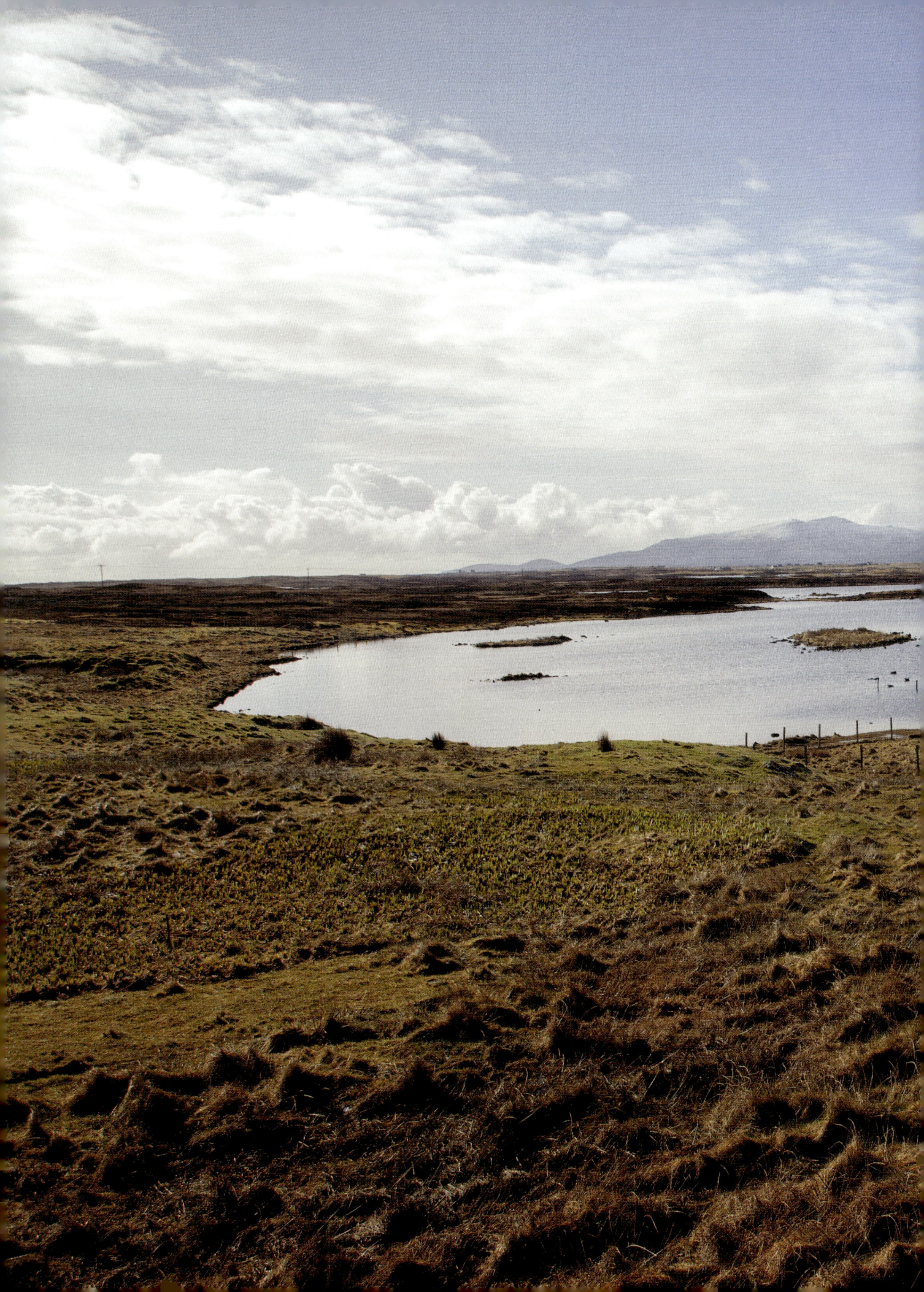

PART THREE
Grimsay and Benbecula

The Boats, Lobsters and Wool of Grimsay

Crossing the tidal North Ford between North Uist and the islands of Grimsay and Benbecula is a magical experience. The entire five-mile length of the causeway travels smoothly over seven islands and three bridges. Low tide reveals the thrilling sandy expanse of the Oitir Mhor, and it is easy to get carried away by the wonder of it all and perhaps accidentally bypass the side road that turns into the Isle of Grimsay, rolling onward to Benbecula. That would be a great shame; gentle

Grimsay, just four miles long by two miles wide, is far too lovely to miss.

Prior to the opening of the causeway in 1960, making a crossing of the North Ford was a tough challenge dictated by the tides of the Atlantic Ocean to the west and the Minch to the east. Traditionally people trekked a four-mile route across the huge sands, guided in all weathers by a chain of tall waymarker cairns indicating the shortest safest passage through tidal channels, heavy mud and shifting sandbanks. The cacophony of drovers accompanying hundreds of cattle bound for island livestock sales resounded across the great open space. Some travellers made the journey on horseback or with pony and trap. At high tide, a small ferry boat crossed between Carinish on North Uist and Gramsdale on Benbecula.

The causeway carrying the A865 touches down on the tip of Grimsay and moves on swiftly to Benbecula. From Balaglas the Grimsay loop road invites discovery of this island populated by fewer than 200 people. A side road reaches Seana Bhaile, a small settlement on Eilean Fraoch, meaning 'Heather Isle'.

The loop road continues towards Loch Hornoray where a rare Iron Age wheelhouse occupies rough boggy ground with views over the romantically named Bagh nam Feadag, 'Bay of the Plover', to the enigmatic smooth slopes of Eaval, the highest mountain on North Uist. The wheelhouse site was uncovered and excavated from 1990 without professional support and examination and so much archaeological information has been lost. Drystone walls, reminiscent of the spokes of a wheel, enclose cells that meet in a central open space. At Loch Hornoray the ruins of Dun Ban, an Iron Age island fort, connect to the south shore by a submerged causeway.

Tracts of dark, rich earth through the Uist group of islands are fertile terrain to which traditional crofting communities applied a mosaic system of agriculture, dedicating small areas of land to potatoes, hayfields and cornfields. Through the 20th century, this traditional land management system has declined, often giving way to rough grazing for sheep. Skills and wisdom, passed down through communities over generations, have been lost.

Crofting is labour intensive and long hours are required to care for crops and livestock. What was once a way of life throughout the Outer Hebrides has become a subsidiary to work providing more reliable income streams. Modern crofters are passionate about their role, but many describe it as an expensive hobby because they are unable to make a viable living from it. Rather than waste the potential of the fertile black earth, many island communities are exploring how traditional techniques and wisdom might be revisited and adapted to work derelict land in a way that responds also to the needs of conservation and production.

The seven-mile loop road soon arrives at lovely Baymore, site of the old harbour, with views to the rugged Isle of Ronay offshore. Ronay, and many smaller islands around it, was inhabited until 1831 when the community was cleared by the laird. Later generations returned but dwindled and Ronay became another of the Outer Hebrides' empty islands by 1931.

Wildlife is abundant in Grimsay. Sleek otters slip through seaweed forests and scamper across tidal saltings that turn from emerald green to candy pink under clouds of thrift flowers in summer. Canny seals await fishers' boats in expectation of tidbits, red deer swim from islet to islet for favourite grazing, sea eagles and golden eagles patrol on high. The road visits the neat hub of Kallin harbour where local crews are joined by fishers from Benbecula and North Uist. The Grimsay Boatshed facility, founded in 2001, is a centre of traditional and new boatbuilding and repair skills. Wildlife boat trips invite visitors to discover island shores from thrilling new perspectives.

The fishers of Grimsay have enjoyed a long worldwide reputation for high-quality catches of lobster, scallops and prawns. Lobsters from the west side of the islands are especially big. Heisker, or the Monach Isles, a chain of five low-lying islands some seven miles to the west, is a rich fishing ground for the Grimsay fleet. Traditionally, from April to September, Grimsay lobster fishers relocated with pots, pans and bedding to small turf-roofed stone huts on fertile Ceann Ear where a community of around 100 residents kept cattle and grew crops including barley, oats and potatoes. The signature island dish of shag soup was a seabird delicacy with an acquired taste. Resident islanders looked forward to the visitors' arrival, relishing the seasonal company and entertainment. The valuable catch of lobsters was held in floating seawater crates for delivery via steamer from Lochmaddy to the mainland and onward to Billingsgate fish market in London and further abroad. Many lobsters died in transit and for these the fishers were not paid.

Shellfish remains important to the island economy. Crab and lobster are caught on the Atlantic seaboard to the west, langoustines and scallops are fished in the Minch to the east. A small processing factory and shop adjacent to the harbour provides employment. On the pier, beyond shelves piled high with fishers' wellies and colourful buoys, the small seafood café at Namara Marine Supplies serves fresh crab, scallops and lobster.

The shores around sheltered Scotvein Bay are frequented by otters and herons. At the water's edge an historic timber shed is part of the fascinating self-guided Grimsay Boat Trail developed by passionate islanders keen to preserve and share the island's extraordinary boat-building heritage.

Uist Mill and Wool Centre in Scotvein is an inspirational creative venue. Here artisan craftspeople produce exquisite and sustainable island yarns, especially wool from Hebridean sheep, one of the oldest native Scottish breeds. The island co-operative operates on a not-for-

Beauty Spot

A rough track leads to St Michael's Point, an atmospheric promontory where the lonely ruins of the eponymous chapel peer across creeks and bays to proud mountains on the Isle of Skye and hills on the small isles of Rum and Canna. According to folklore, the oratory, enclosed by overgrown walls, was built by Amie MacRuari as a place of refuge when stormy weather detained her in the islands. Noblewoman Amie was the first wife of John of Islay, Lord of the Isles. The couple married in 1337 and John immediately assumed her Clan Ruari lands. But this substantial acquisition was not enough for sleekit John, hungry for higher status. He ditched Amie to marry Margaret, daughter of the influential High Steward of Scotland. While John put his energies into courting fame and fortune, more spiritual Amie turned to ecclesiastical building projects in Highland communities.

profit basis, showcasing the work of the immensely talented team. In the sassy rural store, stunning woollen garments and patterns, beautifully displayed, inspire even the most reluctant wannabe knitter. Glorious colours reflect Hebridean land and sea. In the heady fug of wool, a large window overlooks the fascinating production process on the mill floor.

The former Free Church and manse at Scotvein has been transformed into a colourful, cosy, welcoming hub where the island community gathers for social events and tasty local food and drink in the café. This lovely centre also hosts an exhibition space, a post office counter, and the maritime delights of the Grimsay Boathaven celebrating the fascinating history of Grimsay's clinker-built craft and boatbuilding techniques.

Four generations of the Stewart family designed, developed and built strong agile boats for fishing communities throughout the islands. Distinctive Grimsay vessels were designed to be small enough to slip into steep and narrow rocky inlets on the Minch coast and fast and stable enough to ride the powerful waves of the Atlantic Ocean. Moreover, each boat was built individually, by eye, without moulds. Among the restored boats on display is *Morning Star*, small yet majestic. She was constructed in 1928 to deliver mail and supplies to the lighthouse keepers in the Monach Isles and was the first Grimsay boat built for an engine. A celebratory poem by the North Uist Gaelic bard Dòmhnall Ruadh Chorùna described her evocatively with flippers of brass instead of a sail. The renowned island poet also wrote the lyric for one of the most enduring love songs from the Outer Hebrides, '*An Eala Bhàn*', mentioned on page 135.

Inside the Stewarts' large and draughty timber-built boat shed, well-used tools of the trade are set out on the long workbench giving the impression the workers might have popped out for a moment. A boat occupies the workshop floor, out of water to receive loving attention. Wide double doors open to the slipway where the sea calls. I find this time-capsule spine-tingling and especially evocative. My profoundly deaf grandfather Ted Benson worked all his life as a shipbuilder, apprenticed from his teenage years. I remember well his delight in work well done and the importance of the precious hand tools that served all his years in the yard, each stored with care and bearing his scorched initials. How he would have loved this place.

To Atmospheric Benbecula: the Flattest Island Across the Longest Causeway

The causeway crossing the North Ford is the longest in the Outer Hebrides, travelling five miles from North Uist to Benbecula via the Isle of Grimsay. On approach, the landmark slopes of Rueval dominate Benbecula, the flattest island in the Outer Hebrides chain. The island is described sometimes as a stepping stone in the sandy straits between North Uist and South Uist yet there is so much more to it than that. Consider Benbecula a tangy juicy gooseberry between the smoochy Uist couple.

The causeway lands at Gramsdale shore, steeped in ritual. A large circle of ancient standing stones, some 100 feet in diameter, occupies a flat farm field to the east. This northern tip of the island also held significance for the Pictish people who sited a mysterious symbol stone from the sixth to ninth centuries at Strome Shunnamal. The granite monument carved with mysterious circles and squares is on display in the National Museum of Scotland in Edinburgh. Gramsdale is the site of a proposed new distillery and visitor centre for Benbecula that, comparing levels of population, will create the equivalent of 10,000 jobs in Glasgow.

A small road invites discovery of a smattering of isles at Kyles Flodda. A short causeway stitches the tidal island of Flodday into the fabric of Benbecula. From the road end a rough farm path veers toward the headland known as Seal Point. Islets and skerries are the haunt of Atlantic grey seals, among the rarest in the world and the largest living carnivore in Britain.

Beyond Flodday lies Rarinish where flamboyant fugitive Bonnie Prince Charlie took refuge in May 1746. The prince hid in a lowly hut while government forces pursued their man relentlessly through the islands after the brutal bloodbath that crushed his Jacobite forces at Culloden.

Perhaps, in the dank hideaway, the despondent Young Pretender was glad of the warming comfort of Drambuie. According to tradition, the famous blend of whisky, imbued with honey, heather and spices, was his personal tipple and when at last he reached the Isle of Skye, after his flight through the islands, he gifted the recipe to supporters in return for their loyalty.

The royal fugitive famously reached Skye by boat with the assistance of Flora MacDonald from South Uist. Could they have ever imagined, as has been recently proposed, a 17-mile subsea dual carriageway link between low-lying Rarinish and towering Neist Point on Skye, the shortest distance between Scotland and the Outer Hebrides?

The northern district of Benbecula was sold to the Air Ministry in 1942 and a sandy pre-war civilian airstrip became RAF Benbecula. Boeing Flying Fortress planes, equipped with bombs and machine guns for high-altitude missions, scoured the North Atlantic for German U-boats. The solidly built Fortresses were renowned for their ability to stay in the air even after considerable damage.

During the Cold War, the development of RAF Benbecula as the control centre of the Hebrides Inter Services Missile Testing Range required earthworks that might possibly destroy archaeological treasures around the airfield. Sites excavated hurriedly in 1956 revealed a complex of Iron Age wheelhouses occupied by people of high status. Several were destroyed by the expansion of the airfield runways.

Benbecula Airport operates daily flights to Stornoway, Glasgow and Barra. The Island Kitchen Café is popular with air passengers and visitors. A defunct concrete water tower, built to service the RAF station at Balivanich, has become one of the island's most iconic architectural treasures. Visible at a distance

Curiosity

The activity of the military airfield brought a regular influx of new residents to Balivanich. As the community grew, leisure and entertainment facilities expanded. Benbecula Golf Club was instigated by American troops who made an unofficial four-hole links in a patch of green grass on the airfield. In 1984 flat land alongside was formally developed into a nine-hole course with great views to the Monach Isles. The course clubhouse is a former wartime building and visitors are warmly welcome. The Army Saddle Club, founded in 1974, operated at first from three railway carriages with just three ponies. Since then, horse riding has flourished at Balivanich, and a former swimming pool has been transformed into an indoor riding school. The club became Uist Community Riding School with more than 20 horses and ponies. Visitors are invited to experience wonderful beach rides.

across the largely flat island, the 1970s design reminds me of a supersized chalice. Curiously, it overlooks the ruins of Teampull Chaluim Cille, a small ancient chapel dedicated to St Columba in marshy land close by the B982 road. Balivanich is known in Gaelic as Baile a' Mhanaich, meaning 'Town of the Monks'.

While the east coast of Benbecula is watery inlets and islets, the west is sweeping sands and headlands. The arc of Culla Bay inspired an eponymous Scottish country dance devised by Anne Dix for her friend Sheila Jupp. When invited to name the dance, Sheila paid homage to the bay on the island to where she was evacuated as a little girl to stay with family during the Second Word War. The beautiful shore frequented by beachcombers, artists and surfers is backed by the lush pastures of Nunton, known in Gaelic as Baile nan Cailleach or 'Town of the Nuns'.

Nunton House is a grand 18th-century building with a significant contribution to the story of Bonnie Prince Charlie's flight through the Outer Hebrides in 1746. The islands were crawling with some 3,000 soldiers offering the generous reward for information leading to his capture. Anyone suspected of being a Jacobite was executed.

An extraordinary plan hatched by his supporters at Nunton House schemed to disguise the prince as the Irish maidservant of 24-year-old Flora MacDonald, commissioned to accompany the fugitive to the Isle of Skye. Recognising the enormous risk, Flora was less than enthusiastic. Her stepfather, Hugh Macdonald, was captain of a company of militia with orders to find Charles, yet he secretly supported the prince's cause, and was willing to help him escape.

Flora acquiesced and the prince became Betty Burke, decked out in a blue and white frock. The odd couple completed their mission and arrived safely at the Skye headland now known as Rudha Phrionnsa or 'Prince's Point'. Flora was later arrested and imprisoned for her part in the escape. After early release, she married Allan MacDonald and emigrated to North Carolina just as the American Revolution was unfolding. The couple's support for the British side cost them their plantation and livelihood. Flora returned to Scotland and settled in the Isle of Skye where she died in 1790. At Kilmuir, on the island where she famously landed with the prince, a high Celtic cross marks her resting place and bears the commendation of Samuel Johnson, the writer and Jacobite sympathiser who was enchanted by her when they met during his visit to Skye in 1773: 'Flora MacDonald. Preserver of Prince Charles Edward Stuart. Her name will be mentioned in history and if courage and fidelity be virtues, mentioned with honour.'

The history of Nunton House intrigues cyclists, walkers, and other guests at the independent hostel within part of the building. The elegant buildings of Nunton Steading host the production base of the first whisky to be distilled legally in the southern islands of the Outer Hebrides chain. North Uist Distillery is the latest occupant of 17th-century farm buildings on the site of a 13th-century monastery. While the maturing whisky is yet to be released, the small batch range of premium island gin is a roaring success. With a wittily affectionate nod to the moist Hebridean climate, the impressive spirit is not called Downpour for nothing.

The lumpy ruins of medieval Borve Castle, built by Amie MacRuairi, the first wife of John, Lord of the Isles, occupy a ploughed flat field in the village of Torlum. The site has changed since the fortress was constructed, possibly on a tidal island or shore that has since been

Beauty Spot

Rueval is the modest high point of Benbecula, dominating the flat landscape at just 124 feet. The summit overlooks an extraordinary scene of mazey lochs and lochans, island causeways and the shores of North and South Uist. The waymarked hill path reaching this splendour departs from the Market Stance landfill depot on the A865. Allow a couple of hours for the hike on a rough track over flattish terrain. An extension of the walk visits the atmospheric Roisinis peninsula. Further hikes are signed to the lonely yet lovely shores of Scarilode and Meanish on grassy routes tramped by cattle drovers bound for the market stance sales.

infilled by windblown sand. Prehistoric remains discovered in the intertidal zone off Lionacleit shore form one of the best surviving examples of a submerged forest of birch, willow and Scots pine. Here Bronze Age people butchered animals for food, and left their tools behind. Dynamic coastal change is eroding the shore and washing the history away.

The Dark Island Hotel at Lionacleit shares its name with a 1960s BBC Television series set in Benbecula. The drama unfolded around the discovery of a torpedo on the beach. The show's evocative theme tune, composed in 1958 as a pipe lament for a local man under the title 'Dr Mackay's Farewell to Creagorry', is a popular performance piece.

Lionacleit comprehensive school is a vibrant hub where pupils enjoy the rare opportunity to learn the craft of boatbuilding, in association with the Grimsay Boat Shed Trust. The site comprises a community centre with a library, museum and sports facilities. Visitors are warmly welcomed.

Two inviting roads explore spacious south-east Benbecula. The narrow unclassified route to Uisgeabhagh discovers scattered crofts, lochs, islets around the secluded shore from where Flora and Charlie sailed to Skye. The B891 sashays to a teeny port with an extraordinary story. When mail steamers began deliveries to Lochmaddy in North Uist and Lochboisdale in South Uist in the 1880s, Benbecula was overlooked, because the island was unable to offer a suitable west coast port of call. Correspondence arrived in the island via neighbouring islands and was subject to further delay at the north and south fords, sometimes impassable due to wild weather for days. Eventually, a pier was built at Peter's Port on the islet of Eilean na Cille in 1894, however funds did not stretch to a causeway or bridge and so the far-flung landing place remained bizarrely disconnected. The ensuing furore was a right old stooshie further compounded by the harbour approach proving perilous for large boats. When at last a short causeway was

GRIMSAY AND BENBECULA

built in 1906 to connect Eilean na Cille with the Benbecula mainland it was all too late.

The quiet pier overlooks the uninhabited island of Wiay where Hercules the showbusiness grizzly bear last romped before his notorious North Uist escape. Discover his adventures on page 132.

Bonnie Prince Charlie visited Wiay too, though perhaps in not such a romping mood. The royal fugitive slept on an old sail in a secret cave. His hideaway, known as The Prince's Rest, enjoys fresh air views across the Minch to the Isle of Skye. Crystal-clear waters and sheltered bays around Wiay make excellent snorkelling sites.

No doubt the Peter's Port pier fiasco was the talk of the Creagorry Hotel bar frequented by locals, holidaymakers on fishing trips, and visitors attending island cattle sales. Before leaving Benbecula, I make a ritual stop at the Co-op on the seashore from where people crossed to South Uist prior to the causeway. The supermarket car park views over the sandy expanse of the South Ford are fabulous.

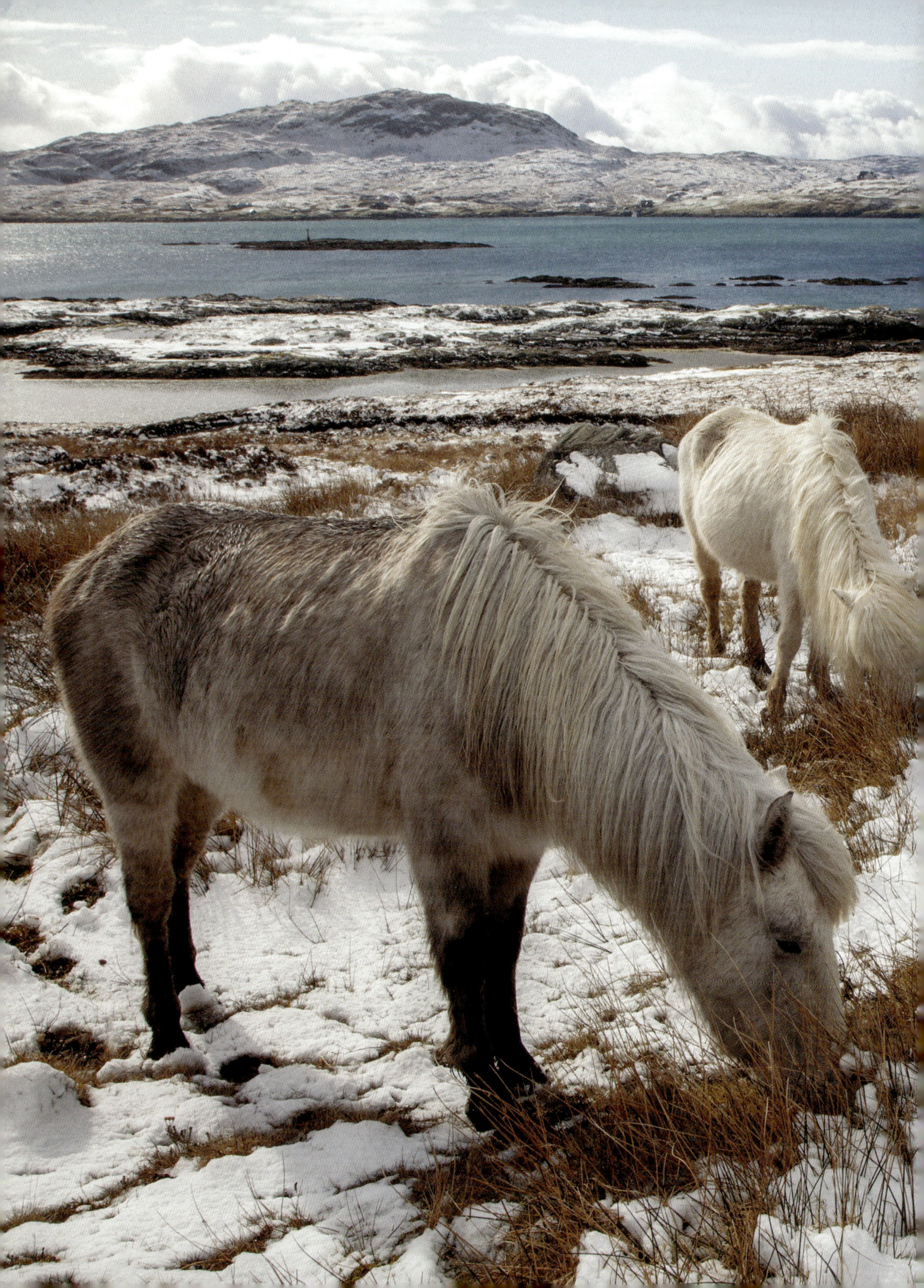

PART FOUR
South Uist and Eriskay

Creagorry
Ardkenneth
Iochdar
Ardivachar
Orasay
Loch Carnan
Loch Bee
West Gerinish
Stilligarry
B890
Loch Skipport
Loch Druidibeg
Howmore
Hecla
South Uist
A865
Glen Corrodale
Beinn Corrodale
Stoneybridge
Bornish Point
Beinn Mhor
Loch Ardvule
Bornish
Kildonan
Milton
Loch Eynort
0
2 km
0
2 miles
n
Askernish
Cladh Hallan
Daliburgh
Lochboisdale
B888
Calvay
North Glendale
Hairteabhagh
Garrynamonie
Cille Bhrighde
South Glendale
Polochar Inn
Ludag
Lingay
Ceann a' Ghàrraidh
Eriskay
Sound of Barra
Acarsaid Mhor
Fuday
to Barra

The Shrines, Shores and Silent Weaver of South Uist

The Outer Hebrides archipelago is imbued with colourful stories of remarkable individuals whose lives were shaped by their inspirational faith, courage and outstanding creative talent. This journey through South Uist celebrates the extraordinary achievements of fascinating characters, determined island priests and an enigmatic silent weaver of grass.

South Uist is the second largest of the Outer Hebrides islands after the single landmass of Lewis and Harris. The summits of Hecla, Beinn Corrodale and Beinn Mhor rise above large sea lochs to the east. Summer wildflowers splash jewel colours through the grassy machair that extends for miles along sandy beaches to the west. The spine of fertile ground between these distinctively different coasts is known as the *talamh-dubh*, the 'black earth'.

In the harsh winters of the 1930s, when the islands were served by only three steamers a week, local priest Father O'Regan campaigned successfully for improved connections, supported by Kenneth MacLeod, headmaster of Balivanich School. When the Air Ministry established RAF Benbecula in 1942 the new single-lane bridge of 82 spans was completed at speed but exposure to fierce winds and waves caused the concrete structure to deteriorate. The replacement, opened in 1983, is a bridge between Benbecula and tiny Creagorry island and a causeway thereafter. The new crossing is still known by some as Drochaid Oregan or 'O'Regan's Bridge'.

There is no mistaking South Uist is a predominantly Catholic community; the A865 reaches a shrine within moments of landing on the island. A multitude of statues and shrines throughout the island express faith and resistance. They remember historical repression of Catholicism and Gaelic language and culture in the islands, especially under threat when, in the wake of the Second World War, the Ministry of Defence proposed to develop a rocket range and vast military training arena, akin to Salisbury Plain, between Sollas in North Uist and Bornais in South Uist. The scheme required the removal of local people and identified Ardkenneth as the site of a purpose-built town to service the vision.

Recognising the imminent threat to his congregation, Canon Morrison of St Michael's Church in Ardkenneth instigated a campaign of resistance for which he became known as Father Rocket. Shrine-building began in earnest and the Blessed Virgin Mary appeared at the side of proposed military routes. Sculptor Hew Lorimer was commissioned to design *Bana Thighearna nan Eilean* or *Our Lady of the Isles*, a towering statue of the Madonna cradling infant Jesus on the slopes of Rueval. The defiant project was supported by people of all denominations far and wide and, ultimately, plans for the military arena and new town were abandoned.

However, the Hebrides range was given the go-ahead. The military facility, consisting of a deep range for complex weapons trials and in-service firings, and an inner range for ground-based air defence test and evaluation, is a major employer. Curiously, the largest area for the live firing of rockets and missiles of any UK range is monitored by Hew Lorimer's embodiment of the Virgin Mary and Jesus. She stands 27 feet high beside the radar station; her boy raises his hand to bless the islands and the ocean while classified signals transmit between Uist and St Kilda.

The sleek, white granite statue is believed to have been inspired by the work of Emile-Antoine Bourdelle. The French sculptor designed the Madonna and Child, known as *La Vierge d'Alsace*, for the Eichstein hill in Alsace. The Scottish National Gallery of Modern Art acquired an intermediary model of this artwork in 1930. The Bourdelle bronze model is on display in the sculpture park of Modern Two in Edinburgh. An intermediary model of Lorimer's sculpture graces the grounds of St Michael's Church in Ardkenneth.

The sandy bays, seaweed heaps, upturned boats, mudflats and island dunes of Gualan in the north-west district of South Uist are perfect for a mooching walk.

From a jetty beside Croft 99 on Carnan shore the small ferry boat crossed to Creagorry on the high tide. Drovers attending horse and cattle sales throughout the islands crossed at low tide. Guiding livestock cavalcades safely across the perilous ford was no mean feat. Community-owned Carnan Stores is a crofting mainstay, selling animal feed, seed potatoes, cattle and sheep tags, pig housing, gas, coal and fertiliser.

The clachan of Iochdar was the boyhood home of an extraordinary man known in Gaelic as *A' Fighe Le Feur*, the 'Weaver of Grass'. Angus MacPhee was eight years old when his mother Ellen died, and his widowed father Neil moved the family from the mainland to his native South Uist. Here the bereft boy turned to the company of animals for solace. Bonding especially with horses, Angus soon learned the craft of fashioning ropes and harnesses from marram, known in the breezy islands as bent grass. Handweaving was an essential skill to produce everyday items for crofting life; wool was made into cloth and twisted marram served for ropes, baskets and grain sacks. Horsehair, hay and heather also made strong ropes.

In the village drill hall, the Lovat Scouts regiment, raised in 1899 for service in South Africa by Lord Lovat, trained Highland and island ghillies, shepherds and stalkers to use their observation skills for military advantage. When Angus enlisted for service in the Second World War, he was sent to the Faroe Islands where he monitored the seas between Shetland and Iceland for U-boats. During this time, his mental well-being declined. His plight became especially apparent after the war when the quiet, gentle man returned to the family croft and found himself unable to care for the animals he had always treated with kindness.

Uprooted again, Angus became an inmate of the farm ward at Craig Dunain psychiatric hospital in mainland Inverness. The Gaelic-speaking islander expressed his trauma with silence. He chose not to converse and found comfort in weaving. From grass, leaves and tufts of sheep's wool snagged on fences he shaped extraordinary costumes that he draped artfully in trees. With woven grass mittens, he picked freshly dug tatties. Stashing his lovingly made creations in hedgerows, he watched on as hospital gardeners tidied them into the fire.

For 50 years, Angus remained a mostly silent inmate, speaking exceptionally rarely. When the 1990s Care in the Community scheme repatriated him to South Uist, Angus reunited with his sister Peggy, but the homecoming was short-lived; he died a year later. The story of his extraordinary woven art lives on because art therapist Joyce Laing recognised his unique talent and brought it to a wider audience. Angus the Weaver of Grass is buried beside the sea in Ardivachar cemetery. His simple epitaph reads, *Fois Agus Sith*, 'Rest in Peace'.

Along the shore, further creativity sparkles in the studio of Hebridean Jewellery where a small team of artisans handcraft designs inspired by island life. The bright café is a welcome refuge after a breezy walk.

The huge inland waters of Loch Bee are shallow and tidal, connecting with the sea to both sides. The experience of crossing the causeway feels different every time, the ebbing tide exposes golden sands and drying skerries thick with seaweed. High water on a calm day creates a beautiful mirror, reflecting clouds and anglers' boats.

A quiet road to the east explores Loch Carnan, indented with creeks, speckled with islets. A house by the shore, known locally as Doctor Louise's croft, is depicted in a collection of 1954 monochrome images of the Hebrides by photographer Paul Strand. His three-month project came after his fellow American Margaret Fay Shaw had already begun her collection of landscapes and portraits. The pioneering female photographer lived in the islands for six years and is far less well known than

Strand; however, the big shot was familiar with her work and, curiously, photographed in several identical locations.

An adventurous cycling holiday through the islands inspired Margaret to move to South Uist and live among the Gaelic-speaking community where she learned the language and achieved extraordinary creative work. But more of this remarkable woman and her place in the hearts of the Hebridean community in the next itinerary. The Loch Carnan road winds onward to the coast, passing traditionally thatched cottages, the community windfarm, Salar Smokehouse, Orasay Inn, the power station and pools of wild white water lilies along the way.

In West Gerinish, a modern bungalow-style church, built in 1966, is dedicated to St Bride whose story is entwined extraordinarily with the pagan goddess Brigid. The Catholic church transformed the pre-Christian goddess of the Gael into a saint in the fifth century. Throughout Scotland she is honoured at sites known as Cille Bhrighde, Kilbride and Kirkbride. Curiously, in the Hebrides, she is known also as the foster mother of Christ. At West Gerinish a large Brigid's cross stands beside the altar. The symbol associated with the fire goddess and saint is considered to protect homes and communities. Traditionally the crosses were woven from reeds on 1 February, the fire festival of Imbolc heralding the return of spring, and the feast day of St Brigid.

The long and quiet B890 escapes the speedy spine road to reach a car park beside Loch Druidibeg. Walks from here explore the National Nature Reserve formed through a partnership of the RSPB, the community estate and local crofters. Interpretation panels indicate three self-guided trails to experience the rare atmosphere of the distinctly less visited eastern shore where South Uist's imposing trio of summits, Beinn Mhor, Beinn Corrodale and Hecla rise in chorus, the happy hunting ground of golden eagles, sea eagles and hen harriers.

The straggly road continues to the shore of Loch Skipport through a blasted gorge and hairpin bends to arrive at the quiet remains of a decaying port that was of great significance up until the 1950s. Steamers from Glasgow landed goods and passengers. Drovers loaded cattle, fresh from island sales and weary from walking, down the perilously steep slope onto boats bound for the mainland. Sit quietly in the ghostly hush and you may be treated to otters at play around the stumps of the old wooden pier.

HEBRIDEAN JOURNEY

The Hebridean Island that Won Margaret Fay Shaw

Journeying south towards Loch Eynort, the A865 Outer Hebrides spine road through South Uist connects with a series of branch roads to the coast, an arrangement on the map reminiscent of a wind-blasted Scots pine. The branches reach into scattered crofting communities beside the ocean, each with a local freshwater loch or two. Cultivated fields merge into rare and precious wildflower machair grassland at the edge of an astounding golden shore some 20 miles long.

Beside croft house ruins at Stilligarry a memorial cairn honours the MacMhuirich bards of Clan Currie, poets who served the powerful MacDonalds of Clanranald. Stones in the cairn were contributed by clan members around the world. The lane to Howmore leads to an ecclesiastical centre of two churches, three chapels and the burial ground of Clanranald chiefs. The ruins formed a significant hub in medieval times and earlier centuries too. The religious community is gone but the neighbouring Gatliff Youth Hostel hosts a lively congregation of walkers and cyclists. Facilities in the traditional thatched and white-washed croft house are cosy and basic; the situation is heavenly. Barefoot evening strolls on the soft sands beside the Atlantic Ocean are unforgettable. The twittering morning call of meadow birds is the sweetest island alarm clock.

However, the Uist firing range extends to the shore and all warning signs and notices should be observed. The almost human form of the prominent Crois Chnoca Breaca standing stone on the Stoneybridge coast seems, to me, a wise and knowing time traveller. The ruins of Ormacleit Castle, home of the chiefs of Clanranald, have been standing far longer than the building which burned down just seven years after completion in 1708; apparently folks celebrating the Jacobite army's victory at the Battle of Sheriffmuir did not pay enough attention to the fire over which a slap-up venison feast was roasting. Construction material to build the castle, of romantic design possibly inspired by a French chateau, may have been transported to the western shore by small boats navigating a maze of inland lochs and stone-lined channels around the district.

Tidal Loch Eynort chomps deep inland; briny waters from the sea to the east almost divide South Uist into two chunks. A narrow road

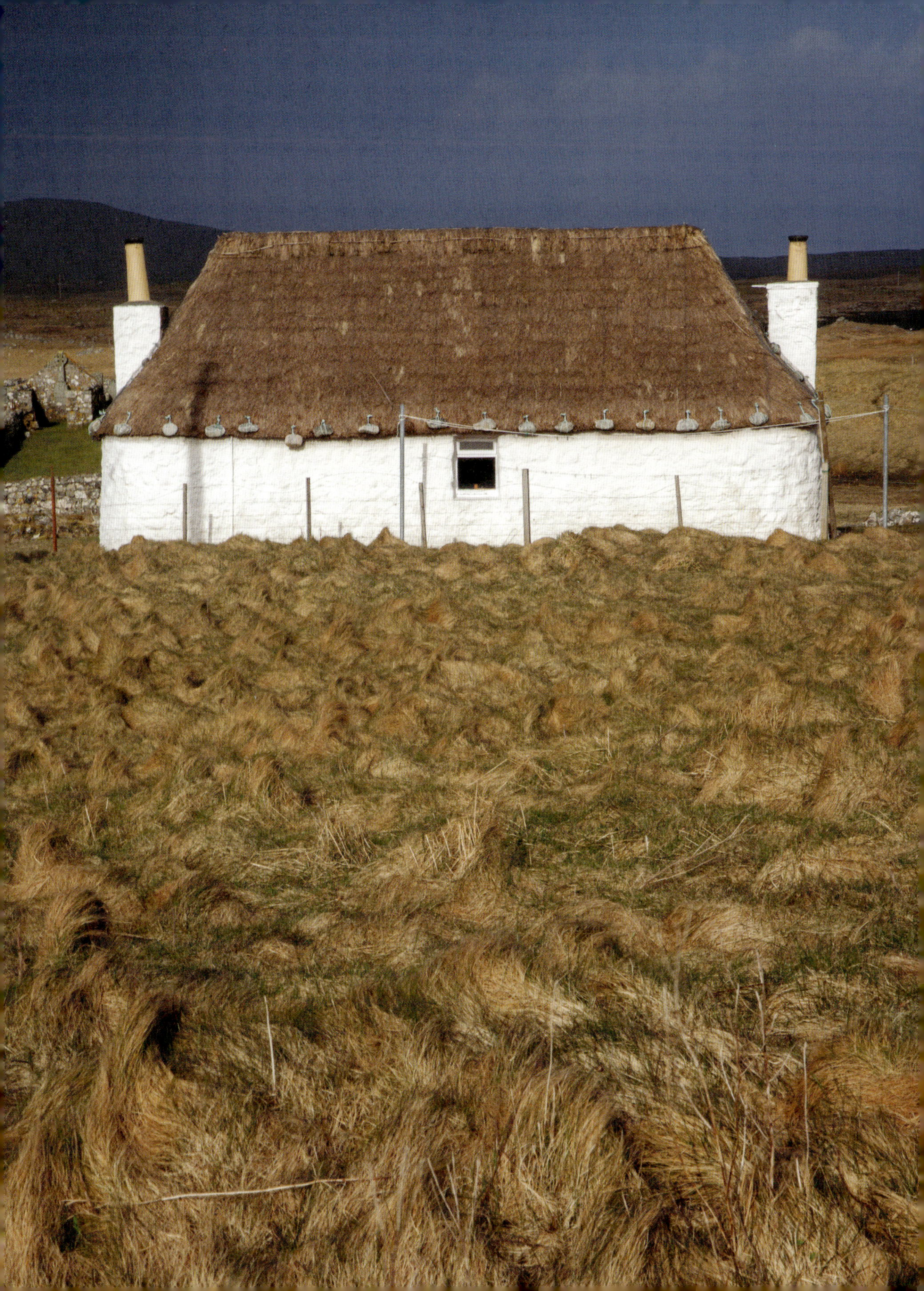

ventures to the inlet and forks, in wide lobster-pincer fashion, not quite keeping a firm grip on Calvay island surrounded by two narrow straits. Scattered homes on the southern shore peer into the imposing heights of Beinn Mhor, Beinn Corrodale and Hecla, where walkers thrill to challenging terrain and the company of eagles. Spectacular vistas scope a multitude of islands beyond: Harris, Skye, Rhum, Jura and St Kilda. Anyone entering this lonely landscape must prepare well; it's not for nothing that fugitive Bonnie Prince Charlie and his men, fleeing from defeat at the Battle of Culloden, sheltered undiscovered in a hut behind a rock in lonely Glen Corrodale. A cave nearby, named Uamh a' Phrionnsa in his honour, provided refuge for shepherds who slept on heather beds.

Traces of an extraordinary Norse-trading settlement at Bornish are faintly visible in the

Beauty Spot

The quiet route along the north shore of Loch Eynort crosses bridges over shallow bays to reach the historic site of a nunnery known as Airidh nam Ban. Here, rare woodland, planted over decades by Archie MacDonald, is full of birdsong. Paths through the croft invite discovery of rocky bays beyond where common seals bask in sunshine. Trees are a rare sight in the Outer Hebrides, yet previously the islands were covered in forests exploited especially by the Vikings. The Croft Woodlands Project, established in 2016, is a community undertaking to plant more than 130,000 native trees through the islands for the benefit of future generations.

landscape, yet awesome reconstruction occurs when the site is viewed in situ through the augmented reality of the *Uist Unearthed* free app, developed by the University of the Highlands and Islands. The tool is a great way to see and understand better outstanding archaeological sites across the islands.

The friendly café in a cultural hub within the former village school at Kildonan is a great place to refuel after adventures outdoors. Here an intriguing museum traces island life through the years with over 700 items from a collection curated by Canon Morrison of Iochdar, aka Father Rocket. Galley Aileach is a commanding clinker-built replica of iconic Celtic vessels known as birlinns in Scots Gaelic. The sleek craft dominated trading routes around the coast of Scotland and beyond between the 12th and 15th centuries. Research for the design of Galley Aileach, some 40 feet long with 16 oars and one sail, was informed by a carving from the period on a Macleod grave at Rodel church in Harris.

Heroic Flora MacDonald was born in 1722 at the family croft of her minister father in the township of Milton. Following his death, her mother remarried and moved to the Isle of Skye, yet Flora chose to stay in South Uist to receive her education. Later she attended classes in Edinburgh, with the daughter of her mother's friend, Lady Clanranald.

Flora became world famous for her part in assisting Bonnie Prince Charlie to flee Scotland in the wake of defeat at the Battle of Culloden, a watershed that changed the course of relations between Scotland and the rest of Britain and ended the Jacobite claim to the throne. With Charlie disguised as Flora's maidservant, the unlikely pair eluded their pursuers. The famous flight across the sea is celebrated in 'The Skye Boat Song', traditionally sung by rowers to maintain the rhythm of the oars.

Curiosity

Bornish Point is as far west as you can go in South Uist. Here Atlantic swell slams a ragged headland with the strange watery eye of Loch Ardvule in the middle. By contrast, the elegant church known in Gaelic as Eaglais an Naoimh Moire is a vision of serenity. Scots Gaelic does not use Mairi for the Virgin Mary, rather she is given the unique name Moire. The sea is known as *cuilidh Moire*, Mary's treasury. The church constructed in 1837 was originally of the same design as St Michael's in Ardkenneth prior to remodelling and extension in 1955 under the supervision of Reginald Fairlie, a pal of sculptor Hew Lorimer who created the towering statue of *Our Lady of the Isles*, and was dedicated in 1958. Inside the chapel, icons by artist Michael Gilfedder celebrate the lives of modern saints Edith Stein and Mary MacKillop. German Jewish philosopher Edith Stein converted to Catholicism and became a nun. She was executed by poisonous gas at Auschwitz. Educator and social reformer Mary MacKillop founded Australia's first order of nuns and is informally regarded as the patron saint of sexual abuse for her role in exposing a paedophile priest. Her personal motto was 'Never see a need without doing something about it'.

I know well the lovely statue of Flora and her faithful hound beside Inverness Castle in the capital of the Highlands, and I have visited her burial place at Kilmuir on Skye, where she is honoured with a splendid high Celtic cross. But at her South Uist birthplace there is no pomp. The roofless croft house ruin contrasts starkly with the birthplace of her partner in crime. Prince Charles Edward Stuart was born in December 1720 to the exiled Stuart King James VII and II at the Palazzo Muti in Rome, a residence bestowed upon the Catholic family by Pope Clement XI. To stand in the tumbledown surrounds of Flora's family croft and consider how the lives of two young people collided momentously in 1746 is quite something.

The Outer Hebrides landscape keeps many secrets, and discovery of them can be astonishing. Take Askernish Golf Course on the far Atlantic shore, a masterpiece of 1890s design by Old Tom Morris, links architect extraordinaire. His lost South Uist project was unearthed from windblown sand more than a century after it was designed. The fantastic links beside the ocean affirm how the game born in Scotland was intended to be played, in tune with nature at large. In winter, local crofters' free-roaming livestock pattern the site with squidgy souvenirs. Summer brings corncrakes sounding their distinctive *crex crex* calls from hiding places in the rough, rough. Atlantic breezes toy with white balls losing their way in crowds of wildflowers and helpful rabbits industriously excavate a zillion alternative holes. Askernish is simply magnificent, and visitors are most welcome to play.

A further Uist mystery emerged from the dunes at nearby Cladh Hallan in 2001 when archaeologists from Sheffield University discovered the intentionally mummified remains of Bronze Age people in a lost settlement. Examination revealed that the skeletons were composed of bones from different people, suggesting they were considered important ancestral figures, held in high regard, and kept in a place sacred to their community. Curiously

---

Beauty Spot

The seashore mound of Hallan burial ground rises at the end of a bumpy track trammelled by crofters' tractors working shallow sandy plots on the machair. Among the island community at peace in this wonderful spot beside the sea is American Margaret Fay Shaw, the pioneering photographer, cinematographer and musician who crossed the Atlantic to begin a new life in Scotland. Fittingly, the woman whose work came from the heart and not the ego, found extraordinary kindness and inspiration among the islanders of South Uist, Barra and Canna. She is buried as requested, alongside Peigi and Mairi MacRae, the sisters who took the young woman into their croft house at North Glendale in 1929. Margaret lived with them for six magical summers before marrying folklorist John Lorne Campbell. From the atmospheric burial ground, a sandy track through high dunes leads to a beautifully situated picnic bench overlooking the ocean.

the stones used to build the walls of nearby Hallan graveyard may be from the site.

The undulating A865 spine road bounces on through South Uist to the junction where it forks eastward to Lochboisdale, passing Hill Side filling station where the fluffy drive-through car wash is a rare novelty in the islands. Nearby, the candy-pink post office and stores cheers the greyest day. The B888 takes up the journey south towards the causeway that connects with the Isle of Eriskay.

Lochboisdale is re-energised with a major upgrade of facilities at the historic port serving fishers, leisure craft and ferries. The former pier is an infilled community garden. The maze of pens at the livestock mart still honours an old tradition.

Since 1880 the handsome Lochboisdale Hotel has looked from the headland to Calvay, the small island that protects the harbour and famously offered shelter to fugitive Bonnie Prince Charlie (him again!) on a June night in 1746. The hotel's facilities, gun room, rod room and drying room, met with estate owner Lady Gordon Cathcart's original brief for accommodation to suit sporting types. The friendly venue is one of those special island places where, in the warmth of a peat fire, folk in transit encounter people they might not otherwise meet. Though the drovers are gone, loyal anglers return to stay where the chef will cook the catch for supper.

It is here that Margaret Fay Shaw first met John Lorne Campbell, the bachelor regarded as one of the foremost scholars of Scottish Gaelic. Accounts of the vivacious American photographer intrigued him, and hotel proprietor Finlay Mackenzie happily facilitated the rendezvous. The couple formed a rare partnership and were married for 60 years.

In the modest hub of Daliburgh, the Church of Scotland hosts a community thrift shop and tearoom, the Borodale Hotel overlooks a memorial to the Gaelic bard Donald J. MacDonald, and the Co-op store and school occupy a strip of land sandwiched between freshwater lochs. Double Mac at Burnside filling station is a rare thing, an island fish-and-chip shop. Black pudding, white pudding and haggis are on the menu. Cnoc Sollier is a vibrant new centre for Gaelic music, dance and culture – the name means 'bright hill'. The exciting venue hosts educational programmes, community-led activities, performance space and recording facilities.

HEBRIDEAN JOURNEY

The smooth, fast B888 travels to crossroads from where a long lane rolls up and downhill to reach the crofting community of North Glendale. It is a quiet landscape of scattered crofts, reedy loch shores, free roaming sheep and hills with views to the harbour at Lochboisdale, a deeply rural environment that attracted the young American Margaret Fay Shaw like a magnet.

Margaret was born in 1903, the youngest of five sisters whose parents tragically died young. The sadness affected her deeply and at 18 years old the forlorn student was sent from steely Pittsburgh in western Pennsylvania to live with relatives in the Scottish coastal town of Helensburgh. Here she attended a life-changing recital of Gaelic folk songs performed by Marjorie Kennedy Fraser at St Bride's School. The music and language hooked her powerfully. On return to America, she studied music in Manhattan, with the intention of becoming a classical pianist, but when her hopes were dashed by rheumatoid arthritis in her hands Margaret needed a new dream urgently. A favourite book of traditional songs in Gaelic from Skye, Eigg and Uist, collected by folklorist Miss Frances Tolmie, inspired her to sail for the Outer Hebrides.

After cycling the entire length of the islands, she chose to settle in South Uist and immerse herself in the Gaelic-speaking community. Writing about this decision in later years, she compared the experience to falling in love. The island won her.

In North Glendale she paid rent to share the modest home of sisters Peigi and Mairi MacRae, a thatched blackhouse without electricity and running water. A hole in the roof served to evacuate the smoke of the peat fire. The young American resided with the sisters for six blissful years between 1929 and 1935, she learned to speak and read Gaelic, and participated wholeheartedly in crofting life. Her musical education enabled her to write down and preserve folksongs passed down through the oral tradition to accompany everyday tasks like spinning, rocking a cradle, rowing a boat and more. The South Uist community opened their hearts completely to Margaret. She wrote in her autobiography that she felt like a strange bird that had flown in from the far west to be honoured with love, trust and affection. She was a courageous pioneer, gathering island songs and becoming also one of the foremost female photographers of the twentieth century. Her huge collection of photographs and films of island life are evocative and important.

Upon marriage to folklore scholar John Lorne Campbell, Margaret left South Uist to live in Barra for three years. In 1938 the couple bought the island of Canna in the Scottish Inner Hebrides. Here they entertained people from all walks of life from all over the world. Margaret died in 2004, aged 101 and, much as she loved Canna dearly, her choice was to be buried in the island that won her heart. Significantly her South Uist grave at Hallan cemetery bears a Gaelic dedication from the islanders and their deep regard for her is not lost in translation. 'You came across the ocean, And you gave respect to our history, You gathered our precious legacy, Riches that will endure.'

Beyond the cottage where Margaret lived with the MacRae sisters, *The Listening Place* is an outdoor sculpture by artist Valerie Pagnell on the site of the former village school. An arc of vintage tractor seats surrounds a whale bone, and a sweeping stone wall is inscribed with the poetry recalling the ceilidh nights when people gathered with friends, illuminating their path through the darkness with a clod of glowing peat.

HEBRIDEAN JOURNEY

A rough track from North Glendale ventures through peat banks to Hairteabhagh bay, a beautiful and yet harsh landscape where a community of 13 families struggled to survive. Overgrown ruins bear witness to hardship and heartache.

The modernist architecture of Our Lady of Sorrows Church beside the B888 at Garrynamonie is a bold 1965 design that met the brief to create an intimate place of worship able to withstand Atlantic storms. An external mural by Michael Gilfedder represents the sorrows of the contemporary world. By night, a huge neon rooftop cross shines bright to guide and comfort distant mariners.

A turning off the B888 reaches the Polochar Inn, a hostelry built in response to Charles I authorising the ferry route between South Uist and Eriskay on condition of an inn to accommodate travellers. The name is derived from the Gaelic Poll a' Charra, meaning 'the Stone Beside the Inlet' with reference to a Bronze Age monolith that serves as a shore mark. A fingerpost indicates the lovely Machair Way path through the National Scenic Area where generations of crofters have

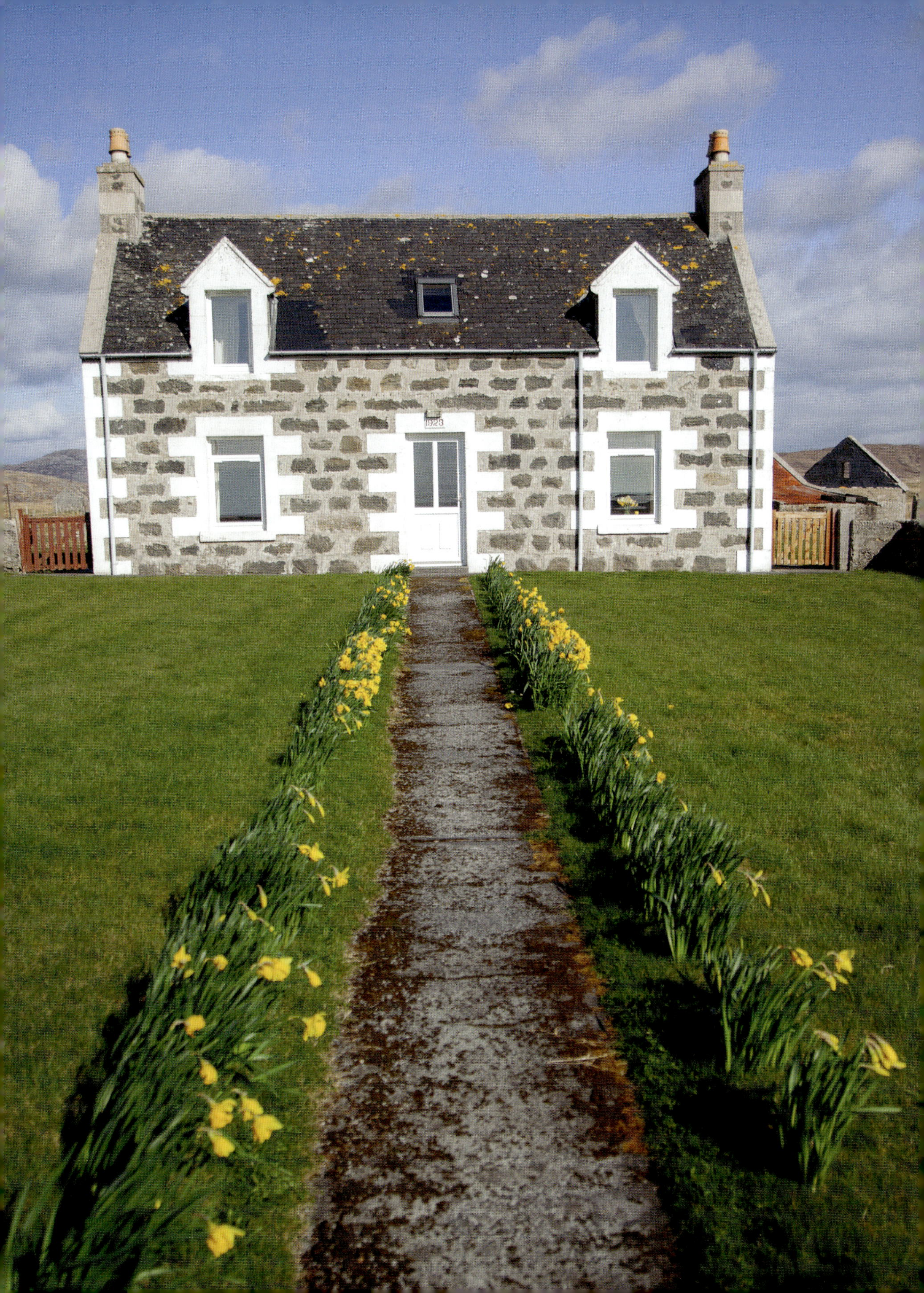
1923

Beauty Spot

The Machair Way visits Boisdale beach and tidal Orasay island. Weary wire fences along the shore are patterned with fishing-net repairs and snagged with knotty wool rubbed by sheep and lambs. On bright breezy days, when the tide is retreating, the huge wet strand mirrors dashing clouds. Seabirds ceilidh at mounds of strappy kelp washed to the shore, their dance steps imprinting the sand. Seaward, the horizon is wide, yet the Uist hills have your back.

dressed shallow sandy fields with seaweed to nourish small oats, bere barley and rye, crops able to withstand the blast of salty winds. Summer's show of wildflowers at the island edge attracts the hum of great yellow bumblebees.

Cille Bhrighde, or West Kilbride, is an ancient site named for the woman who is both fire goddess and Christian saint. But Brigid's seashore chapel is without trace; most likely the stones were repurposed, as is often the case in the islands. A handsome walled garden is all that remains of Kilbride House, a rustic Georgian mansion. The beckoning hills of Eriskay and Barra draw ever nearer and the sensation of leaving South Uist is bittersweet. The gentle shore offers the opportunity to pause and reflect, and perhaps even stay longer, Kilbride Café and campsite are beautifully situated at the water's edge.

The B888 travels to East Kilbride around boulders of coastal armour designed to defend the low-lying island. Prior to the opening of the causeway in 2001, the crossing to Eriskay was made by ferry from the quiet harbour at Ludag. Before quitting South Uist, the road traces a horseshoe with an offshoot to South Glendale. Eriskay awaits across the one-mile-long causeway that supports communities on both shores, especially fishers from South Uist who work from Eriskay's natural harbour at Acarsaid Mhor. Young people on Eriskay benefit from attending school in South Uist without having to board away from home. The causeways of the Outer Hebrides are indeed precious connections.

Irresistible Eriskay

Eriskay is a bijou island of immense character, and it has always intrigued that me some of the most fascinating aspects of the island's story all begin with the letter P: the Prince, the *Politician*, the Priest, the Pitch, the Poem, and the Ponies. It is a curious thing.

Let's begin with Prince Charles Edward Stuart who arrived in Eriskay on 23 July 1745, on a mission to raise funds and an army to depose Hanoverian King George II and restore his exiled father King James VII and II to the throne. His plan was in vain. Defeat by the ruthlessly efficient Hanoverian forces at the Battle of Culloden on 16 April 1746 brought dire consequences, designed to quell any further rebellion among Gaelic-speaking island and Highland people.

In honour of the dandy's derring-do, the cockleshell beach where he first set foot on Scottish land is known as Coileag a' Phrionnsa, the 'Prince's Shore'. A memorial cairn, built with the assistance of island children on the 250th anniversary of his arrival in July 1995, enjoys views to the rolling hills of neighbouring Barra and the uninhabited islands of Lingay and Fuday. Blush-pink bindweed flourishes on Eriskay's dunes with a romantic, if unlikely, tale of provenance. The original seeds are said to have fluttered to ground from the prince's silken pocket.

Eriskay celebrates a special connection with a politician too. The

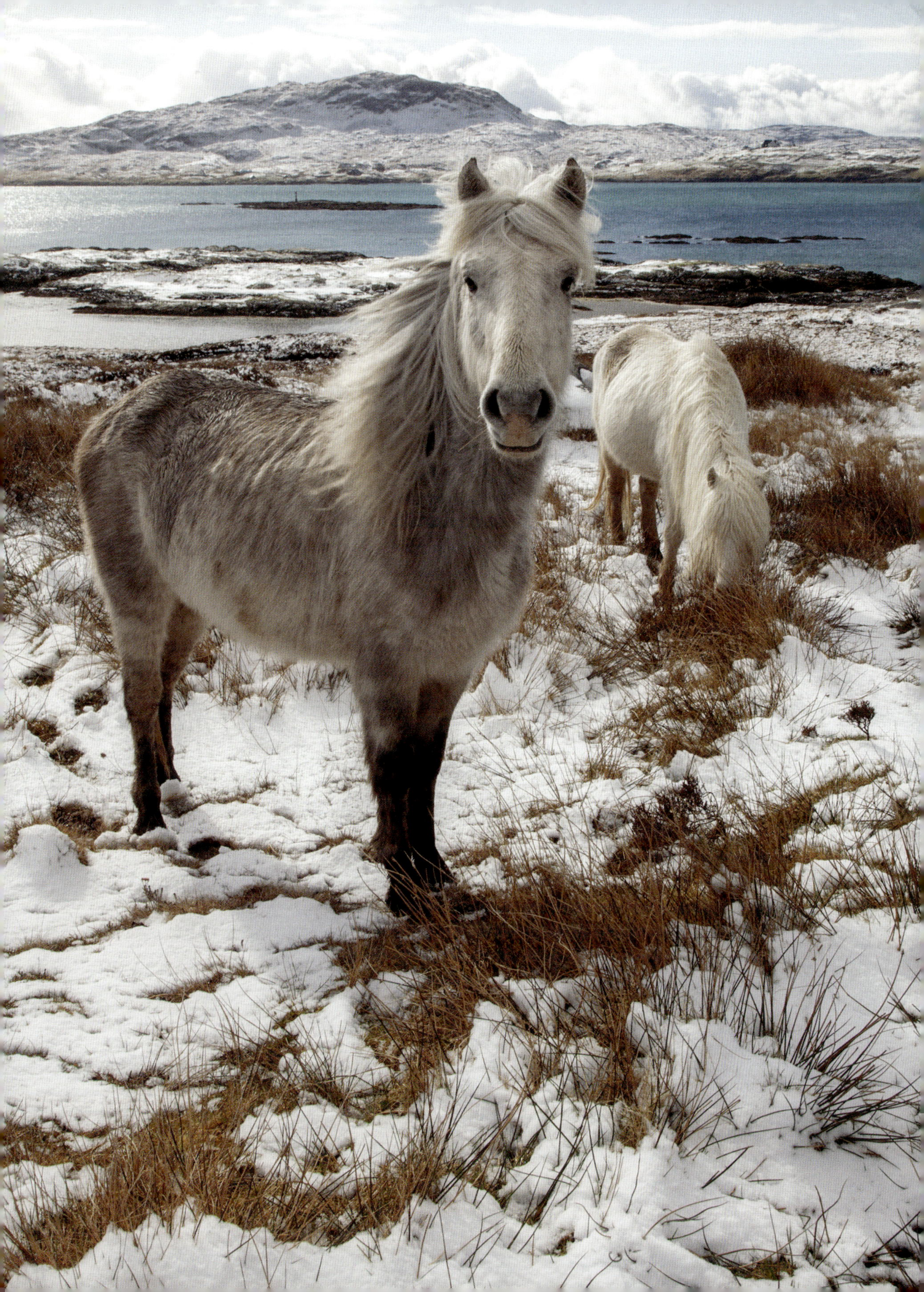

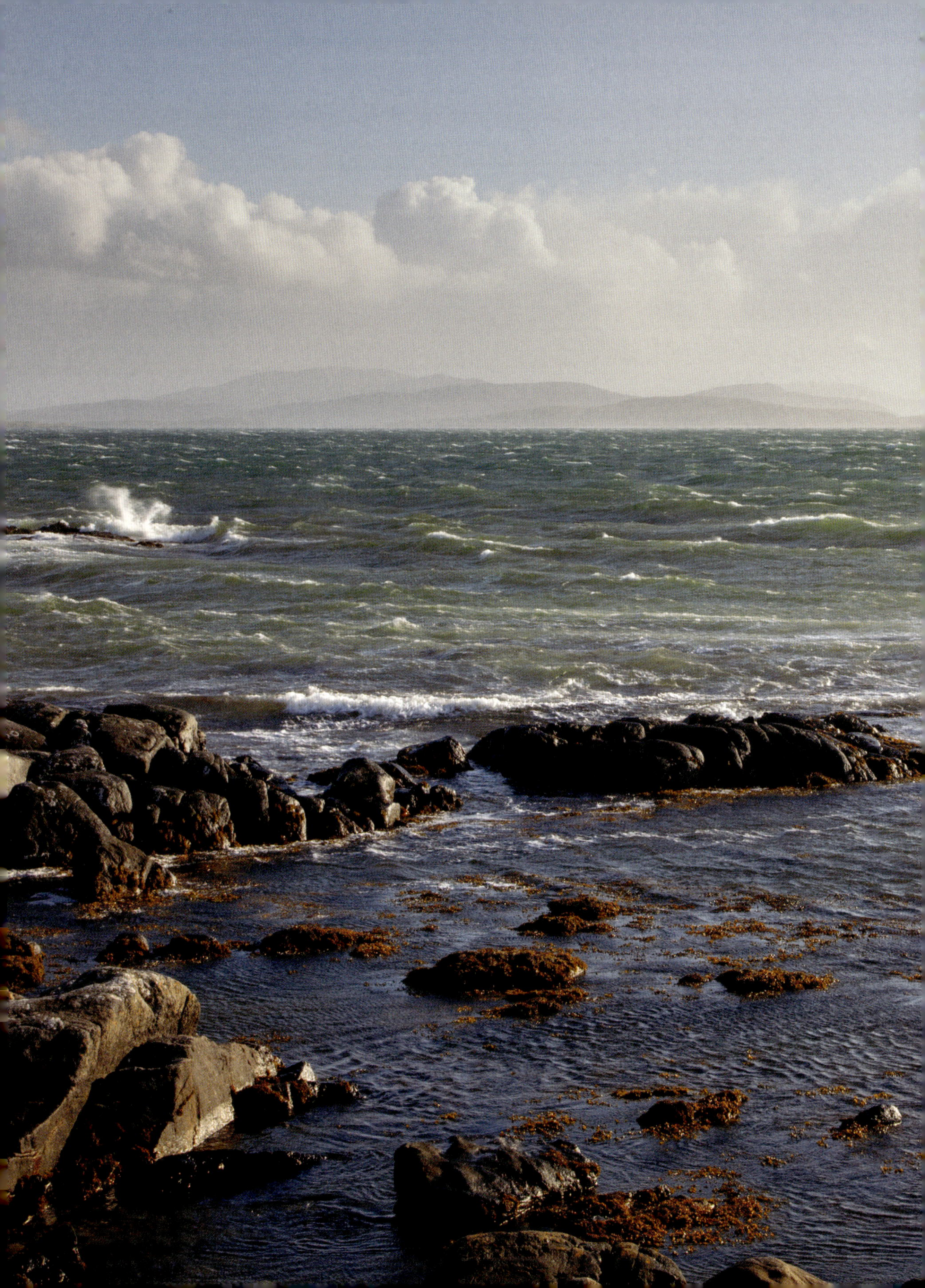

cargo ship ss *Politician* sailed from Liverpool docks on 3 February 1941, bound for New Orleans and Kingston, Jamaica with a hold full of cotton, stoves, cutlery, medicines, biscuits, baths, bicycles and cases of fine whisky. Taking a wrong turn, the vessel ran aground on Calvay island off Eriskay. Islanders rescued the crew; HM Customs and Excise salvaged much of the cargo, however oily water fortuitously deterred the authorities from reaching the whisky. Rising to the challenge, a doughty flotilla of local boats rowed back and forth until 24,000 cases of illicit Highland spirit had evaporated into the islands, leaving more than a residual whiff around the happy communities of Eriskay, Barra and Uist. Customs officer Charles McColl requested the ship be exploded to prevent any further shenanigans.

Author Compton Mackenzie was resident in Barra when ss *Politician* ran aground and the rumbustious events that unfolded spurred him to write his classic novel *Whisky Galore*, published in 1947, after he relocated to London. The author begins with a wry note, 'By a strange coincidence the S.S. *Cabinet Minister* was wrecked off Little Todday two years after the S.S. *Politician* with a similar cargo was wrecked off Eriskay; but the coincidence stops there, for the rest is pure fiction.' His use of 'galore' in the title derives from the Gaelic term for abundance, *gu leòr*.

The priests of Eriskay are renowned for their commitment to improving island life. Gaelic bard and scholar Father Allan MacDonald served the parish between 1894 and 1905, and while ministering to his parishioners he also undertook research to ensure that island traditions and stories were recorded for posterity. Generously, he shared his research into the tradition of second sight among islanders with clairvoyant Ada Goodrich Freer, who went on to claim much of it as her own and was later exposed as a fraudster, cheating at seances, and leading her husband to believe she was 17 years younger than her true age.

During Father MacDonald's tenure, the island population increased; families arrived in crisis, shunted from other islands by lairds keen to clear them from the land. When the island chapel grew too small, Father Allan contributed funds raised by the sale of his books to the building of a bigger church. The fishing community pledged the proceeds of a night's work. St Michael's of the Sea is a meaningful testament to the combined efforts of the priest and parishioners who became fundraisers and builders. The architectural flair of the church has a touch of Spain about it, imbued by Father Allan's time in Valladolid.

Ships are in the very fabric of the church building; it is constructed with timber from wrecks. The prow of a lifeboat from HMS *Hermes*, the world's first ship to be designed as an aircraft carrier, supports the altar, under a heavenly blue canopy glittering with gold stars. A poignant ship's bell was recovered from German battle cruiser SMS *Derfflinger*, interned in Scapa Flow after the end of the war. To prevent the vessel being seized by Allied powers, orders were given to scuttle her on 21 June 1919.

SOUTH UIST AND ERISKAY

Beyond the village, the site of Eriskay's former parish church is a hillside garden where a statue of *Our Lady of Fatima* is protected by a gleaming white picket fence. She casts blessings upon the island football pitch further below, recognised by FIFA as one of the eight most remarkable places in the world to play football. The turf appears deceptively flat when spied from the hill, but this is no level playing field. Closer inspection reveals stony bumps causing wonky white lines in places and one of the corners is slightly uphill. But it is a great improvement on the era when the haphazard lines made for five corners until an offending rock was gouged out. Further natural hazards are rabbit holes and poo deposited liberally by grazing sheep; cleaning the pitch is a necessary precursor to kick-off.

Eriskay FC play between March and September in the fiercely contested Uist and Barra league. Islanders hope the beautiful game has a beautiful future on the rock, known fondly as Eilean na h-Òig, the 'Island of Youth', after a poem by priest and folklore collector Father Allan MacDonald but as older players retire, fewer young people fill their boots; the island population hovers precariously around 150. Eriskay's only pub, named after the beleaguered ss *Politician*, sponsors the club's distinctive green-and-white hooped shirts, an echo of Celtic FC, supported by most of the players. In the hostelry known locally as 'the Polly', highly prized bottles of shipwreck whisky are trophies for display only.

One of the great joys of Eriskay is the roaming herd of eponymous native ponies. They forage freely on the beach, the hill and around the village. Their stamina, strength, thick waterproof winter coats and canny character made them perfect partners in a traditional crofting family's endeavour, capable of carrying baskets of seaweed to nourish vegetable plots and peats from the moor for the fire. They drew carts and carried the children to school, island doctors and nurses travelled on horseback too. When the Ministry of Agriculture offered alternative breeding stallions with the intention of improving island stock, Eriskay crofters resisted because the costs of raising larger animals would be prohibitive on a small island. And so Eriskay's ponies remained,

Curiosity

Aristocratic German film-maker Werner Kissling poured his passion for Eriskay into the 1935 film *Eriskay: A Poem of Remote Lives*. Revenue from the premiere funded an improved island road, known for many years as Rathad Kissling.

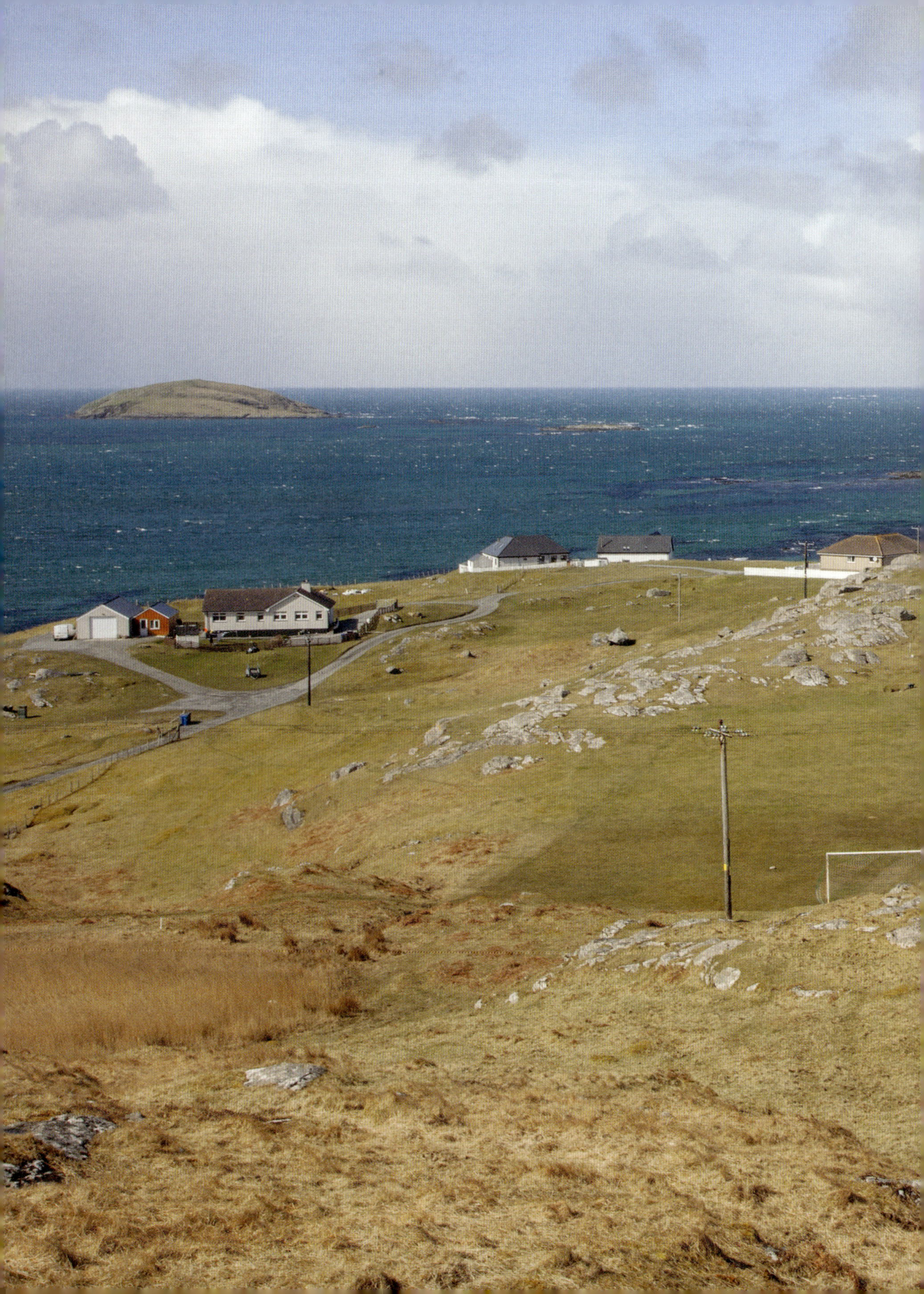

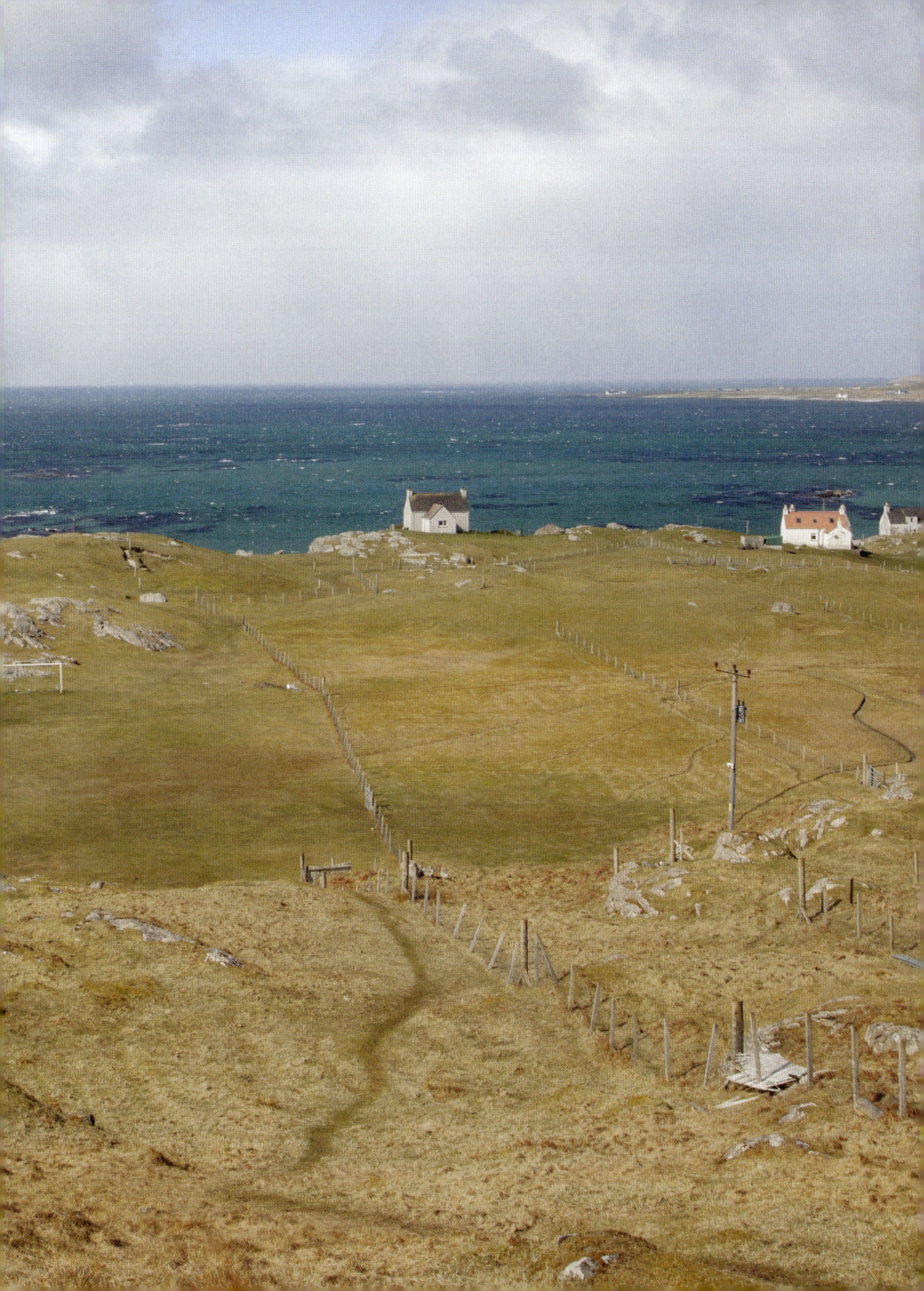

HEBRIDEAN JOURNEY

becoming increasingly rare and precious. The Eriskay Pony Society works hard to increase the breed beyond the islands and warmly welcomes new members, wherever they may be.

Eriskay has three piers around the island; the lesser-used anchorage of Haun, which derives its name from the Viking for harbour, the upgraded haven at Acarsaid Mhor and the ferry slipway at Ceann a' Ghàrraidh, protected by a curving breakwater to ensure the safety of the overnight berth. Shower facilities in the waiting room are much appreciated by cyclists and walkers on the long-distance Hebridean Way.

The poetic Hebridean air '*Gràdh Geal Mo Chridh*', known as the 'Eriskay Love Lilt', was made world famous by Marjorie Kennedy-Fraser who reworked it from a popular traditional version by Mary Macinnes. Hugh S. Robertson's programme notes describe the setting, painting quite a scene. The action takes place 'at the time of the new moon, and at a time when love thoughts are ripest, and the brown eyes of Morag are gazing over murmurous lapping waters'. Although many renowned singers have performed this island song of longing, my grandmother, Victoria, would entertain only the version by Scottish tenor Robert Wilson. Attending a concert to hear his performance of the heart-rending 'Eriskay Love Lilt' in person absolutely thrilled her.

Beauty Spot

Walking is the best way to discover Eriskay. The island circular requires around three hours, but allow plenty more time if inclined to stop, stare, swim, picnic and perhaps snooze to the sound of the sea. The great community shop stocks all you need for a memorable feast. The store also offers handcrafted goods made by islanders, including Eriskay jerseys with unique patterns that honour the tradition of womenfolk stitching designs to identify their seafaring men in case of drowning. Walking through yellow flag iris to secret coves with views to shimmering islands near and far is magical. Castle ruins on Stack Island recall dastardly pirates who ruled the roost. Encounters with the Eriskay herd of gentle ponies feel very special. Please do not feed them, it encourages bad behaviour and can make them unwell. On approach to the harbour at Acarsaid Mhor an outdoor *Stations of the Cross*, painted in 1970, is presented on slates otherwise redundant when the church roof was replaced. They lead to a beautiful hillside viewpoint.

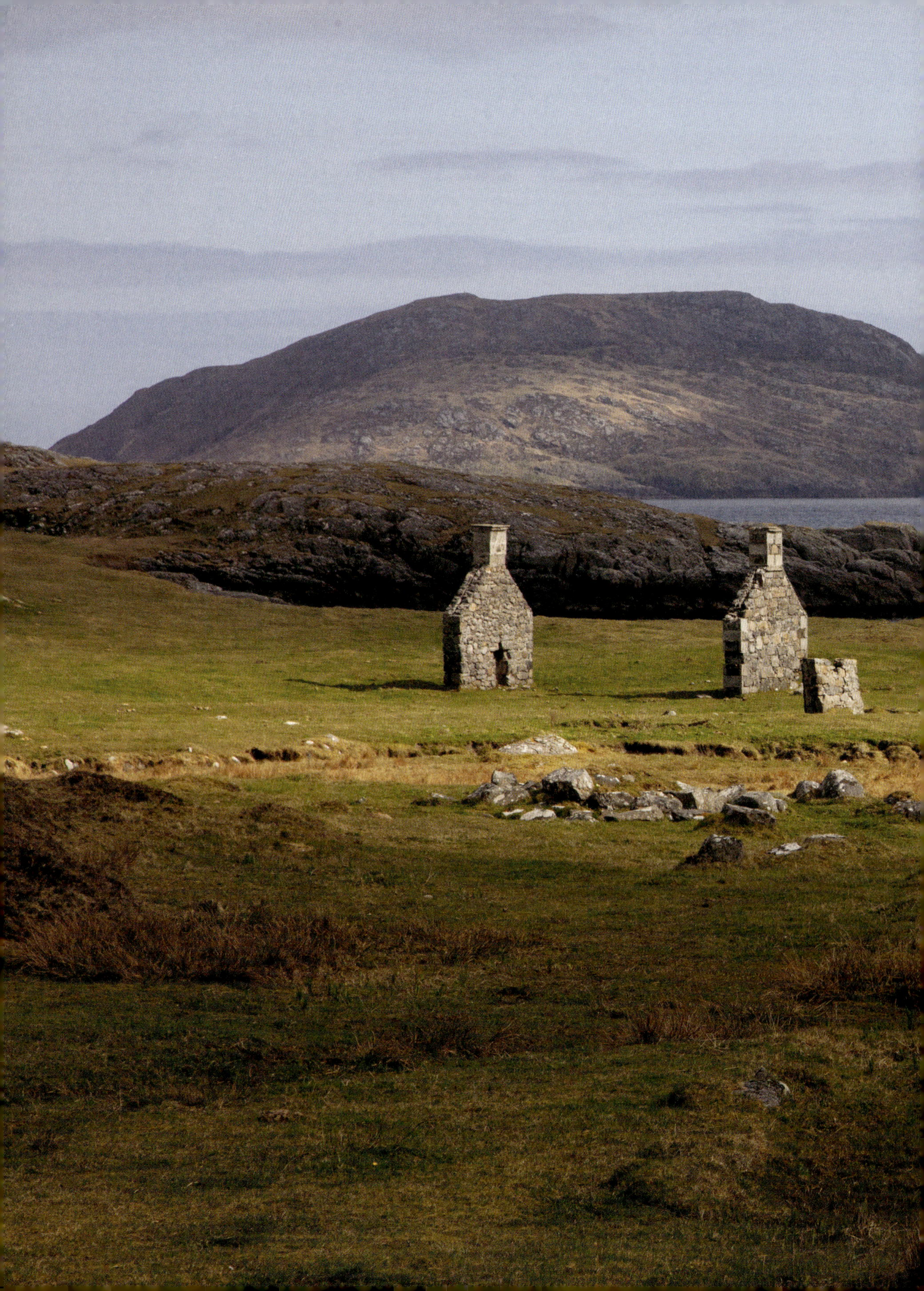

PART FIVE
Barra and Vatersay

Sound of Barra
Fiaraidh
Scurrival Point
Eoligarry
Port na Cille
Traigh Eais
Fuday
Orosay
Vaslain
Barra Airport
to Eriksay
Gighay
Greian Head
Cleat
Ardmore
Northbay
Ardveenish
Hellisay
Allasdale
Barra
Bogach
Bruernish
Halaman Bay
Craigston
Balnabodach
Loch Ob
Borve
Tangasdale
Loch
Tangasdale
A888
Heaval
Earsary
to Lochboisdale
Sound of Vatersay
Castlebay
Brevig
Beannachan
Rubha
Glas
Vatersay
Uidh
Vineasan
to Oban
Vatersay
Eorisdale
0
4 km
0
4 miles
Sandray
Pabbay
Mingulay
Barra Head
Skate
Point

To Barradise and Beyond

The ferry crossing from Eriskay to Barra, the most westerly inhabited island in the United Kingdom, weaves a 40-minute journey through dumpling islets, rocky reefs, sandbanks and shallow channels in the scenic Sound of Barra. Here Hellisay, Fuday and Gighay are among the many Outer Hebrides' uninhabited islands that formerly supported communities. Depopulation remains a threat throughout the archipelago, especially because young people are priced out of an overheated housing market in scenic areas. Future well-being depends on many factors, not least affordable homes, transport links and the economic success of the internal market. The Sound of Barra ferry, introduced in 2003, plays a vital role.

The ferry landing place on the quiet shore at Ardmore is the playground of otters. A joyous sculpture by Iain Brady shapes two of the sleek acrobatic hunters in pursuit of a hapless salmon. The twin otters remind me neatly of the planes using Barra's extraordinary beach airfield at Traigh Mhor. In the cosy refuge of the timber-built ferry waiting room, a small café offers great coffee and extensive views of the Sound.

The sandy shores and relaxed atmosphere of easy-going Barra have earned it the luscious nickname Barradise, far sweeter than the historical alternative, 'Island of Skate Eaters'. Skate are traditionally plentiful in the seas around Barra; the lighthouse on uninhabited Barra Head, the most southerly island in the Outer Hebrides chain, was built in 1833 by Robert Stevenson on Skate Point. However, urea waste in the skin prevents the fish being preserved like herring, with salt. In Barra the winged creatures were hung out to dry on croft walls, for up to two weeks, to improve fermentation, texture and flavour before they were smoked or boiled as required. A more gruesome preparation was to cure the *sgat ghoirt*, 'soured skate', in pits of cow dung.

Skate decorations are no more, yet the refrigerated lorries of Barratlantic are a regular sight, transporting the quality Scottish catch around the world from the fishing pier at Ardveenish. Discover freshly landed and frozen seafood in the quayside factory shop.

Eoligarry refers to the northern district of Barra, an astounding coastline of white sands, turquoise water and verdant islands beyond. The vista from a stupendous rock on Ardmore hillside is thrilling. Low tide reveals the vast apron of Traigh Mhor. According to folklore, if Clach Mhor nan Gleannan, the 'Big Rock of the Little Valleys', some 18 feet high, 25 feet wide and 30 feet long, ever tumbles from the hill, Barra is doomed.

The single-track road to the airport and Eoligarry hugs the shore closely toward Vaslain machair and Suidheachan, the 'sitting-down place', where Compton Mackenzie, author of *Whisky Galore*, built the island home he occupied with his mistress between 1935 and 1948. His wife lived on the mainland. The villa's design echoes faintly Nunton Steading in Benbecula.

Whisky Galore! became an Ealing Studios movie in 1949 starring

Basil Radford, Joan Greenwood and Compton Mackenzie himself, in the role of fictional Captain Buncher, whose fictional ship the *Cabinet Minister* ran aground off the fictional isle of Little Todday. Filmed on Barra rather than Eriskay, the production hit bad-weather delays and overran the ten-week schedule by five weeks. Curiously, the writing retreat became a cockleshell-crushing factory before renovation in the 1990s.

Sprawling sands at Traigh Mhor fulfil multiple roles, much like many island folk. The strand is a happy hunting ground speckled with people carrying rakes and buckets to excavate bait and cockles on a retreating tide, yet access is permissible only when windsocks around the shore are lowered. When the orange fluorescent signals fly high above the sand dunes, wildflowers, cattle grids and sheepfold, Traigh Mhor becomes a unique airfield for commercial and private flights.

The airport operates subject to the tide, the runways to be cleared of seaweed heaps, driftwood, and debris between flights. Twice daily the purr of the Loganair Twin Otter plane from Glasgow carries on the wind. With just 19 seats, a low ceiling, and no door between the pilots and the passengers, the flight is intimate. Gliding over island jewels in a turquoise ocean is unforgettable; touchdown and take-off over juddering ridges of firm wet sand are extraordinary. For passengers and plane spotters alike, the experience of Barra's beach airfield is magical.

A favourite circular walk in the spectacular coastal scenery of Eoligarry tracks from the jetty and the seals to the small medieval parish church of St Barr, with two ruinous chapels, akin to Howmore on South Uist. The traditional burial ground of MacNeil clan chiefs is also the resting place of Compton Mackenzie. The little church held the imposing Kilbar Stone, a mysterious grave slab inscribed with Scandinavian runes, dating from 900 to 1100, dedicating the beautiful memorial to Thorgeth, daughter of Steinar, about whom nothing is known. A convincing replica stands in place of the original, which was removed to Edinburgh; nonetheless, this intriguing Christian Nordic memorial bears witness to the fascinating and potent fusion of beliefs that runs deep in the islands.

At the tip of the peninsula, Scurrival Point peers into the small island of Fiaraidh, reputed to be the home of a fairy woman. The hilltop remains of Dun Scurrival hint at the strategic importance to Iron Age people of this Hebridean observation post with commanding Atlantic views. The gentle slopes of Ben Eoligarry, strewn with wild primroses in spring, are a wonderful picnic spot to view the activity of surfers riding Atlantic white horses onto the long shore of Traigh Eais and the dinky control tower of Barra airfield at the edge of Traigh Mhor across the dunes. The route descends to the machair where Eoligarry School has fishing boats in the playground and fishing nets in the goalposts. The airport café is a welcome pit stop before skirting the coast back to the jetty, with magical views of islands and islets along the way. This circuit can be achieved in a few hours, but, in my experience, anyone unable to resist sploshing in crystal-clear water, lounging around in sand dunes and lazy picnic lunches should allow plenty of extra time.

A rare road encircles the hilly interior of Barra; the coastal A888 is unusual in that it does not connect with any other classified route. The importance of the 14-mile loop connecting crofting and fishing communities was recognised by Compton Mackenzie who organised an island protest in 1939 to express frustration at road-tax demands for inadequate surfaces.

The spur road from Eoligarry connects with the A888 at Northbay, a sheltered haven on a sea loch. On a small islet, a monumental sculpture of St Barr, the island patron saint, blesses the comings and goings of the fishing fleet. Artist Margaret Somerville also created the striking shell mosaic of St Barr on the exterior wall of the Catholic church in his name beside the fishing pier. Golden-coloured windows in the church cast warm soothing light upon the congregation. From the harbour, travelling in an anticlockwise direction, the road reaches a green corridor where the Northbay Woodland Walk explores ferny magic and the Marie Curie Field of Hope brims with golden daffodils in spring.

The spur road to Cleat arrives at a wonderfully rugged shore indented with secret coves, tidal caves and quiet sandy beaches. From here mourners carried coffins on the historic track through the hills for burial at Cille Bharra, resting at Suidheachan along the way. The most westerly golf course in the United Kingdom perches on Greian Head, amid scant remains of the Second World War early-warning Chain Home Low Radar Station that surveyed the skies for low-flying enemy aircraft. The headland home of Barra Golf Club is a magnificent place to play the game, whether novice or veteran. Salt-laden winds blasting straight off the Atlantic are great levellers.

The road curves to Allasdale on the exposed western shore. From the car park at Cuier cemetery a waymarked path climbs to the remains of an Iron Age fortress with spectacular views of Atlantic beaches and bays and the distant shores of South Uist.

Barra is rich in prehistoric archaeology and the dynamic coast reveals and destroys much precious information. In 2007 Channel 4's *Time Team* television crew broadcast the discovery of a Bronze Age roundhouse and burial site in the wake of a powerful storm that smashed sand dunes to reveal 4,000-year-old skeletons crouched in simple stone graves known as cists.

To discover the reefs, rock pools, natural swimming pools and wildlife of Seal Bay, park opposite the post box at the North Allasdale junction and cross the grassy track through the wildflower machair to the shore where the songs of beguiling selkie folk carry on the wind.

The sandy beaches of Traigh Hamara and Traigh Tuath announce the community of Craigston. Here one of the most respected priests in the Hebrides is buried beside the whitewashed church of St Brendan the Navigator, where he served the community of his birthplace between 1936 and 1943. Father John MacMillan is renowned for his commitment to Hebridean people, demonstrated by his decision to emigrate voluntarily in 1923 with impoverished Gaelic-speaking families to ensure their spiritual needs were met in the new Canadian community of Clandonald, Alberta. Frustrated by the authorities' failure to keep promises, he returned to Barra where he made the acquaintance of author Compton Mackenzie and inspired the character of Father James MacAlister in the novels *Keep the Home Guard Turning* and *Whisky Galore*. Father John was a collector and composer of Gaelic songs; among his most popular works is 'Fàilte do Bharraigh', 'Welcome to Barra'. When he died in 1951, some 1,200 islanders attended his funeral. His grave bears an inscription from Compton Mackenzie: 'He loved alike the language of his forefathers and the conversation of his fellowmen. Out of the abundance of his vitality he gave so much to life. Priest, poet and humanist, of all the sons of Barra none was better loved.'

On lonely slopes overlooking the crofts of Craigston and Borve, and the wide Atlantic Ocean, a huge mound of stones rises from rough ground to honour the dead. Dun Bharpa is considered one of the best-preserved chambered cairns in the Outer Hebrides, some 20 feet high and 100 feet in diameter, backed by dark hills and the historic pass of the Beul a' Bhealaich coffin road. This heritage path from Craigston to Earsary served islanders cleared in 1840 by the Barra estate from fertile west coast land to less productive ground on the east coast. Until the church of Our Lady, Star of the Sea opened in Castlebay on Christmas Eve in 1888, St Brendan's in Craigston was the only island church, thus the devout Catholic community of Barra's east coast tramped to mass on the pass through the hills. Today the route serves hikers exploring the island. The nearby dam and reservoir at Borve are within the grounds of Barra's proposed whisky distillery.

Sea cliffs along the west coast of Barra attract climbers who thrill at the challenge of impressive chasms gouged by the might of a tireless ocean; the outpost of Borve Point is a favourite haunt. Eras and cultures collide around Port na Cille shore where a walled cemetery is contained by a stone wall perilously close to the ocean edge. The remains of a chapel lie in the machair grassland, shared with a ruined dun, a Viking burial mound and partly submerged standing stones that perhaps served as navigation marks for people arriving from near and far by boat.

Onward to Halaman Bay where the Isle of Barra Beach Hotel enjoys sunset views in a prime location above Tangasdale beach. From a parking spot opposite Tangasdale phone box, an adventurous circular walk crosses the machair to reach the scant remains of Dun Ban, a 2,000-year-old tower perched on a dramatic headland ravaged by the hungry sea. The hardy occupants enjoyed fabulous panoramic views. A further ruined tower, Dun Macleod, stands in the freshwater of Loch Tangasdale; the square medieval dwelling occupies an Iron Age crannog.

The three-mile walk visits the beach before returning to the phone box. Allow around three hours to explore the indented coast safely and be sure to take a detailed map.

Towards Castlebay, a hilly spur known as the Nasg road climbs to the strikingly triangular Barra and Vatersay war memorial, dedicated in 1993, atop Rubha Glas headland overlooking both islands. I especially appreciate the care taken to show the formal and patronymic names of the war dead. The Gaelic patronym is the first name or nickname followed by the father's name or nickname. From the war memorial the road slips around and down the coast to cross the Sound of Vatersay causeway, but more of that lovely journey later.

Continuing the Barra loop, a further spur drops to Horve, a historic hub, although just one traditional fisher's cottage remains in the cluster of contemporary amenities including the Co-op store, fire station, hospital, sports pitch, marina and distillery where the tang of island seaweed lends a kick to Barra Atlantic Gin. Dualchas community and heritage centre celebrates the history of Barra and Vatersay and it is not unusual to meet visiting descendants of people who left the island generations ago; their stories and discoveries are invariably fascinating. The museum and café are seasonal.

Castlebay is named for the extraordinary island fortress perched on a rock in the wide sheltered harbour. Kisimul is the 15th-century stronghold of the MacNeil clan, whose historic power is summed up neatly in an old saying: 'they had a boat of their ain at the flood'. When a MacNeil was in residence, mealtimes were followed by a castle constable hollering from the high walls in all directions to inform all within earshot that the MacNeil of Barra had dined and so the kings and princes of the world might now be permitted to eat. Happily there's no such nonsense at Café Kisimul on Castlebay's Main Street where a cheery mosaic cites the inclusive Gaelic proverb, *Chan fhiach cuirm gun a còmhradh*, 'a feast is no good without good talk'.

If I could have Hebridean wishes granted, among the first would be to time travel to the

---

Curiosity

Hebridean seascapes especially stir creative individuals from all disciplines. When Samuel Peploe, one of the quartet of artists known as the Scottish Colourists, visited Barra to paint, he found love and his future wife Margaret at work in the Castlebay post office. A small Peploe seascape, simply titled *Barra*, is among my favourite pieces in Kelvingrove Art Gallery and Museum in Glasgow.

1800s to witness the height of the great herring boom that brought prosperity and crowds of workers to island harbours. The herring season began in Shetland in May and ended in Great Yarmouth in autumn. A huge fleet followed the shoals, accompanied by an overland cavalcade of workers enlisted to prepare and barrel the catch for customers in Britain and abroad. In May and June, the population of Castlebay swelled, boats crammed into the harbour, and curing stations around the shore thronged with activity. Through the summer months, Gaelic-speaking Hebridean women and girls migrated to herring ports around Britain. They were pioneers, travelling with their kists, or trunks, to work away from home in arduous and unhygienic conditions. In teams of three the herring girls grafted on the quayside, gutting, sorting and curing the fish in barrels, working with bandaged hands to protect them from wounds and salt; it was back-breaking labour at a time when British women were not even considered eligible to vote. It took until 1928 for all women over the age of 21 to receive that right on the same terms as men. The Herring Walk around the Castlebay shore celebrates the skilled workers who contributed to the silver darling economy. The seashore deck of Hebridean Toffee is a happy spot to refuel with views to Kisimul Castle and ferry activity.

Island stores are at the heart of Hebridean life. In a scattered community local shops and services often provide important social care too, checking in with people, arranging deliveries, responding, and often pre-empting, the needs of islanders. The care, kindness and friendship of people who work in island stores is inspirational, they keep folk connected and I urge visitors to support them. Bùth Barraigh co-operative specialises in local produce from the land and sea. Crafts, art materials, books and maps are for sale, laundry services and visitor information are available and the Bùth team can arrange for the hire of bikes, pushchairs and golf clubs, as well as advise on sea kayak adventures and boat trips to Kisimul Castle and around the uninhabited islands of Mingulay, Pabbay and Sandray, known as the Bishop's Isles.

Castlebay's church, Our Lady, Star of the Sea, rises from a rocky knoll beyond the handsome former kelp store in The Square. St Brendan's Road climbs the slopes of Heaval, Barra's highest hill, to reach a monumental white statue of the Madonna looking across the harbour to surrounding islands. *Our Lady Star of the Sea*, known also as *Stella Maris*, carries infant Jesus. He holds a star aloft to shine spiritual light and encouragement, especially to seafarers who traditionally sail by the stars. The monumental statue was erected in 1954, three years prior to *Our Lady of the Isles* on the slopes of Rueval in South Uist.

The Castlebay Hotel, built when the herring fishery boom was its height, is adjacent to the Castlebay Bar where The Vatersay Boys, a much-loved island band with a huge international following, have

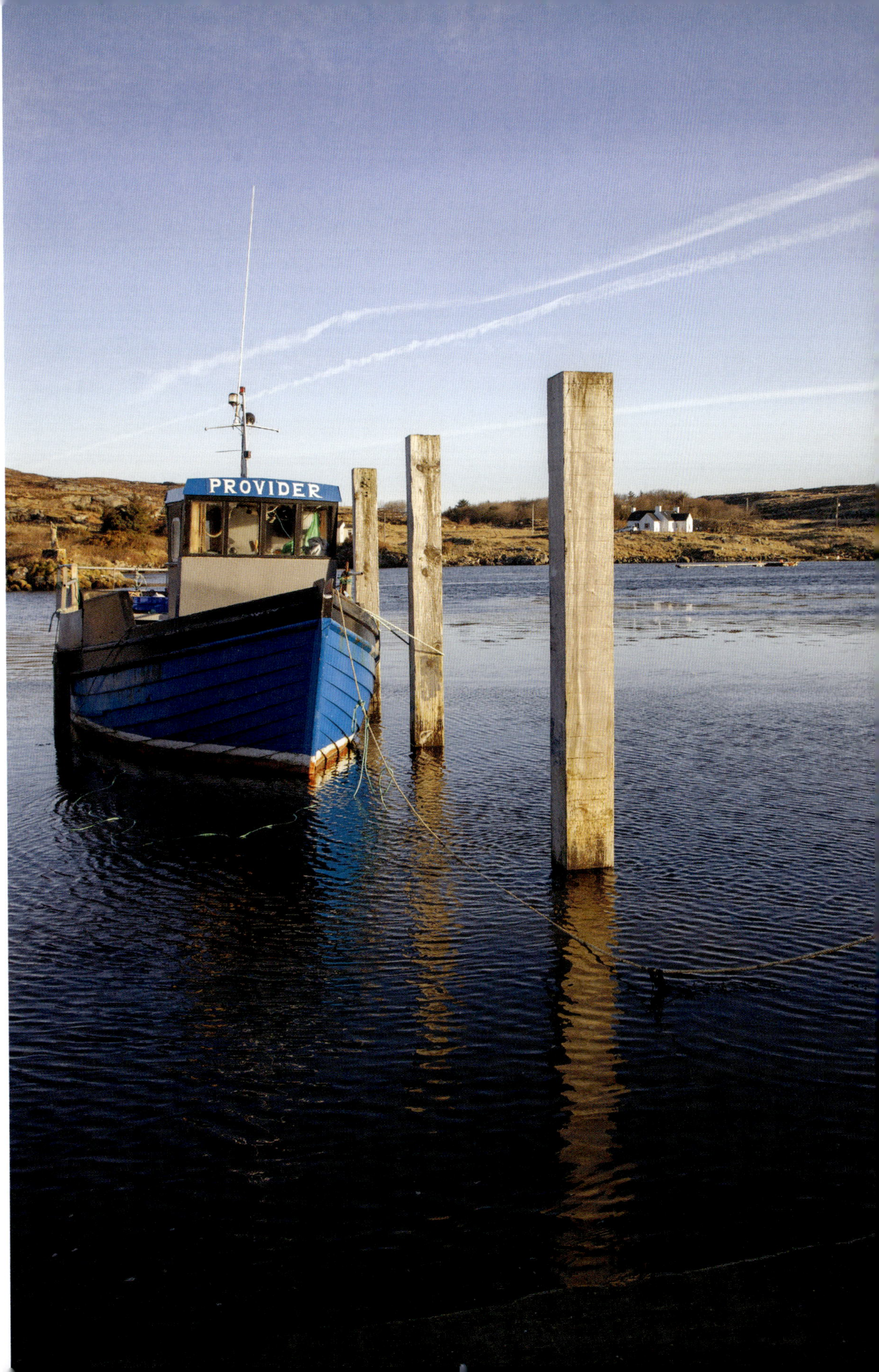
PROVIDER

Beauty Spot

On the coast at Balnabodach a narrow sea dyke pierces dramatically inland to create an easily guarded safe haven in Loch Ob. Here, in 1851, a community of 11 families were forced from their crofts by the landlord, Colonel Gordon of Cluny, in response to the poverty caused throughout the islands by the failure of the potato crop. The people of Balnabodach were dispatched to Québec on an immigrant ship to relieve the colonel of the pressing problem. Traces of their homes remain; simple blackhouses with thick stone walls occupy the grassy loch shore where carpets of sea pinks and clumps of yellow flag iris bloom in their memory.

performed while at home. In the words of the hotel management, the fabulous atmosphere ranges from tranquil to vibrant. The Craigard Hotel also offers the friendly island vibe and comfortable rooms with harbour views.

A gentle stroll of around an hour explores the shore of Ledaig, a lovely spot to observe at a distance the increased activity that comes with the arrival and departure of the CalMac ferry linking Castlebay with Oban and the mainland. The track leads to the island of Orosay with views to sandy beaches on Vatersay.

From Castlebay the island road climbs to the bays of the east coast. The remains of a standing stone group beside a derelict building on the slope of Heaval suggest this was an area of Bronze Age ritual. Boats, buoys and mounds of nets jostle with vegetable and flower beds in croft house gardens, lending a colourful zing to overcast days. The road weaves on to lovely Earsary through a series of sandy coves where moored boats find shelter from stormy seas. Mounds of lobster creels await the call of the sea. At the water's edge whitewashed cottages peer across grassy islands offshore into the grandeur and mystery of mountains on Skye and Rhum. The intriguingly named settlement of Balnabodach derives from the Gaelic Buaile nam Bodach meaning 'Place of the Old Men'. Who were these lads? Local people suspect a lost Viking village may yet be discovered.

The loop road rounds the shore to the head of Loch Ob and the handsome buildings of Northbay House that formerly comprised the junior school, secondary school and teacher's residence, built in 1879. The spur road from Bogach junction travels to the Bruernish peninsula, another island place with a lingering air of Viking times, deriving its name from Old Norse. Otters, seals, porpoises and sea eagles visit ragged promontories with magical views to a glorious smattering of uninhabited islands offshore. After all the exploring, warm cheer, good food and drink at the Heathbank Hotel, a former church, is most welcome.

Vatersay

The islands of Vatersay and Barra connect across a causeway opened in 1991 to prevent depopulation, alleviate hardship and increase safety and opportunity. The hugely important crossing, just 600 feet long, straddles straits where fast-flowing tides of the North Atlantic Ocean and the Sea of the Hebrides meet in turbulence.

Prior to the causeway, the relatively small gap between Vatersay and Barra dictated the timing of island activities. Berthing the small ferry proved impossible at some states of the tide. Visiting priests from Castlebay were sometimes detained for days, even weeks. Pity the island livestock bound for market in faraway Oban, whose epic journey began with an enforced swim across the perilous narrows. Sadly, losses were inevitable. When a prize Aberdeen Angus bull by the name of Bennie drowned in 1986 the clamour for a causeway grew louder. The eventual opening in 1991 was a massive relief.

Vatersay feels much more than one island and the lie of the land backs that up; two distinct slabs are connected by a sandy tombolo, a natural causeway. Towards Uidh, the upper slab of Vatersay puffs yet-smaller chunks of rock into the Sea of the Hebrides. The ruins of Dun a' Chaolais may be reduced to a mound of stones, but the strategic spot still offers an impressive panoramic view, especially towards Traigh Bharlais where roaming island cattle enjoy time at the seaside.

When Colonel Gordon of Cluny set about clearing impoverished islanders from his Barra estate in 1851 after the catastrophic failure of the potato crop, some were removed to Canada aboard the emigrant ship *The Admiral*. Others migrated to outposts in Bishop's Isles group of Mingulay, Sandray, Pabbay and Barra Head. Without adequate farmland to sustain a growing population, the inhabitants of these congested islands took ever-increasing risks. Many who had previously farmed turned their hand to fishing. Working with little experience, and in small boats, they scoured isolated and dangerous shores. Safe harbours and landing facilities were few. Tragedy was inevitable. In 1897 four men died when their boat capsized in the Sea of the Ghosts off Barra Head. The lost fishers represented the entire male population of the island of Pabbay, leaving widows and children to fend for themselves.

A desperate band of landless cottars arrived on Vatersay in 1906, the fertile island farm previously cleared of people by the estate owner. Near the former fish-curing station, the men planted potatoes and erected temporary huts. Others in search of fertile ground soon joined them.

Failing to clear them from her island, absentee landlord Lady Gordon Cathcart, who visited Vatersay only once in 54 years, charged the cottars with resisting eviction. The appearance of ten Vatersay raiders in court in Edinburgh in 1908 was a defining moment in Scottish land reform. People throughout the British Isles read front-page news of landless people living in abysmal poverty, cleared from their islands. The court case heard how fishers with small boats struggled to make a living working from inadequate harbours with poor transport links in the face of competition from trawlers with nets scooping vastly bigger catches in the same fishing grounds. The landmark case concluded with two months' imprisonment for the raiders and the accusation of a failure of duty of care by the island estate. The government bought the island and shared the land to establish a new crofting and fishing community. The four townships, Caolas, Uidh, Vatersay and Eorisdale are testament to the raiders' achievement.

The first crofters returning to Vatersay attended open-air church services at Mass Rock on the Beannachan hillside. The new community took delivery of a corrugated iron church building in 1913. Our Lady of the Waves and St John occupies a plot of land offered by Uileam Boyd, one of the ten raiders. Island churches are frequently melting pots, full of unexpected surprises. Vatersay does not disappoint. The confessional door was salvaged from *The Maple Branch* sailing ship, wrecked off the Isle of Sandray in 1897, and the altar rail was made originally for St Columba's Church on Mingulay.

The Vatersay coast road passes a bench beside shattered fragments of a Catalina seaplane, a poignant, graphic scene. On a night-flying exercise in May 1944, the flying boat and amphibious aircraft that served to hunt U-boats and protect convoys of merchant ships transporting food to nations under wartime rations crashed into the slopes of Theiseabhal Beag. Despite the courage of islanders racing to rescue nine airmen aboard, three of the crew died. Upon completion of investigations, the smashed Catalina was dragged to the shore where the wreckage remains, honoured as a war grave and respectfully untouched.

Vatersay community hall snuggles between the wondrous beaches that gild the tombolo. Islanders serve homemade soup and cake to walkers and cyclists at the end, or the beginning of the Hebridean Way long-distance trail. The hub is aglow with bright bunting flags, each designed and made by a visitor from

Beauty Spot

The tidal islet of Uineasan lies beyond Station Brae where the Vatersay raiders launched their island claim. Low tide exposes secluded sandy coves with views to Castlebay and Heaval. The tumbled remains of Cille Bhrianain, a tiny medieval chapel, form bumps in a cloak of golden buttercups. This haven is a favourite with sea kayakers especially.

Curiosity

When Father Allan MacDonald of Eriskay visited Mingulay in 1898 to celebrate the first mass in a new chapel dedicated to St Columba he noted in his diary that the altar was strewn with wildflowers. The joyous occasion promised much yet without adequate facilities to support fishing especially, the future of the community of around 160 people was in jeopardy. The island occupied steadily since the Bronze Age was economically adrift. Just 14 years after Father Allan's mass of dedication, the entire population had left. Today Mingulay is in the care of the National Trust for Scotland. Shifting sands threaten the empty village at Skipsdale, seabirds rule roosts in perpendicular cliffs, and seals patrol the coast. Boat trips from Castlebay pier offer visitors the experience of a few hours ashore, weather depending.

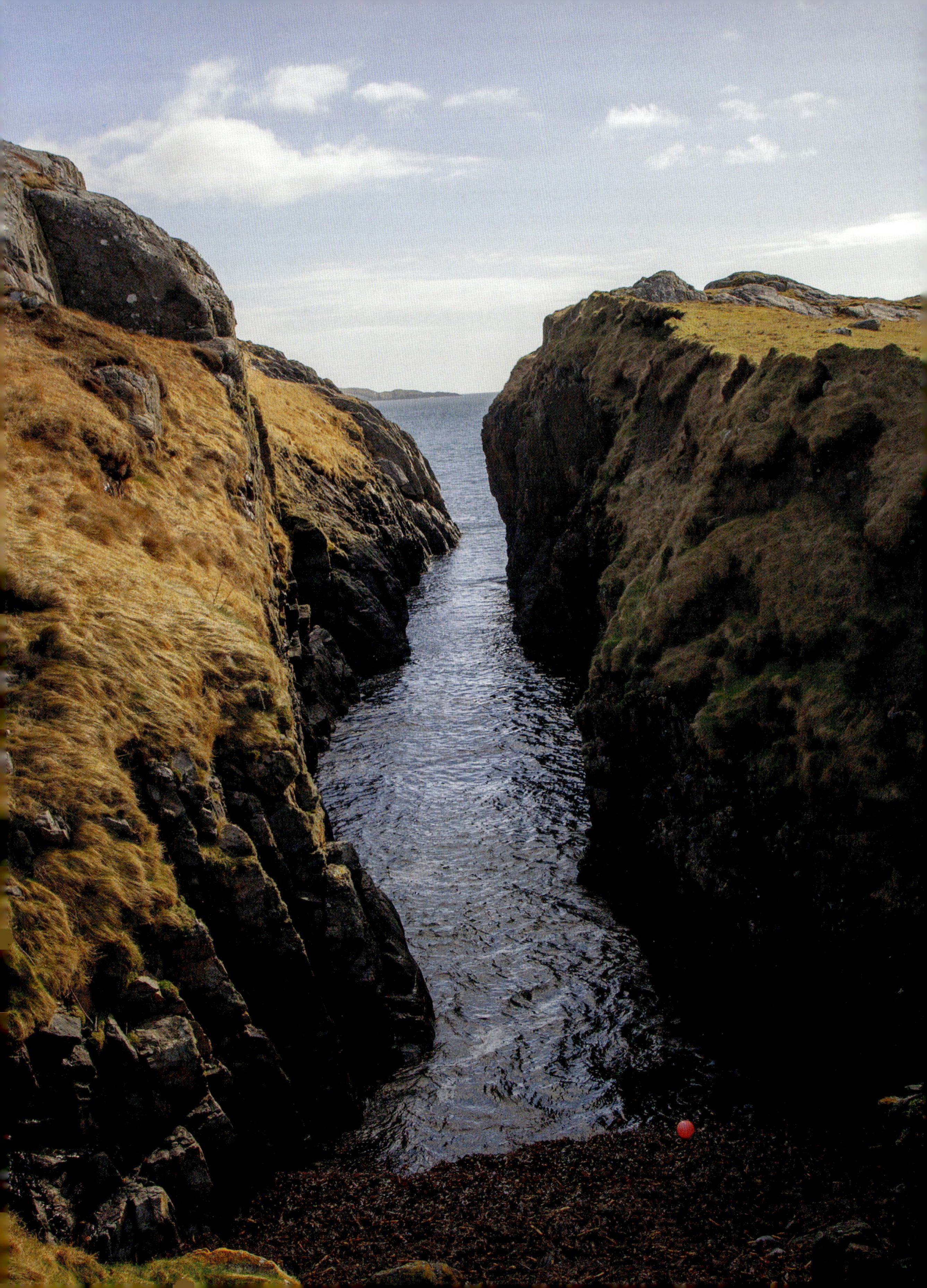

around the world. To the west, the bay of Traigh Shiar hosts summer sunset surfers riding transparent Atlantic waves. To the east, the calm anchorage of Traigh a' Bhaigh entertains visiting yachts.

On the hill above, a simple granite obelisk honours a desperate tragedy. The *Annie Jane*, a three-masted merchant ship, set sail from Liverpool for Montreal in September 1853 with a cargo of iron and a passenger list of hundreds of Scottish and Irish emigrants who had converged on the banks of the River Mersey for the cramped voyage to a better life. Many of the impoverished passengers were classified as redemptioners, people unable to afford the cost of the voyage upfront who contracted to pay by instalments upon arrival at their destination, where they determined to find work.

In atrocious weather, the vessel turned back once before sailing again but the storm had not quietened; an almighty wave washed passengers overboard and damaged the vessel. The stricken *Annie Jane* drifted for several days; in desperation the captain succeeded in grounding her on rocks off Vatersay, but tumultuous waves again washed tragic emigrants overboard. A minimum of 350 people lost their lives: the death toll was not exact because any children travelling were not required to be listed on the ship's manifest. While islanders rescued 102 survivors, the dead continued to wash up on the shore. Without timber for coffins, traumatised islanders buried the victims in a mass grave. The ensuing investigation into the tragedy revealed the average age of the passengers and crew was just 23 and 24 years old, respectively. Survivors of the disaster set a legal precedent for public enquiries following major incidents.

Beside the Pier Master's house at the Royal Albert Dock on the banks of the River Mersey in Liverpool, *The Legacy* sculpture depicts a family of four, two adults and their children bound for new lives abroad. The artwork honours some 9 million people who emigrated through the port, many of them from the Outer Hebrides.

Beauty Spot

One of the great joys of Vatersay is the opportunity to explore much of the island on a wonderful circular walk that starts from the village hall. Allow at least three hours for the circuit of some five miles and more if you are inclined to picnic, paddle and perhaps swim, you will not regret it. The walk visits the gable ends of former homes in Eorisdale, an unofficial island sculpture, like so many dwellings through the islands. Secluded Bagh a Deas, a shallow swimming beach with views to Sandray, is backed by a rainbow of wildflowers in summer, dainty harebells dance to sea breezes. Ceilidh nights in the village hall are joyous fun, and the welcome is warm. A perfect Vatersay day closes with the setting sun dipping into the North Atlantic beyond the shore.

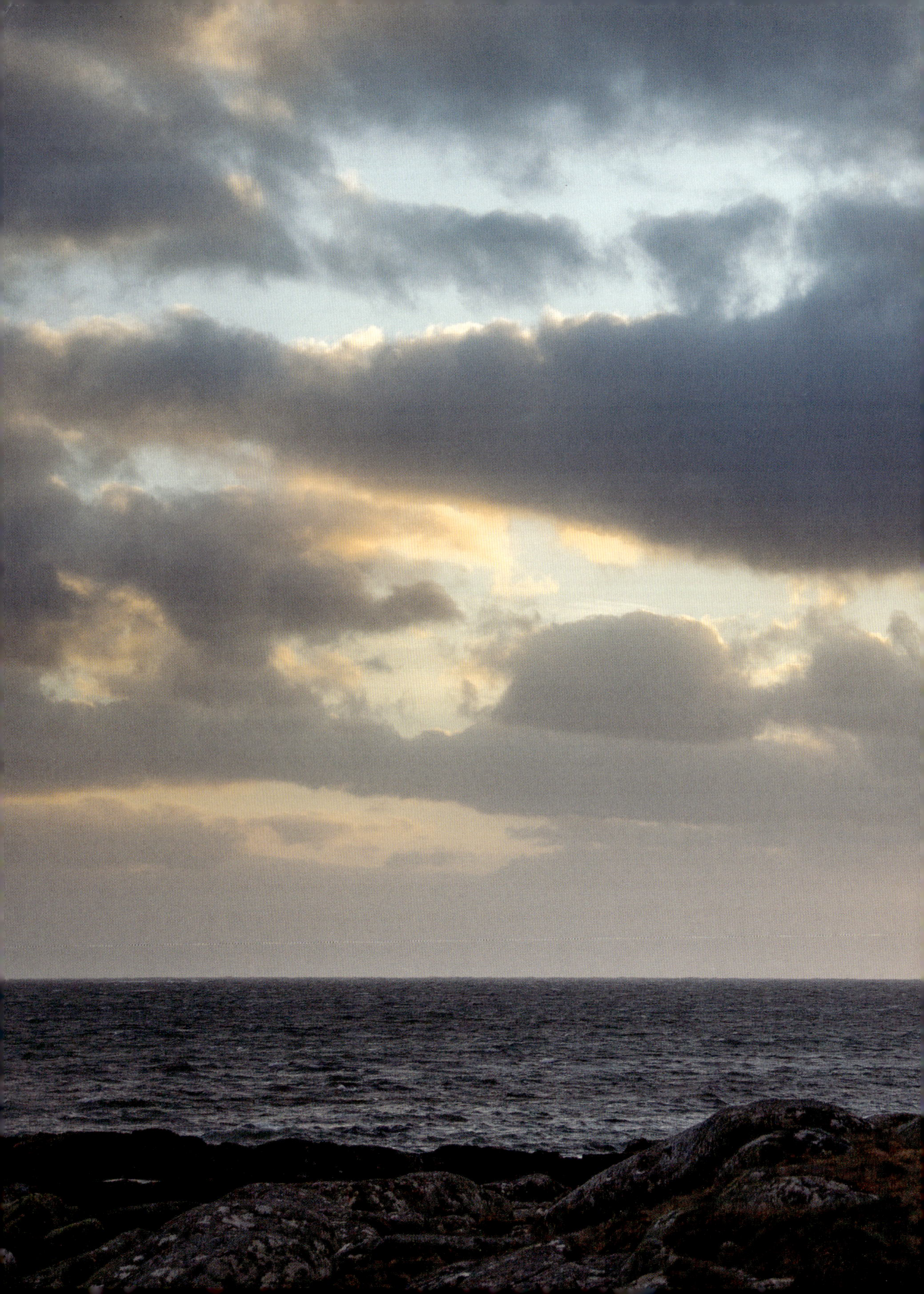

Beyond all things is the sea
SENECA

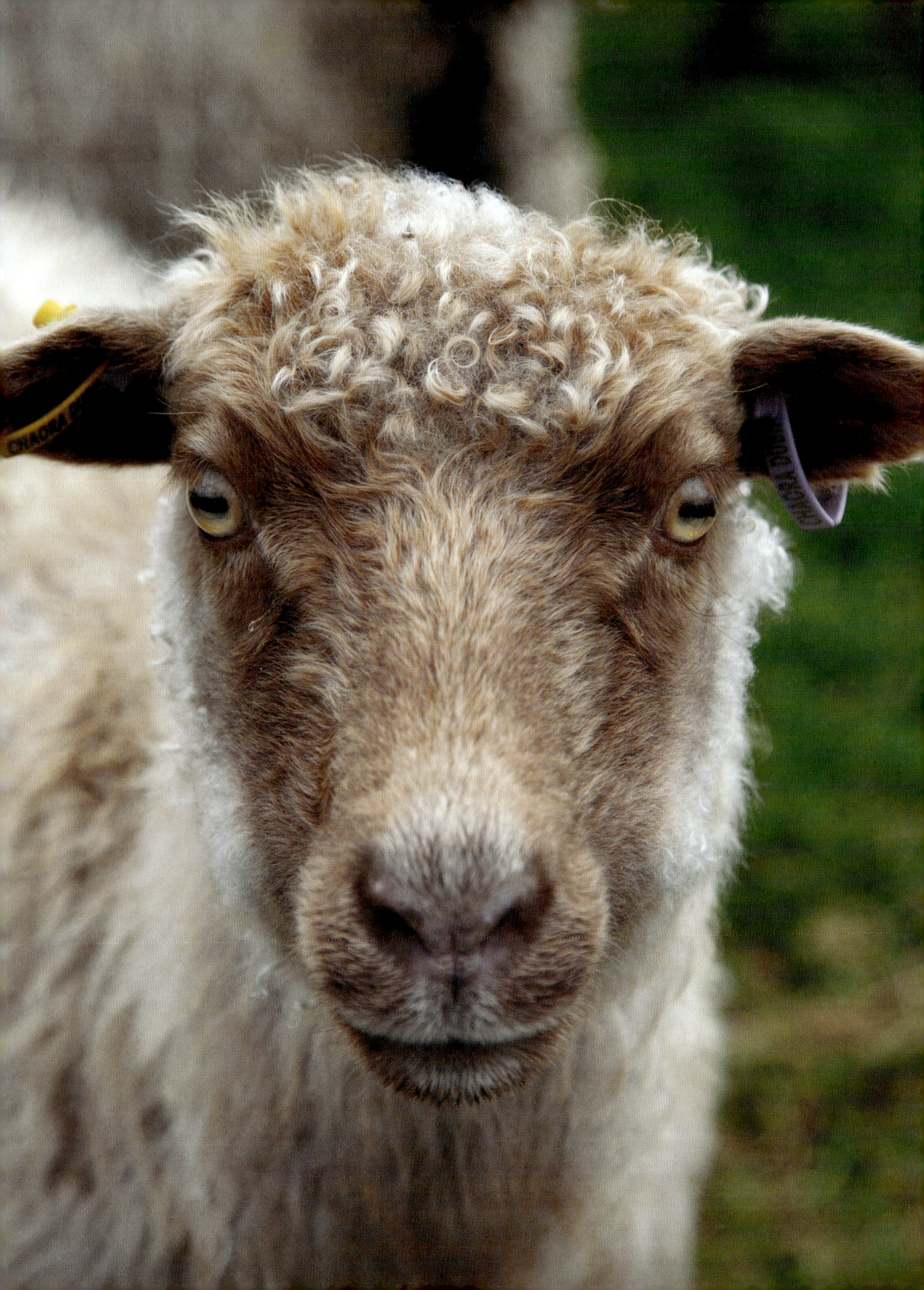

List of Illustrations

Front cover: North Uist sunset
2–3 View to Luskentyre, Harris
4–5 North Uist sunset shore
6 Reef beach, Lewis
10–11 Late summer morning, North Uist
12 Slipway, boat and creels, Great Bernera
14 A warm welcome in the Bays of Harris
15 Hebridean ocean blues
16 Seaweed and stone
19 South Uist flock
21 Trusty companion, Brigid's well-travelled rug
22 Single-track road, Lewis
24–25 Beckoning Harris hills across Lewis moorland
27 Quayside and castle, Stornoway
29 Stornoway fishing boat
30 Stornoway kipper house
34 Stornoway quayside
37 Cut peats drying on the moor
39 The Clach an Truseil standing stone
40 Moorland sheiling
41 Eoropie winter swell
The Cunndal memorial
42 Crofter Donald MacDonald, Eoropie
43 Harbour and shore, Port of Ness
45 Tolsta Chaolais
46–47 The Callanish stones
49 Flannan Isles memorial, Breasclete
51 Drystone wall and thatched roof
53 Murdo Morrison's whalebone arch, Bragar
54 Island views from the Eye peninsula, known locally as Point
55 Detail from the *Iolaire* memorial at the Beasts of Holm rocks
57 Aignish Raiders memorial cairn
59 Tiumpan Head lighthouse
62 Bosta sands and tide bell
64 Seashore picnic bench
65 The narrow road to Mealasta
66 Einacleit telephone box
67 Crofters' sheepfolds, Cliff
68 *An Suileachan* monument
69 Uig Lodge
70 The Carry bus shelter artwork, Glen Valtos
72 Sea cliffs and stacks at the wild Atlantic edge, Lewis
73 Crofters' tattie patch on the sandy shore, Lewis
77 Balallan crofts
78 Seaweed forest at Kershader shore
81 Bonnie Prince Charlie memorial, Arivruach
82 Morning mist, Clisham heights
83 Sunshine yellow Tarbert Stores
84–5 The iconic hills of Harris rise beyond remnants of the shore-based whaling station at Bunavoneader
87 Isle of Scalpay croft houses
91 Bunavoneader tennis court on the rocky road to Huisinis
93 A seat in the hills
94 Island views from the Huisinis road
97 East Loch Tarbert
99 The rocky, watery landscape of the Bays of Harris
101 St Clement's Church, Rodel
102–03 Horgabost shore
106 An t-Ob, or Leverburgh
109 Camping at Horgabost
111 Scarista shore and Toe Head
113 Highland cow from the Luskentyre herd
114 On the road to Luskentyre
116–17 North Uist sunrise
120 Berneray harbour
122 Isles and islets in the Sound of Harris
123 The Sound of Pabbay from West Beach, Berneray
125 Seal Bay, Berneray
126–27 Distant squall, on the road to Lochmaddy

213

HEBRIDEAN JOURNEY

128	Comann na Mara dolphin at Lochmaddy pier
129	Caledonian MacBrayne ferry leaving Lochmaddy
130	Baleshare island causeway
134	*Sanctuary* sculpture, Uist Sculpture Trail
136	*Reflections* sculpture, Uist Sculpture Trail
139	Creels, Houghharry shore
140	Island light, RSPB Balranald shore
141	St Kilda viewpoint, South Clettraval
142–43	Folly tower, Loch Scolpaig
145	Lingay strand, North Uist
146–47	Island view from the Benbecula war memorial
151	Grimsay island scene
153	Boatbuilder's shed, Grimsay
154	Saline lochs and lagoons, Benbecula
157	Culla Bay, Benbecula
159	Croft house in Hebridean light, Benbecula
160–61	Eriskay native ponies
164	South Uist croft, shrine and cattle
169	Howmore Gatliff Trust Hostel
170	The winter shore of tidal Loch Eynort
175	The road to North Glendale
176	The B888 highway near Garrynamonie
177	South Boisdale croft house and daffodils
178–79	Boisdale shore and Orasay island
180	Hebridean skies, South Uist
181	Eriskay native ponies
182	Towards Eriskay and Barra
183	Ferry and breakwater, Eriskay
184	Croft house, Eriskay
186–87	FIFA favourite, Eriskay FC
188	Crofter Barbara MacDonald
189	The serene Sound of Eriskay
190–91	Eorsdale gable ends, Vatersay
193	Traigh Mhor sunset, Barra
195	Traigh Mhor, Barra's spectacular beach airport
199	Barra croft house
202	Kisimul Castle, Barra
203	Fishing boat, Northbay, Barra
205	The golden tombolo, Vatersay
208	Seaward gully, Vatersay
210–11	Polochar standing stone, South Uist
212	Island sheep
220	Off-duty tractor, Lewis

Ways to Visit and Useful Addresses

A favourite Gaelic proverb reflects that too much rush causes delay, or *luathaid gu deanamh maille*. I find that any opportunity to prepare well makes a great difference to my journeys and so I have drawn together a selection of useful contacts to share. I trust this will prove helpful as you navigate these islands.

I wish you much safe and happy exploring!

Visit Outer Hebrides

The archipelago is beautifully presented on the informative Visit Outer Hebrides website: www.visitouterhebrides.co.uk.

Caledonian MacBrayne

Caledonian MacBrayne ferries serve the islands and the website (at www.calmac.co.uk) provides essential sailing updates, links to the travel centre team, timetables and tickets. I urge you to book well ahead and to monitor the status of your routes once in the islands. They are subject to change, dependent on tides and weather conditions.

Logan Air

Logan Air operates scheduled commercial flights to Barra, Benbecula and Stornoway airports. See www.loganair.co.uk for more information.

Scottish Outdoor Access Code

Whichever way you intend to explore the islands, please make yourself familiar with the Scottish Outdoor Access Code. Visit the website (www.outdooraccess-scotland.scot) for practical advice regarding many important aspects of island life, including hillwalking in stag-stalking season, how to prevent accidental wildfire, how to cross military ranges safely and essential wild-camping considerations.

Single-track Roads

The web of single-track roads that criss-cross the islands is a lifeline for the local communities and I urge you to reduce your stress (and theirs) by knowing, well ahead of your travels, the etiquette and rules of driving on roads with passing places. This neat video explains it all beautifully: www.youtube.com/watch?v=8RWwKgCVhuQ. It is easy once you know how, and your kindness and consideration will be appreciated massively by local road users.

Western Isles Council

Offering updated information and cameras showing the latest situation for causeway crossings and road closures, especially in poor weather, check the Western Isles Council webpage at www.cne-siar.gov.uk.

Weather on the Western Isles

Weather conditions on the Atlantic seaboard change swiftly – be sure to check the forecast before setting off on any adventure (www.metoffice.gov.uk). If you are exploring the coast, check surf conditions and times (www.magicseaweed.com) so that you can return safely before the high tide comes in.

Coastguard

If you see someone in difficulty at sea or around the coast, call 999 and ask for the Coastguard.

Mountaineering Council of Scotland

The Mountaineering Council of Scotland provides safety advice to those venturing outdoors in Scotland. Have a look at the website for more details: www.mcofs.org.uk.

Hebrides Search and Rescue

Hebrides Search and Rescue, the local mountain rescue team, also offer useful information. See www.hsar.org.uk.

First Aid

The Red Cross app (www.redcross.org.uk/app) provides great advice. Take a good first-aid kit on your travels because pharmacies and doctors are few and far between. Remember that mobile phone signals can be patchy in the islands, so don't rely on them.

Ticks and Lyme disease

Ticks carry many diseases that affect animals or humans (or both). In Scotland, Lyme disease, also known as *Lyme borreliosis*, is the most common transmitted by ticks. To reduce the risk of tick bites, ensure that skin which may come into contact with vegetation is kept covered. Tuck trousers into socks and wear long sleeves. Check clothing regularly and brush off any ticks.

Check skin folds regularly, too, especially knees and elbows, and remember that disease-carrying ticks may be as small as a pinhead. It is important to examine children and pets also. Removing a tick must be done with great care; buy a tick remover and always keep it with you. For further information about ticks and Lyme disease, visit www.hps.scot.nhs.uk.

The Hebridean Way

The Hebridean Way offers two long-distance routes through the islands for walkers and for cyclists. For more details, see www.hebrideanway.co.uk.

Wildlife on the Islands

For information about the wildlife reserves in the islands, visit the Scottish Wildlife Trust (www.scottishwildlifetrust.org.uk) and the Royal Society for the Protection of Birds (www.rspb.org.uk).

The Outer Hebrides Bird of Prey Trail is a self-guided journey through the islands, introducing you to fantastic sites to observe magnificent raptors, including sea eagles and golden eagles. For details, see www.hebridesbirdofpreytrail.co.uk.

The Hebridean Whale Trail identifies shore-based sites where you can experience the wonder of passing whales and dolphins: www.whaletrail.org.

The Scottish Marine Animal Stranding Scheme provides support and gathers data on strandings around the Scottish coastline of whales, dolphins and porpoises (collectively known as cetaceans), seals, marine turtles and basking sharks.

Should you discover a stranding, information you provide will be valuable for trained rescuers and for data-gathering. However, please remember not to interfere, even if the animal is alive. Keep your distance, and keep other people, dogs and gulls away. For wild animals in distress, contact with or proximity to humans compounds their trauma. Direct contact can also transmit disease. Please call trained rescuers on 07979 245893.

Further agencies offering support include the British Divers Marine Life Rescue (hotline: 01825 765546) and the Scottish Society for Prevention of Cruelty to Animals (hotline: 03000 999999).

Harris Tweed Authority

The Harris Tweed Authority shares the story of the unique island cloth, protects the standard and authenticity, and promotes the brand around the world. See the website for further details: www.harristweed.org.

A Soundtrack to the Hebrides …

The diverse soundtrack of my Hebridean journey is a thing of rare beauty, as it weaves through eras and styles, but if I had to choose just one tune that sums up the magic, then 'My Island' by Peat and Diesel is sure to set my heart racing. The official video, of outstanding coastal scenery, is a joy.

Detailed Maps

Among my top tips for experiencing the islands is a supply of great maps of the areas you intend to visit. Not least because the diverse spelling of Gaelic place names can sometimes be confusing. It is not unusual for local signage to present a name quite differently to the map and so the bigger picture of the routes and surroundings is immensely useful for context.

The maps in this book are for outline only, to make the most of each itinerary; a detailed map is invaluable.

I prefer physical maps – fascinating treasure sheets that pique my curiosity and often reveal secrets and connections that are not immediately obvious in the landscape. Without doubt, my well-worn annotated stash has rewarded the investment repeatedly. Some of my happiest discoveries have emerged from truly seeing the lie of the land on a map.

Plenty of Cash

Enterprising islanders offer all kinds of treats to passing folk, from freshly laid eggs (and I assure you that you will not want for eggs in the islands – they are almost ubiquitous, whether duck, goose or hen) appearing beside honesty boxes at gateways throughout the Outer Hebrides, to cakes, savouries, knitted goods, hand-loomed tweed items, plants, jams, chutneys, home-grown vegetables and unique craft work. Without cash, it is impossible to indulge in the fun of these delightful Hebridean roadside stalls.

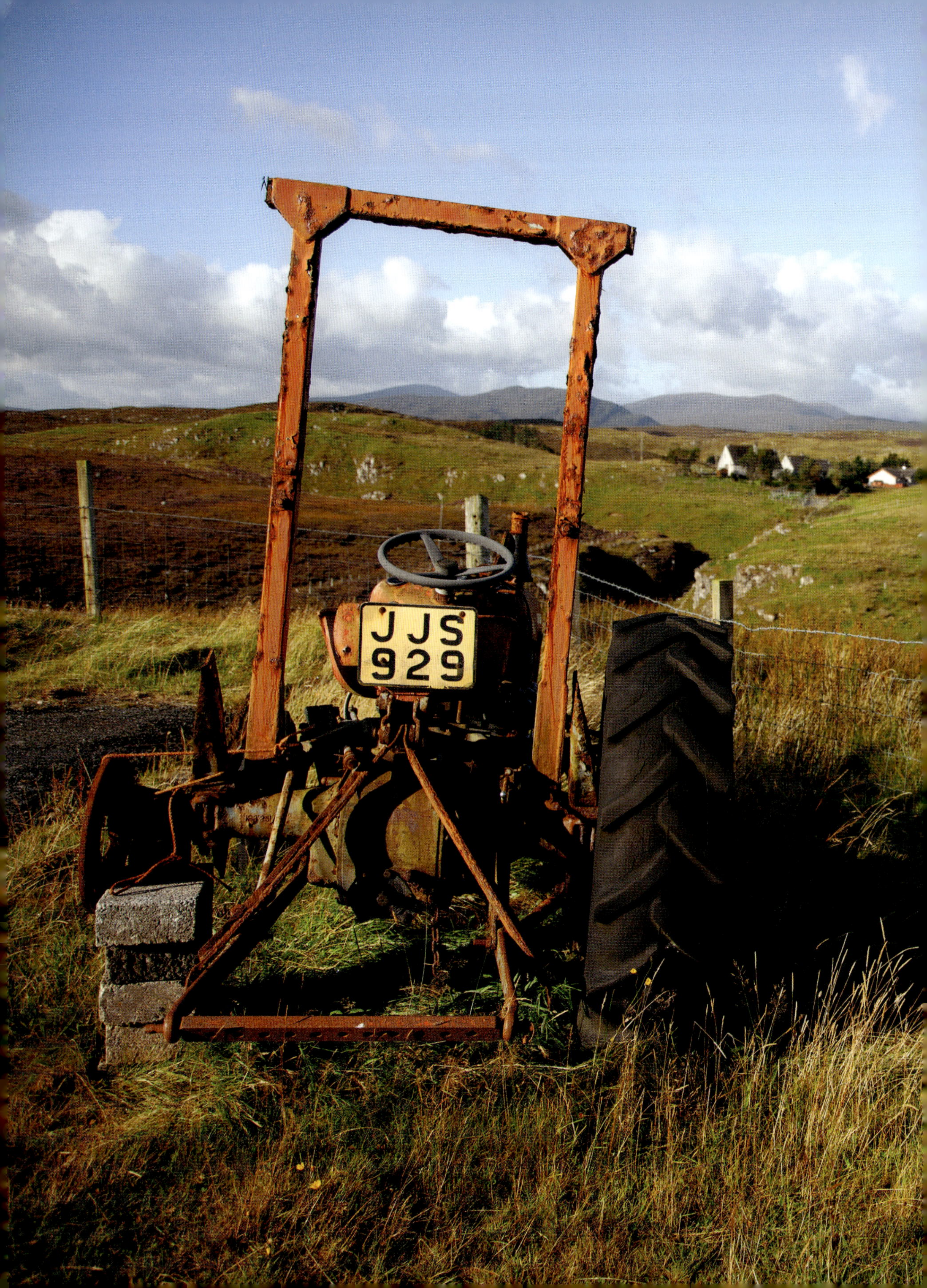
JJS
929

Index

References to text boxes are indicated by the suffixes 'B' (Beauty Spot) and 'C' (Curiosity). Entries in **bold** refer to photographs.

2001: A Space Odyssey 97

Achamore 44
Aignish Raiders cairn 56–57, **57**
air ambulances 136–37, 144
Aird Niseabost 112
Airidh nam Ban 170B
airstrips and airports 144, 155, 195–96
Aline Community Woodland 81
Allt na Brog burn 31C
Amhuinnsuidhe 93–95
'An Eala Bhàn' (song) 135C
An Lanntair, Stornoway 29B
An Rubha (Eye peninsula) **54**, 56–58
An Suileachan (sculpture) 68–69, 68B, **68**
Annie Jane (ship) 209
Ardhasaig 83
Ardkenneth 163–65
Ardmore 194
Ardroil 71
Ardvourlie Woodland 81
Arivruach 81, **81**
Arnol 53–54
Askernish Golf Course 172
Aunt Julia (Norman MacCaig) 90C, 114–15

Backhill 122
Bagh Steinigidh 112
Baile 123
Balallan 77, **77**
Baleshare **130**, 135
Balivanich 155C, 155–56
Balnabodach 204, 204B
Balranald 139–40, **140**
Barpa Langass Community Wood 132
Barrie, J.M. 83C, 93
Barvas Moor 36–37
Barvas Ware pottery 38C

Bayble Exchange 58C
Bayhead 137
Bays, the **14**, 99, **99**
Benbecula 153–59, **154**, **157**, **159**
Benbecula Golf Club 155C
Bernera (Great Bernera) 12, 61–65
Bernera Riot 62–63
Berneray 120–24, **120**, **123**, **125**
Beul a' Bhealaich coffin road 198
Beveridge, Erskine and George 141–44
Bhaltos Community Trust 68, 68B
birlinns 171
black pudding 39–40
blackhouses 50, 53, 123–24
boatbuilding 152–53, **153**
Boisdale beach 178B, **178–79**
Bonnet Laird walk 49
Boreray 145
Bornish 170–71
Bornish Point 171C
Borve (Barra) 198–99
Borve (Harris) 112
Borve (Lewis) 38–39
Borve Castle (Benbecula) 157–58
Bosta **62**, 63–64
Both nam Faileas (sculpture) 127
bothies 71
Bragar 52–53, **53**
Breaclete (Great Bernera) 61–62
Breasclete (Lewis) 45, 48–49, **49**
Breinis 73
Brevig 33
Bride (saint) 39, 167, 178
bridges
    Borve (Lewis) 38–39
    Bridge to Nowhere 35
    Great Bernera 61
    O'Regan's Bridge 163
    Scalpay 87–88
Brigid (saint) 39, 167, 178
Broad Bay 58
Bronze Age 158, 197
Bruernish peninsula 204
bulb growing 138–39

bulls, swimming 66–67, 67C, 205–06
Bunavoneader **84–85**, 91–92, **91**
bundling 54C
bus shelters 70C, **70**
Bùth Barraigh 201
Butt of Lewis 40–42

Caledonian MacBrayne 215
Callanish 44–45, **46–47**
Callanish VIII 61C
Campbell, John Lorne 173, 175
camping 112B
Carinish 134–35
Carishader 67–68
Carloway 50, 52
Carnan 165
Castlebay 200–204
Catalina seaplane crash 207
cats, Leverburgh 107C
causeways
    Baleshare **130**
    Barra–Vatersay 205–06
    Berneray–North Uist 125
    Eriskay 179
    North Uist–Benbecula–Grimsay 136, 148–49
    South Uist–Creagorry–Benbecula 163
Ceann an Ora 91–92
Chair Stone 124C
Charles, HRH Prince 124C
Charlie, Bonnie Prince (Charles Edward Stuart)
    Benbecula 154–55, 158, **159**
    Eriskay 180
    and Flora MacDonald 156, 171–72
    Lewis 80, 81, **81**
    South Uist 170, 173
Cheese Bay 126
Cille Mhoire, North Uist 140
Clach an Truseil 38, **39**
Clach Aonghais Greum 55
Clach Mhicleod (the Macleod stone) 112
Clach Stein 42C

221

Clachan 136–37
Clachan Sands 126B
Claddach Kirkibost 137
Claddach Knockline 137–38
Cladh Hallan 172–73
Cladh Maolrithe 121
clearances
    Barra and Vatersay 204B, 206
    Highland 17, 28
    Lewis 68B, 73
    North Uist 144
    Scalpay 88–89
Cleat (Barra) 197
Cliff **67**, 68, 70
climate change 125, 145
Clisham 82, **82**
Coastguard 216
coffin routes 97C, 114, 197, 198
Cold War 70, 155
Committee Road 137C
Comunn Eachdraidh Nis 40
Congested Districts Board 66
corncrakes 37–38
Craigston 198
Creagorry 159, 165
crofting 17–18, 149–50
Croir 64
Crois Chnoca Breaca 168
Cromore 79
Crosbost 76C, 76
Cross Stores 39–40
crosses, stone 141, 143C
Cubbin, Robert Alfred Colby 31C
Cubby (stockman) 67C
Culla Bay 156, **157**
Cunndal memorial 41B, **41**

Daliburgh 173
dance, Culla Bay 156
depopulation 17, 28, 73, 193–94
Disraeli, Benjamin 30
distilleries 71, 83, 157
Ditch of Blood, Carinish 135
dolphin, Comann na Mara 128, **128**
dolphins 58, 218
Dòmhnall Ruadh Chorùna 135C, 152
Donnan (saint) 145
Drambuie 155
Drinishader 97B
drones 112B
droving 129–30, 165
Dun Bharpa 198
Dun Carloway broch 50
Dun Eistean 42C
Dun Othail 35

Dune Tower and Chapel 36C
Dunmore, Countess of 107
Dunmore, Earls of 94

Eaglais an Naoimh Moire, South Uist 171C
eagles 81–82, 92–93, 120B, 218
East Loch Tarbert 97B, **97**
Eilean Chaluim Cille 79B
Eilean Glas lighthouse 88, 89–90
Einacleit 66, **66**
Eishken 80C, 80
emigration 73, 88–89, 198, 209
Eoligarry 194, 196
Eoropie 40–41, **41**
Eorsdale **190–91**
equipment for visitors 20–21, 86
Eriskay **160–61**, 179–89, **181**, **183**, **184**, **186–87**, 189B
Eriskay Football Cub 185, **186–87**
'Eriskay Love Lilt' (song) 189
Eye peninsula (Point) **54**, 56–58

family history 108
ferries
    Eriskay to Barra 193–94
    Leverburgh to Berneray 118–20
    Ullapool to Stornoway 27–28
ferry terminals 120–21, 128–29
Filiscleitir 35, 36C
Finsbay 100
Fionn mac Cumhaill 133
first aid 217
fisheries 28–30, 89, 150–51, 201
fishing (angling) 33, 71, 99
Flannan Isles 45–49, **45**
Flodabay 100C
Flodday 154
football 42–43, 76, 131, 185
Foshigarry 141

Gaelic 14–16, 62, 171C
Gallan Head 70
Galson Estate Trust 38
gannets (guga) 43
Garrynamonie 176, **176**
Garyvard 79
Gatliff Trust hostels 83B, 123–24, 168, **169**
Gearrannan 50
Geocrab 98C, 98
Geshader 66–67
Gleann Lacasdail 82, 83B
Gleann Miabhaig observatory 92–93

Glen Valtos 70C, **70**
Golden Road, the 96, 97
golf courses 111, 155C, 172, 197
Graham, Angus 55
Gramsdale 154
Gravir 79–80
Great Bernera **12**, 61–65
Great Bernera Trail 61–62
Grenitote 145
Gress 33
Griminish Point 141
Grimsay 149–53, **151**, **153**
Grimshader 74–76
guga hunting 43

Habost 40
Hairteabhagh bay 176
Hallan burial ground 172B, 175
Harris Tweed 52, 76C, 107, 113C, 218
Harris Walkway 97
Hattersley looms 76C
Hebridean Way 217
Hebrides Search and Rescue 217
Heisker (Monach Isles) 138, 150
Hercules the bear 132–33, 159
herring fisheries 28–30, 89, 201
herring women 28–29, 201
Highland cattle 54, **113**
Horgabost **102–03**, **109**
Horve 200
Hosta 141
hostels and bothies 83B, 123–24, 168, **169**
Houghharry **139**, 140
Howmore 168, **169**
Huisinis 90, 95
'Hut of the Shadow' (sculpture, see also *Both nam Faileas*) 127

Innse Gall 28
Iochdar 165
Iolaire (ship) 29B, 55–56, **55**, 74
iris, yellow flag 80
Iron Age 63, 69, 149
Islibhig Chain Home Low Radar Station 72–73

James Bond 63C
Johnson, Samuel 156–57

Keose 76, 79
Kershader 77–79, **78**
Kilbar Stone 196
Kilbride 178–79

INDEX

Kildonan 171
Kilpheder 141
Kirkibost 61
Kisimul Castle 200, **202**
Kissling, Werner 185C
Kneep 68, 69

land raids 32, 33, 68B, 139, 206–07
Laxay 76–77
lazy beds 50, 97
Leac an Righ 124C
Leathad Ard 50
Legacy, The (sculpture) 209
Lemreway 80
Leurbost 76
Leverburgh (An t-Ob) 105–07, **106**
Leverhulme, Lord 31–32, 35, 92, 98C, 105
Lewis chess pieces 70–71
Lews Castle **27**, 30–31
lighthouses
    Butt of Lewis 41–42
    Eilean Glas 88, 89–90
    Flannan Isles 45–49
    Shillay 138
    Tiumpan Head 58, **59**
Lines (sculpture) 131C
Lingarabay super quarry 100
Lingay strand **145**
Lionacleit 158
Listening Place, The (sculpture) 175
livestock sales 129–30
lobsters 64–65, 95, 150–51
Loch an Sticir 125–26
Loch Bharabhat 61C
Loch Carnan 166–67
Loch Druidibeg 167
Loch Erisort 76–77
Loch Euphort 133
Loch Eynort 168–70, **170**
Loch Hornoray 149
Loch Lacasdale 86–87
Loch na Muilne 53
Loch Roag 44, 49, 61
Loch Scolpaig 141, **142–43**
Loch Skipport 167
Lochboisdale 173
Lochmaddy 127–31, **128**, **129**
Lochs Church, Lewis 76
Logan Air 215
Loomshed Brewery 86
Ludag 122
Luskentyre **2–3**, 113–14, **113**, **114**

MacAskill, Angus 121–22

MacCaig, Norman 90C, 114–15
MacDonald, Father Allan 184, 207C
MacDonald, Annie 98
MacDonald, Flora 156–57, 158, 171–72
Macdonald, Jessie 104
MacFisheries 31–32, 105
Machair Way 176–78, 178B
Mackay, Donald John 113C
Mackenzie, Compton 183, 194–95, 196, 197, 198
MacKillop, Mary (saint) 171C
Macleod, Alasdair Crotach 100–01
Macleod, Captain Alexander 101–04
Macleod, Catherine and Marion 107
MacLeod, Mary Anne 33
Macleod, Sir Norman 123
MacMillan, Father John 198
MacNeice, Louis 104
MacNeils of Barra 200
MacPhee, Angus 165–66
MacRuari, Amie 152B, 157
Mangersta 72
Manish 98
Maraig 82
Mary Rose (J.M.Barrie) 93
Matheson, James 30–31, 44, 62–63, 76
Mealasta **65**, 65, 73
Melbost Borve 39
Miabhaig 97
mills 52, 64
Mingulay 207C
Mirrlees, Count Robin 63C, 63
Molinginish 82, 86
Monach Isles (Heisker) 138, 150
Morrison, Canon (Father Rocket) 163–64, 171
Morrison, Christina 88
Morrison, Malcolm 79
Morrison, Murdo 64–65
Mountaineering Council of Scotland 217

Ness Fishery Memorial 43
Ness Football Club 42–43
Nicolson, John 36C
Nike 113C
Norgrove, Dr Linda 71–72
Norse influence 16–17, 74 *see also* Vikings
North Glendale 174, **175**
North Lee 131, 132
North Lochs 76
North Uist Distillery 157

Northbay 197, **203**
Northbay House 204
Northton 108
Nunton 156–57

Oban (Harris) 86
opium trade 30–31
Ormacleit Castle 168
Otter, Captain and Mrs 108–10
Otternish 125
Our Lady of Sorrows Church, South Uist 176
Our Lady of the Isles (sculpture, South Uist) 164–65
Our Lady of the Waves and St John (Vatersay) 207
Our Lady Star of the Sea (sculpture, Barra) 201–02
oystercatchers 39

Pabbay 108B, 206
Pabbay Mor 69
Paiblesgarry monument 139
Pairc Niseabost 112
Pairc Raiders 33–35
Pairc Raiders Monument 80–81
Pairc Trust 79
passing places 21–23, 90–91, 216
Peat and Diesel 16, 77, 219
peat cutting 18, 36, **37**, 44
Pentland Road 50
Peploe, Samuel 200C
Peter's Port 158–59
Pobull Fhinn ('Finn's People') 133
Point (Eye peninsula) **54**, 56–58
Politician (ship) 180–83
Polochar Inn 176
Polochar standing stone **210–11**
ponies, Eriskay **160–61**, **181**, 185–88, 189B
Porcupine (ship) 108
Port na Cille 199
Port nan Long 125
Port of Ness 43, **43**
Portnaguran 58B
Postman's Path 82, 83B
Princess of Thule, The (William Black) 64
psalm singing 33

radar stations 141B, 197
RAF Benbecula 155–56
rain stone, Cille Mhoire 140
ranges, military 38C, 163–65
Rarinish 154–55

Reef **6**, 68–69, 68B
Reflections (sculpture) 135, **136**
Reid brothers 89C
Rhenigidale 82, 83B
roads, safe use of 21–23, 90–91, 216
rocket mail, Scarp 95
Rodel 100C, 100–04, **101**
Rodel Hotel 104
Roineabhal 100
Ronay 150
RSPB
    Balranald 140, **140**
    corncrakes 38
    Loch na Muilne 53–54
Rueval 158B, 164

Sabbath observance 17, 33
safety
    coastal 110C, 112
    roads 21–23, 90–91, 216
    walking 86
Sanctuary (sculpture) 133–34, **134**
Scalpay 87–90, **87**
Scarista 111–12, **111**
Scarp 94B, 95
Scholar's Path, The 98
Scottish Marine Animal Stranding Scheme 218
Scottish Outdoor Access Code 216
Scotvein 151–52
Seal Bay 123, **125**
seals 123, 154, 218
seaweed 49, 63, 66, 126–27
Sgalabraig 124C
Sgoil Uibhist a Tuath 137
Shader, Upper and Lower 38
Shaw, Margaret Fay 166–67, 172B, 173, 174–75
Shawbost 52
Sheela-na-gigs 100C
Sheshader 58
Shiants, the 90
shielings 18, 35–36, **40**, 54–55, 66
Shillay lighthouse 138
shipwrecks
    Annie Jane 209
    Ersa 67–68
    Pabbay fishermen 206
    Politician 180–83
    St Michael's of the Sea 184
shrines 163–65, **164**
Shulishader 58
skate 194
Skigersta 36

Slochd a' Choire (the 'Spouting Kettle') 141
Sollas 144
songs, Gaelic 14–15, 135C, 140–41, 189
Sound of Eriskay **189**
Sound of Harris 105, 108, 118–20, **122**
South Clettraval 141B, **141**
Sponish 127
St Barr, Barra 196, 197
St Clement's Church, Rodel 100–01, **101**, 123
St Kilda 72, 91–92, 110
St Kilda viewpoint, South Clettraval 141B, **141**
St Michael's Chapel, Grimsay 152B
St Michael's of the Sea, Eriskay 184
St Moluag's Church, Lewis 42
Steimreway 80
Stein, Edith (saint) 171C
Steinacleit 38
Stewart family 152
Stilligarry memorial cairn 168
stone lifting 55
Stornoway 28–32, **34**
Stornoway Museum 31C
Strome Shunnamal symbol stone 154
Strond 107
Struparsaig 98
Stuart, Charles Edward *see* Charlie, Bonnie Prince
Sulasgeir 43
summer walkers 70C

Taigh Chearsabhagh, Lochmaddy 127, 130–31, 131C
Tangasdale 199
Tarbert 83, **83**
Tea Field (Dail Beag) 52B
telephone boxes 66, **66**, 100
Temple Bakery 108
tennis courts **91**, 92
They Are Forsaken (film) 100C
ticks 21, 217
tide bells **62**, 63–64
Timsgarry 70
Tiumpan Head lighthouse 58, **59**
Tobson 63, 64B
Toe Head 108B, **111**
Tolsta 33–35
Tolsta Chaolais **49**, 49, 50C
Tolsta Heritage Trail 35

Tom Mor Urrahag 54
Traigh Dail Mhor and Beag 52B
Traigh Mhor **193**, 195–96
Trump, Donald 33
twins, Miss Harris and Miss Lewis 95

Udal 144–45
Ui Church, Lewis 57–58
Uig 70–71
Uig Lodge **69**
Uineasan 207B
Uist (collective name) 124
Uist Community Riding School 155C
Uist Mill and Wool Centre 151–52
Uist Sculpture Trail 127, 133–34, **134**, 135, **136**
Uist Unearthed app 125C, 171
Ungeshader 66
Urgha Beag 82, 86

Valasay 62
Vallay 141–44, 143C
Valtos 68, 69
Vatersay **190–91**, 205–09, **205**, **208**, 209B
Vatersay raiders 206–207
Vikings 16–17, 69
Visit Outer Hebrides 215

walking safety 86
war memorials 29B, 32, 50C, 134, 200
weather 20, 216
Weaver of Grass, the (Angus MacPhee) 165–66
West Beach **123**, 124
West Gerinish 167
West Harris Trust 112B
Western Isles Council 216
Westford Inn 137
whalebone arch 52–53, **53**
whales 58, 92C, 218
whaling stations 91–92
wheelhouses, Iron Age 69, 149, 155
Whisky Galore (Compton Mackenzie) 183, 194–95
Wiay 159
willow 80
woodlands 80C, 81, 132C, 132, 170B
World War I 28, 32, 134, 135C, 138
    see also Iolaire; war memorials
World War II 72–73, 76, 79, 155, 197, 207